The Lardners

The Lardners

My Family Remembered

Ring Lardner, Jr.

Harper & Row, Publishers
New York Hagerstown San Francisco London

Grateful acknowledgment is made for permission to reprint the following:

Quote from *The Letters of F. Scott Fitzgerald* edited by Andrew Turnbill. Copyright © 1973 by Frances Scott Fitzgerald Lanahan.Reprinted by permission of Charles Scribner's Sons.

Lines of lyric from "As You Desire Me." Words and music by Allie Wrubel. Copyright © 1932 and renewed 1960 Words & Music, Inc. and Essex Music, Inc., New York, N. Y. Used by permission.

Lines of lyric from "Hello Tokio." Words and music by Ring Lardner and George S. Kaufman. © 1976 Warner Bros. Inc. All Rights Reserved.

Lines of lyric from "Prohibition Blues." © 1919 Warner Bros. Inc. Copyright renewed. All Rights Reserved. Used by permission.

Lines of lyric from "There's a New Star in Heaven Tonight." Copyright 1926 by Mills Music Inc. Copyright renewed. All Rights Reserved. Used by permission.

Photo reproductions by Jim Kalett

FIRST EDITION

Designed by Gloria Adelson

Library of Congress Cataloging in Publication Data

Lardner, Ring, Jr. 1915–
　　The Lardners.
　　Includes index.
　　1. Lardner, Ring, Jr. 1915–　　—Biography. 2. Lardner family. I. Title.
PS3562.A72Z515　　818'.5'209 [B]　　74–15837
ISBN 0–06–012517–9

76 77 78 79 10 9 8 7 6 5 4 3 2 1

For the next generation:

Peter, Susan, Ann, Mary Jane,
Katie, John, Joe and Jim . . .

And the next:

Karin, Donald, Eric, Carlo, David,
Ellis, Caleb and Simeon

Illustrations

PART THREE

Part One

Ellis Abbott, Smith College, Class of 1909

My family lasted as a family till 1960, when my mother and last surviving brother died within six weeks. But my most frequent image, waking and sleeping, of the time when there were six of us goes back to the mid-1920s and the big house on Manhasset Bay in Great Neck, Long Island.

Dad was just past forty then, a tall, dark, balding, solemn-faced man who entertained millions of readers in a hundred and fifty newspapers but never found a better audience than his wife and four sons. At home he said funny things as well as wrote them, remaining deadpan through our laughter; he also played the piano and sang for us, or for himself with us as incidental beneficiaries. He was at the height of his fame, one of the best-known people in America, when he decided in 1926 to stop writing for newspapers after twenty years, and concentrate on fiction and the theater.

Mother was a couple of years younger, small, pretty and vivacious. She could make us laugh, too, when she wanted to, and she lined us up to meet guests with such pride we never knew she felt surrounded by a sheer mass of masculinity.

Mass is not an overstatement. John, at fourteen, was several inches taller than she was and I, while only eleven, outweighed her. Jim at twelve was comparatively slight and David was only seven, but even they tended to plumpness in those days. The only sister any of us ever had was exclusively David's when he was three. Her name was Alice Henry Heinzie Blue.

A Ring Lardner collection, *The Love Nest and Other Stories,* was published that year with an introduction by Sarah E. Spooldripper, who "lived with the Lardners for years and took care of their wolf. She knew all there was to know about Lardner and her mind was virtually blank." Dad was reprimanded for not taking his work seriously enough by several reviewers who had no idea how much effort he actually put into it. What he avoided at all costs was taking himself seriously in public. I read he was something called a humorist and asked him if it were true. He said it was a loaded question. "If I said yes, it would be like if you asked a ballplayer what position he played and he answered, 'I'm a great third baseman.' "

Actually, and this is a phenomenon among portraits of the artist as a young man, he didn't start out with any conscious purpose of becoming a humorist, or a fiction writer either, before he wrote his first short story at the age of twenty-eight. His motive for getting into what was to be the major occupation of his later life was not any compelling urge to create but the added expenses involved in the imminent birth of my brother Jim.

There was no accumulation of manuscripts or rejection slips. In fact, nothing he ever wrote for publication went unpublished, and it wasn't till ten years after he started writing for magazines that he received a definite rejection. That was from the *Saturday Evening Post;* the story was "The Golden Honeymoon"; and the advice from George Horace Lorimer, the editor, was that he stick to sports subjects; "which act," wrote Dorothy Parker, "should send the gentleman down to posterity along with that little band whose members include the publisher who rejected *Pride and Prejudice,* the maid who lighted the hearth with the manuscript of Carlyle's *French Revolution,* and Mrs. O'Leary's cow." My father recovered from the blow by switching to *Cosmopolitan,* which paid more money.

The most conclusive evidence of his lack of ambition to be anything beyond a baseball reporter and part-time songwriter is to be found in his marathon correspondence with Miss Ellis

Abbott of Goshen, Indiana, who became his wife after nearly four years of his persistence, her vacillation and their common deference to the proprieties of the day. (It was two and a half years from first meeting to engagement and first kiss, and well over a year after that to their marriage in 1911.)

Their letters were precious to each other and they saved almost all of them, which was especially remarkable in his case because he threw away everyone else's as a matter of course, including Scott Fitzgerald's side of a sustained correspondence. When Mother died, these more than seven hundred surviving letters became family property and they are my main source in reconstructing a courtship that took place within our century but seems to belong to the previous one.

(In view of the degree of devotion expressed by my father in this correspondence, it was pretty startling, after I quoted some of them in *Esquire* for March, 1972, to receive a letter from a woman in San Francisco revealing that he had conducted a simultaneous, hitherto unknown correspondence with another girl, the woman's mother-in-law. But she had the letters, nearly forty of them, and I have since read and copied them, and they will come into this narrative in due time.)

The Ring-to-Ellis letters are concerned in large measure with his effort to make her, and then her parents, see him as a suitable husband and, although there are frequent references to his "prospects," he never once raises the possibility of eventually increasing his income by creative writing. The reason, I'm quite sure, is that it never occurred to him.

The courtship had to be conducted principally by mail because he was traveling with one or the other of the Chicago baseball clubs during the greater part of each of those years, while she was completing her last two years at Smith College, living with her family in Goshen and Lake Wawasee, Indiana, and the last year, teaching at a school for the children of faculty member–officers at Culver Military Academy in Indiana. There were occasional meetings, usually separated by many months, at the large house of her large family; in Niles, Michigan, only thirty miles away, where his parents lived and where Ring and Ellis had first met at a marshmallow roast; on the Smith campus in Northampton, Massachusetts, the one time his job took him to Boston while she was still there; and in Chicago, where Ring and his brother Rex boarded with their married sister Anne Tobin. But at each of these, by his own account, he would fail to say all he had intended and would have to clarify and expand on his feelings in the greater ease of written communication, often in the form of verse.

The long, tortuous path of this particular courtship may seem a little less strange in the 1970s if we consider the special stratum of American society to which the Lardners and the Abbotts belonged.

Both families had gone through two stages of pioneering in the New World. They had been early and prominent settlers in colonial days, the Lardners in Pennsylvania and the Abbotts in Massachusetts. Then in the nineteenth century, as the Middle West was cleared of forests, Indians and other impediments to progress, they had moved on to new frontiers. But this second migration must not be confused with that of the propertyless pioneers in their covered wagons, or the trainloads of European immigrants escaping a life at subsistence level. For those groups the goal was free land . . . a hundred and sixty acres that could, with enough hard work, support a family.

Land was a major inducement for my nineteenth-century forebears, too . . . as the very best investment for their capital, which it continued to be throughout the century. As an added, ego-bolstering attraction, instead of being one among hundreds in the upper classes of Boston or Philadelphia, they shared their elite status in Goshen or Niles with another half-dozen families at most.

Lardner and Abbott are pre-Norman English surnames derived from occupations, like Miller, Hunter and Smith. A lardiner was in charge of the larder in a castle. How a practicing abbot initiated a line of descendants is lost in history.

6

Lynford Lardner emigrated to America in 1740, wisely choosing to seek his fortune in Pennsylvania, into whose governing Penn family his sister had married. He moved right into the governor's house and a place on the public payroll. At thirty-four he married Elizabeth Branson, seventeen, whose father was the "iron baron" of the colony, and then, when she succumbed after twelve years and seven children, Catherine Lawrence, whose uncle served a record five terms as mayor of Philadelphia. With this combination of connections he accumulated a home on Second Street, a country seat, "Somerset," at Lardner's Point on the Delaware, an estate in Bucks County and a shooting box known as "Grouse Hall" in Northampton County.

His son John served with a cavalry troop that was General Washington's bodyguard during several battles of the Revolution, married into a prominent family and had eleven children. It was the generation of his offspring that became allied with an old Maryland family named Wilmer. The Wilmer girls were regarded as prize catches, and the oldest son, Lynford the second, who married Elizabeth Wilmer, was outdone by a younger one, James Lawrence, later an admiral in the Civil War. James not only married Elizabeth's sister Margaret but, when she wore out after only five children, took as his second wife still another sister, Ellen, who bore him two sons. The older was named after a fellow admiral and relative of the Wilmers, Cadwallader Ringgold, and it was his name, Ringgold Wilmer Lardner, that passed to my father and then to me.

The family relationship of that admiral, James Lawrence Lardner, to my brother James Phillips Lardner is that the first was the brother of the second's great-grandfather. But there is a more interesting relationship in the small parts each of them played in American history. By way of preface a completely coincidental item appeared in my father's daily column in the Chicago *Tribune* for March 19, 1918. Jim, approaching four, was a notable menace to all the breakables in the Lardner household, and Ring accordingly addressed Woodrow Wilson's Secretary of the Navy, Josephus Daniels:

Dear Sec:

If the Navy wants another Destroyer may I not offer my son James.

Respy.,
R.W.L.

Quite unknown to Ring, the navy actually had in the works on or about that date a destroyer named after the previous James Lardner, for on November 23, 1919, the Milwaukee *Journal* ran the following news story alongside the syndicated Sunday column to which Ring had meanwhile switched:

RING PROUD OF SEA DOG FOR WHOM DESTROYER IS NAMED

The Milwaukee naval recruiting station has solved a problem which has been on the minds of a sizable percentage of the nation's citizenry, viz.: "What relation is the new oil-burning destroyer Lardner to the humorist whom the Americans have nicknamed Ring?"

The destroyer was named for Rear Admiral James L. Lardner, hero of the capture of Port Royal and Fort Walker during the Civil War, who received the honor of having his name sent to Congress by Abraham Lincoln for a national vote of thanks. Besides this, the rear admiral escorted Lafayette back to France in the Brandywine after the great Frenchman's last visit to the United States. At one time Admiral Lardner commanded the West Indies and East Gulf blockading squadron.

Having all these things in mind, the local navy recruiting station wrote Ring a letter to find out if the navy could lay some claim to him. This is the reply:

"Greenwich, Conn., Nov. 14

"DEAR SIR:

"I don't know the proper method of addressing a lieutenant commander, hence the Dear Sir.

"The picture of Admiral James Lardner adorns our walls. He was my grandfather's brother, making him my great uncle or something. My father had tons of clippings concerning him and all my relatives were proud of the relationship, he being one of the few members of the family imbued with the fighting spirit. I didn't know there was a destroyer named after him and I'm grateful to you for telling me.

Sincerely
RING. W. LARDNER"

In September, 1938, at the age of twenty-four, James P. Lardner was killed in Spain as a volunteer in the International Brigades fighting for the elected government against the insurgents and their Italian and German auxiliaries. The battalion in which he served was named after James L. Lardner's commander-in-chief in our own Civil War. And two years later, at another stage in the struggle against fascism, Roosevelt and Churchill negotiated the transfer of fifty overage American destroyers to British control. One of them had the same name as the most widely publicized of our dead among the "Lincolns" in Spain.

The Lardner coup that proved much more meaningful than escorting Lafayette back to France was the marriage of the admiral's brother, John Lardner, Jr. to Mary Perot Downing. Their son, Perot Lardner, became the only surviving descendant of the wealthy Philadelphia Perots, and when he died a childless widower at the age of forty, the fortune that had fallen his way was divided among the heirs of his five paternal uncles.

It was one of those uncles, Henry Lardner, who migrated to Michigan. Settling in Niles, he invested in land, started a lumber business and married a girl of eighteen named Mary Ann Keys, who lasted another year and left him with an infant son and a handsome dowry of ten thousand dollars. When that son, my grandfather Henry, was five, his father took him back to Philadelphia to be educated. Heading for a destination almost due east, they traveled northwest to St. Joseph, Michigan, by wagon; thence to Chicago by steamboat; Peoria, Illinois, by stagecoach; St. Louis by steamboat; Cincinnati by steamboat; Wheeling, West Virginia, by steamboat; Cumberland, Maryland, by stagecoach; Baltimore by railroad; and finally Philadelphia by railroad. Traveling time was two weeks.

The second Henry returned to Niles at the age of eighteen and took over his parents' prosperous farm four miles outside of town. In 1861 when he was twenty-two, he married Lena Bogardus Phillips, eighteen, who bore him nine children and yet survived as he did to the age of seventy-five. Her father, Joseph Flavius Phillips, was rector of the Protestant Episcopal church and one of Niles's most distinguished citizens, but his greatest influence may have been on Long Island real estate prices. Early in his career he changed the name of a parish there from Mosquito Cove to Glen Cove after a friend named Colonel Glen.

It was through her mother's family, however, that Lena Lardner once claimed membership in the Daughters of the American Revolution. She heard that an ancestor, Jacob Thomson (who married a girl named Freelove Phinney), had been a captain in that war, but a check with the Massachusetts archives revealed he was a part-time private who put in five days' service in 1776 and nine in 1780, both on occasions when his home was directly threatened by British troops.

My grandmother was a remarkable woman with an outgoing personality and a far greater influence on my father than her husband, a quiet man who was over forty-five when Ring, their last child, was born. She was intensely religious but in an affirmative, optimistic way that celebrated life by trying to get as much fun as possible out of it. The six of her children who survived to maturity were divided into two groups of three so separated in age that the older ones seemed to the younger to belong to a different generation. The younger trio, born within a period of three and a half years, consisted of Reginald (Rex), Anna (Anne) and Ringgold (Ring).

"I have known what it was like to be hungry," Ring said in a newspaper interview when he was forty, "but I always went right to a restaurant." Actually he was born into considerable luxury. Henry and Lena Lardner left Niles at the end of the Civil War but returned after a number of years in Cincinnati and bought a large house on several acres that sloped down to the

St. Joseph River. My grandfather's income, which came from investments, mainly mortgages, supported them comfortably in a fast-growing area during a boom period. Then in 1880, the year before Rex was born, Perot Lardner died and his cousin Henry became a rich man. His share of the nine-hundred-thousand-dollar estate was a hundred and eighty thousand, the equivalent of several million in the 1970s. The inheritance came mainly in the form of securities, most of which Mr. Lardner gradually sold and reinvested in mortgages, real estate, especially in Kansas, and later on in more speculative ventures.

The new prosperity was reflected in the rearing of the three youngest children. Each of them had a separate Irish nursemaid and their elementary education was conducted at home, in the beginning by Mrs. Lardner and then, as they advanced to such subjects as Latin and algebra, by a private tutor. The property, enclosed by a rail fence, contained a tennis court, a baseball diamond and a coach house with stables. The three youngest Lardners were not allowed to go outside the yard without a servant or a member of the family, but they were frequently driven around town by the coachman in what was closer to a horse-drawn wagon than the more formal carriage of an equivalent household in the East. They were also taken cruising on the river in the family launch. And selected children from the better Niles families were invited into the enclosure.

Most of their education came disguised as entertainment in the forms of books, music and amateur theatricals. Mrs. Lardner was a part-time writer whose florid poetry and rigidly moral essays appeared in a number of periodicals and were collected into two small books. But her literary tastes were wide enough to include the Brontës and Dickens and other standard novelists of the day; the Lardner library was large and catholic; and my father acquired a good background in classical literature without ever reading anything under compulsion.

Without exposing the reader to samples, I will concede a few degrees of reservation about my grandmother's published work, but by all accounts her musical aptitude was undisputed. She had perfect pitch and could play her own piano arrangement of any piece of music she had heard, both of which gifts my father also possessed. So did his older sister, also called Lena, who later supported herself by giving piano and singing lessons in the Niles house, which became hers after her parents died. The younger Lena, who assisted her mother in Ring's musical education, also succeeded her as organist of Trinity Church and between them they held the title for one hundred and one years. When my Aunt Lena visited us during my childhood and the members of the household would sit in the living room after dinner or on a rainy afternoon, each reading his own book, Lena would silently turn the pages of a musical score.

A good ear for music is often combined with facility in speaking a foreign language properly. Ring never became a linguist (on a German ship once he said "Dry martini" to the bartender and was surprised at, though quickly reconciled to, being served three cocktails at once), but it seems reasonable that the same rule would apply to reproducing the spoken variations of one's own tongue, for which he became famous. At any rate the perfection of his ear and the imperfection of mine sometimes led to his anguish and my chagrin. "That should be a G natural in the treble chord!" he might shout in protest from his upstairs workroom during my piano practice.

Rex and Ring had the job of pumping the organ their mother played in church. They also sang in the choir and on every other occasion, formal or impromptu, that came up. Ring had a natural baritone voice, but in quartet singing, which was one of the great pleasures in his life, he usually took the bass by default. The piano was the primary piece of furniture in any house he ever lived in, but he also liked to teach himself to play other instruments and I can recall a period when he simultaneously owned a saxophone, accordion, French horn and cornet. In the summer of 1927 we rented a house in Lake Placid, New York, that had belonged to Victor Herbert. My father tried to have the piano moved from one room to another and, after the men he engaged for the purpose couldn't get it through the door, learned from the composer's daughter that the house had been built around it. To him that seemed fitting and proper.

The Niles Lardners had not only a piano but a pipe organ in the house, and when Ring began to work out two-piano arrangements for his sister Anne and himself, his mother obligingly bought a second piano.

Mrs. Lardner also went in for charity on an equally lavish scale, and, in the only biography of Ring so far, Donald Elder reports that "her servants were kept busy taking baskets of food all over town"; a third way of getting rid of the income was an exceptionally lavish hospitality that featured musical entertainment and an abundance of food and drink. The latter was supplied by a local saloonkeeper named Billy Casey, who later showed his appreciation in a gesture that is almost inconceivable today. Once a week during her last widowed and penniless years, he had delivered to the house a bottle of whiskey for which no payment was ever asked or made. My grandmother had a degree of dependence on the stuff by that time; she was moved no longer by the hospitable imperative to share that bottle, but by the practical one of making it last the week.

Mrs. Lardner wrote plays for her own and neighboring children to perform; she made the sets and costumes herself and directed as well. Though the youngest, Ring was the first to compete with his mother by writing plays himself, and both dramatists seem to have worked the same vein of broad comedy. You wouldn't think so from reading one of her sentimental poems or turgid essays, but Mrs. Lardner was capable of the same wild nonsense as her three youngest children. What seems a contradiction to us is more a reflection of a time when convention called for moral uplift in anything written for publication by a leading force in the church and the community.

She also had the advanced ideas that children should be raised without punishment, and education so blended with play and fantasy that they were never sure which was which. She viewed the world through such a rosy filter that when the boys started frequenting local saloons in their teens, she preferred to believe

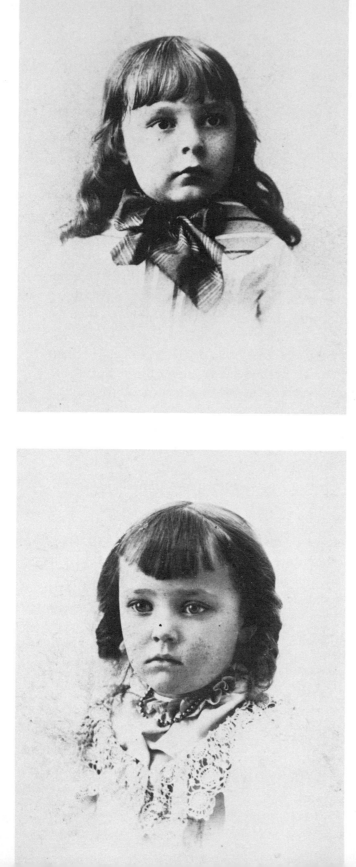

Ring at about five

Ellis at about five

Reginald, Anna and Ringgold in their high school days

Ring when he was courting Ellis

they were putting in extra hours at choir practice.

She was their sole teacher until Ring was ten, when the function was taken over by one Harry Mansfield. It can hardly have been a desirable job since the children regarded the whole idea of formal learning as hilarious and, as Ring later wrote:

> . . . on acct. of it taking him 2 and 1/2 hrs. to get us to stop giggling, why they was only a 1/2 hr. left for work and that was generally always spent on penmanship which was his passion.
>
> The rules of penmanship at that time provided that you had to lean your head over to the left, wind up like they was nobody on second base, and when you finely touched pen to paper, your head followed through from left to right so that when you come to the end of the line, your right ear laid flat on the desk.

Mr. Mansfield didn't notice any special gift in Ring beyond the ability, probably unique at his age level, to list the batting orders of all the twelve baseball teams that then comprised the National League, but all three children were bright and well read, just lacking the formal details of a primary education. This remained true after two years of his tutelage, and when they took entrance examinations for Niles High School, all of them failed. Mrs. Lardner applied as much of her influence as was needed and they were admitted on probation, Rex as a sophomore, Anne and Ring as freshmen. Once in they had no trouble catching up and getting good marks, even though, as Ring wrote later, "Most of we boys done our studying at a 10 × 5 table with six pockets in it."

Ring was born with a deformed foot, which was corrected by an operation in infancy and a metal brace he wore till he was eleven. The fact that he played tackle on the high school football team in his junior year would be an impressive indication of his recovery, except for the supplementary fact that his graduating class consisted of eleven girls and five boys. But he did stop limping after the brace was removed and the only trace of the affliction was that his left leg remained somewhat thinner than his right throughout his life. This was not noticeable on a golf course or, in the days of long white flannels, a tennis court.

He graduated along with his sister three months after his sixteenth birthday, delivering the class poem, of which Elder says, "It was so bad that one can suspect Ring of satirical intentions." This is wishful thinking on the part of an admirer, however. It happens I also wrote a class poem at Andover when I was sixteen, but was not so careless as to save a copy for my children to attack. But my father's was preserved in a scrapbook by his doting sister Lena as it was published in the Niles *Daily Star* at the time, and there is clearly no slyness behind its banality. It's a conventional, unoriginal high school poem, right down to the sprinkling of puns and inside jokes, from the opening:

> Up Learning's ladder, round by round
> We've climbed with many a fall;
> But, through the toil, companionship
> Has made amends for all . . .

all the way through to:

> At last your poet ends his lay,
> He's nothing more to tell,
> But leaves the class of nineteen-one
> With blessing and farewell.

My father published quite a lot of verse in his time, mostly in the column "In the Wake of the News" he conducted in the Chicago *Tribune,* and wrote a good many song lyrics, both to his own tunes and to those of other composers. And starting with the courtship letters to my mother, he wrote hundreds of verses never intended for publication. Birthday and Christmas presents generally came with a rhymed message, like one I remember accompanying a gift of money to my youngest brother:

> Here's wealth for you, David;
> You'll spendid?
> How splendid!
> I feared you would savid.

There was always something special, usually funny, about them, a quality that made them uniquely his, and they gave the impression at least of being practically effortless. But it was an acquired talent and it came rather slowly. What intrigues me about that is the contrast with my brother John, who achieved publication at the age of ten in the column "The Conning Tower" conducted by F.P.A. in the New York *World* with

> Babe Ruth and old Jack Dempsey,
> Both sultans of the swat.
> One hits where other people are,
> The other where they're not.

John was precocious, Dad was not, at least not as a writer. Before he started high school John wrote verse and lyrics that had a more finished, professional quality than Ring's graduation poem or even his first produced "comic opera" two years later. The difference may be explained in part by the physical phenomenon that some intelligent people develop their powers later than others. James Thurber was a striking example of such retardation in a brilliant writing man. But in Ring's case, and in Thurber's, too, conditioning was also an important factor. For Ring, right up until he became, by accident, a newspaperman, writing was a pastime, demanding no more serious attention than pool or serenading Niles girls as part of a quartet. Though his mother hoped he would go into the ministry and his father somehow visualized him as an engineer, Ring in his teens was apparently ambitionless. John, and to varying degrees the rest of us, thought of ourselves as writers at a very early age, set high standards and worked to live up to them. The difference was between an amateur attitude and a semiprofessional one.

My father went to high school from one of the area's wealthiest families and graduated in 1901 into genteel poverty. When Henry Lardner first inherited his fortune from his cousin Perot, he put almost all of it into small mortgage loans. In 1884, for instance, he had sixty-five of these outstanding, ranging from four hundred dollars to five thousand and secured by mortgages on property assessed at several times the amount he lent. The interest at 7 or 8 percent supported the family splendidly, and in a period of rising land values his debtors exerted themselves to pay off their obligations rather than lose their property by foreclosure. In my grandfather's ledger of his transactions, there is only one sheriff's sale recorded.

About 1887 a distinct change took place in his investment practices. In the fall of that year his oldest son William, not yet twenty-three, was already established in Duluth in the banking house of Paine and Lardner, for which Henry Lardner appears to have put up 70 percent of the capital. An increasing proportion of the Lardner fortune was channeled through this firm into Duluth real estate and Western mining claims. In 1889 the Security Bank of Duluth was founded with one hundred thousand dollars' capital, of which Henry Lardner put up thirty-one thousand. My uncle Billy's name was on the stationery as cashier. In 1895 Henry Lardner bought into something called the Duluth Barytes Company, which had a mine on a Canadian island in Lake Superior and a plant in West Superior, Wisconsin. William P. Lardner is listed as secretary and treasurer of the corporation.

Barytes is the same as barite or barium sulfate, "an insoluble white precipitate used in the arts." What the company found insoluble was the problem of bringing the stuff economically from island to mainland. It kept borrowing more money from the bank until the collapse of one precipitated the collapse of the other. McKellar Island remained a useless possession until my grandfather's death in 1914, when it was sold. According to Elder, he liquidated almost all his other property to pay off the creditors of the bank.

Neither my grandfather nor my uncle ever recovered from these calamities. In 1911, before they were married, my father explained to my mother that he sent ten dollars, from a salary of forty-five, home to his parents every week. And Rex contributed the same amount. In later years my father sent his brother Billy a hundred dollars every month, which was reduced to seventy-five in 1932 as part of a general Depression retrenchment. Billy was nineteen years older than Ring and they had never been close. When Ring died at the age of forty-eight in 1933, we sent telegrams in my mother's name ending with the words "No services." Aunt May, Billy's wife, shot back a wire protesting this omission and reminding us of Ring's religious upbringing.

The collapse of the family fortune failed to rouse any dormant ambition in Ring. A small Michigan college, Olivet, offered him a scholarship, but he showed no interest in further education. During the summer after his graduation he went to Chicago, boarded with family friends and landed a job as telephone boy with the McCormick Harvesting Machine Company. Fired after two weeks, he found a similar berth with another concern, and again failed to satisfy his employers. Back in Niles he became a freight hustler for the Michigan Central Railroad at a salary of a dollar a day, once more fell short of expected standards and was fired.

It seems to have been Henry Lardner's solitary decision that both Rex and Ring should go to Armour Institute in Chicago to study mechanical engineering, of which Ring later wrote: "I can't think of no walk in life for which I had more of a natural bent unless it would be hostess at a roller rink . . . and was in accord with the dean when he told me I had progressed as far as I could in the subject"—after one semester.

For a whole year after that he had no job but was deeply involved in an amateur theatrical organization called the American Minstrels, which put on the typical and, by present standards, offensive blackface shows of the period. Ring was a star performer and his favorite numbers were borrowed from the great black vaudevillian Bert Williams, of whom Ring wrote when he died: "In my record book, he leads the league as comedian and can be given no worse than a tie for first place as clown, pantomimist, story-teller, eccentric dancer and a singer of certain types of songs. Otherwise, he was a flop."

On April 14, 1903, at the Niles Opera House, the group produced a show with "A Grand Spectacular First Part" featuring Harry Schmidt, Ring Lardner and Tom Swain, followed by *Zanzibar,* a comic opera in two acts, book by Harry Schmidt, lyrics and music by Ring Lardner, and principal roles performed by Ring Lardner, Tom Swain and Harry Schmidt. It might seem enough to report that my father played a comic black valet who is mistaken for the Sultan of Zanzibar, but complete candor leads me to add that the character's name was Shylock. I have never heard the music, but I have read the book and lyrics, and the best I can say for the defense is that the lyrics stand up a little better than the book.

I don't believe my father gave any serious thought at that time to a professional career in the theater or as a songwriter. Instead, after a year of unemployment he was moved to take a Civil Service examination that qualified him as a postal clerk and mail carrier, and during the ensuing year he served occasional stints as a substitute mailman. (His older brother Harry spent much of his life as a clerk in the Niles Post Office despite a law degree from the University of Michigan. Both Uncle Billy and Uncle Harry had drinking problems but survived, as did Lena and Anne, into their eighties.)

Then, the spring he became nineteen, he went to work for the Niles Gas Company reading meters, trying to collect bills and keeping accounts. This job lasted nearly two years, with his salary going from five to eight dollars a week. But "meters are usually in dark cellars, where my favorite animal, the rat, is wont to dwell. When I entered a cellar and saw a rat reading the meter ahead of me, I accepted his reading and went on to the next house."

Rex had meanwhile become a reporter for the Niles *Daily Sun* and Niles correspondent for the Kalamazoo *Gazette* and South Bend (Indiana) *Tribune.* The editor of the other South Bend paper, the *Times,* came looking for him to offer him a job, and was referred to Ring at the gas office. Ring told him that Rex was bound by a contract, which was true, and that he, Ring, often helped his brother with his work. "This was far from the truth, but I was thinking of those rats." The editor agreed to give him a trial, and thus was launched, my father wrote two years before his death, "a journalistic career so lucrative that I can almost support a day nurse and a night nurse in the hospital to which they have become accustomed."

He worked in South Bend for two years, living at home and traveling across the state line on the "interurban." His title was "sporting editor," but he also covered crime, general news and the theater in a city of fifty thousand people. He started at twelve dollars a week and rose to fifteen, supplemented by a fee of one dollar a game as official scorer of the South Bend baseball club's home games.

His passion for baseball increased with his knowledge of the finer points of the game and no other sport ever approached its place in his affections, though he also became known as a football expert and was fascinated by the strange customs of the boxing world. He liked to watch tennis and to play golf, remained neutral toward horse-racing and apathetic about track and swimming meets. Basketball he regarded with the distaste of a true conservative for a sport that had been invented during his lifetime.

His vacation toward the end of his second year in South Bend coincided with the 1907 World Series between the Chicago Cubs and the Detroit Tigers. At the time, he wrote twenty-five years later, he was "heartbroken . . . because the only girl I could ever care for had announced her engagement to somebody decent," and as a result he wanted to leave home and move on to big-time journalism in Chicago or New York.

The girl referred to seems to have been Ethel Witkowsky of Niles, and their romance had never quite surmounted the obstacle that she was Jewish and both families disapproved. In gauging the weight of the blow to my father and his youthful resilience, it is worth noting that before this vacation trip he had already met my mother and written her at least three letters, in the last of which he called her "my affinity."

In Chicago he met Hugh S. Fullerton, who wrote baseball for the *Examiner,* and they sat together through three Series games there and the final two in Detroit. Fullerton was so impressed with Ring's expertise he pushed him into a vacancy as a sportswriter on the Chicago *Inter-Ocean*. During the courtship correspondence Ring went on to similar jobs with the *Examiner* and the *Tribune*, and a brief stint as managing editor of the *Sporting News* in St. Louis.

2

The founder of the Abbott family in America arrived in this country a whole century before the first Lardner. George Abbott settled in Rowley, Massachusetts, in 1642, and his descendants remained in the northeastern corner of the commonwealth for more than two hundred years, mostly in the town of Andover, where the family homestead was built in 1685. A William Abbott, who enlisted in the Revolution the morning after Paul Revere's ride, married Experience Bixby, who ranks with Freelove Phinney as one of my favorite ancestors. A second William Abbott took his family west in 1862 when his son, Frank Parker Abbott, my grandfather, was four. They settled in Goshen, Indiana, where Frank Abbott grew up and married Jeannette Hascall, who claimed *Mayflower* descent through both her parents.

Even the reader who has skimmed my genealogical data lightly may have noted my inability to find a single ancestral line that wasn't Anglo-Saxon. (Those rich Philadelphia Perots were not lineal relatives; what the Lardners derived from them was money, not blood.) This phenomenon may be reflected in manifestations of character or temperament in my family that might have emerged differently had some Italian or African or Jewish or Slavic been thrown in. The main effect, however, of family backgrounds like the ones I've traced is not the actual inheritance of the descendants but what they assume it to be. A certain sense of where we belonged on the American scene was transmitted to my brothers and me with the knowledge of whom we came from, and it was different from the sense of identity that some other children had, also growing up in well-to-do households in Great Neck, Long Island, in the 1920s, whose parents or grandparents were, for instance, Russian-Jewish immigrants.

The assurance and self-importance we got from our background in my generation were diluted through the comparatively enlightened attitude of our parents toward such matters. The way they had received it in the bosoms of their families, it was a more compelling force to resist. An indication of Waspish attitudes in our American heartland in those days lies in an obituary notice in the Goshen *Democrat* around 1900. An aunt of my grandmother's had gone out to California in 1874 as part of a group that founded the "Indiana Colony" there and later changed its name to Pasadena. Her daughter had married Don Arturo Bandini, who "saw Los Angeles grow from a pueblo" and whose health broke "under the strain of managing the $7,000,000 estate of his sister." Now the newspaper was reporting the death of Don Arturo for his wife's many relatives back in Goshen, and to make clear what manner of man he was, stated: "He was of pure Castilian blood and looked down upon the Mexican as a southern planter despises the negro."

Jeannette Hascall Abbott, the only grandparent I can remember, was a cultured woman, for which her mother rather than her father must have been responsible. For in him the proud New England heritage emerged in the tradition of the Yankee trader rather than that of such contemporaries as Emerson and Thoreau. Arriving in Goshen in 1836 at the age of twenty-four, Chauncey Hascall was at first partner in a tavern and then established himself in "the general mercantile business." Almost all I know of him is from a flamboyant ad in the *Democrat* for May 15, 1850, which is headlined "OLD HASCALL FOREVER!" and offers "direct from New York, by Rail Road one of the most ASTONISHING STOCKS OF GOODS ever brought to this, or any other country."

He was thirty-eight years old then and I don't know how long before that he had taken for himself the name "Old Hascall," but it is used twenty-one times in the ad, often in a laudatory way. Among the products advertised are bonnets, hats, parasols, salt in barrels, window curtains, paper hangings, horses, wagons, buggies, harness, coffee, windmills ("The only Man in town that keeps a good article of Wind-Mills is Old Hascall. Morris cant hold a Candle to them"), door locks, pine sash, plaster, iron, nails, glass, boots and shoes, and ready-made clothing. The paragraph of text dealing with this last category reveals a few things about my great-grandfather:

> Let the word go forth, that Old Hascall has got one of the greatest lots of Ready made Clothing ever brought to this place. The people may depend upon every article being made in a workmanlike manner. My clothing is not the miserable trash, that is made and peddled through the country by the Jews. Come and see for yourselves.

Having become quite rich through the store and Goshen real estate, Chauncey Hascall lost his fortune as a railroad contractor and spent the last years of his life in the home of his daughter and son-in-law (my grandparents) in East Chicago, where they had moved for business reasons. My mother was thus exposed to him till about the age of seven. Nearly fifty years later, despite a pretty good record of freedom from most of the vulgar prejudices, she said to my first wife Silvia, discussing the price of a piece of furniture they had just looked at: "I think you can jew him down." Because Silvia is Jewish and because Mother quickly realized what she had done, she never used the term again, at least in my hearing. It's even possible she had never used it before; but it had been implanted in her at an uncritical age and she could only expunge it after giving voice to it in circumstances that made her consciously aware of its implications.

My father would not have been as likely to commit such an overt indiscretion. He had absorbed a full set of prejudices along with the rest of his background, but his lifelong forays into songwriting and the theater brought him into close professional contact with Jews. Many of the people he most admired in these fields were Jewish, and a few of them became good friends. When we lived in East Hampton, Long Island, he took Ed Wynn to play golf at the Maidstone Club there as his guest. A director of the club asked him not to repeat the offense and he responded by offering his resignation. We boys became aware of the issue only because it temporarily kept us from the tennis courts, and were greatly relieved when it was resolved. I don't know exactly what the settlement was except that my father didn't retreat from his position, so presumably the club did from its.

I can also remember hearing him speak, in a burst of justified indignation, of "that damn Jew Ziegfeld." And his attitude toward blacks was even more contradictory. He had participated in minstrel shows based on racial stereotypes, and even when he wrote lyrics for Bert Williams, he accepted, as Williams himself did in his public image, cliché conventions like the black man's fear of ghosts. He somehow kept on believing, as he had been brought up to believe, that blacks in general were inferior, even after he had come to admire individuals like Williams and Paul Robeson and the composer J. Rosamond Johnson.

I recall the night Johnson, accompanied by a younger black man, a singer, I believe, named Taylor Gordon, came to our house in Great Neck for dinner. I still remember it because of the musical entertainment afterward and because the two Finnish women servants we had at the time quit in Nordic dudgeon over being obliged to serve such conspicuous non-Aryans.

There must have been another occasion on which my parents had black guests because Ellis told her friend "Tee" Wheeler of a different servant reaction from a married couple who functioned as butler and cook. They had no objection to serving such people, the butler assured Ellis; the only distasteful thing would be to sit down with them, and that, fortunately, was the employers' problem.

My Grandfather Abbott was in the lumber business, working his way up to be president of the "only exclusive wholesale manufacturers of walnut in the world." His buyers scoured the country for stands of rare black walnut and his agents sold the finished product (in eight thicknesses ranging from three-eighths of an inch to two inches) to predominantly European customers.

His house in Goshen was "the handsomest and most costly residence in Elkhart County," and when he died in 1912, his life insurance claim was the largest paid in Indiana that year. He was a slight but distinguished-looking man with an impressive mustache and a manner that intimidated the young men who came courting his five daughters. For some five years until he retired from lumber when my mother was about fourteen, to become president of a bank in Goshen, he spent five days a week near the site of his mill in East Chicago, returning to Goshen for family life on weekends only. He also traveled extensively in America, Mexico and Europe, generally in the company of a business partner, almost never with his wife, who had ten pregnancies and eight surviving children to console her during his absences.

The children were obliged to say their prayers every night and sat each Sunday with their mother in a select pew down front in the Presbyterian church, to which their father contributed money but never his own presence. Religion, including the temperance movement which was strong at the time, was mandatory for women and children, but for himself Mr. Abbott preferred a quiet Sunday at home with his Canadian Club. He was a widely admired man and his children in later life were unanimous in their praise of him.

Jeannette Abbott shared with Lena Lardner the conviction that her children were better off at home with their friends visiting them than the other way around. Accordingly, the number of people who sat down to dinner, which was fourteen with just the family, including a grandmother, two maiden aunts and a seamstress in residence, might be expanded well beyond that. But nothing seemed to disturb Mrs. Abbott's serenity, to which the deafness that came to her as a young woman undoubtedly contributed. A walnut buyer from Europe, whom Mr. Abbott brought home as a surprise guest for lunch, congratulated him on his wife. The children all had sniffles and the little ones were sobbing and complaining, and clearly it was not a proper time to have a guest. But, the visitor told my grandfather approvingly, "your wife never apologized for anything."

She maintained her faith and serenity to the end. Just before she died in Indianapolis in 1926 at the age of seventy-three, lying in a plaster cast on a hospital bed, she wrote:

> When the sun of life is low
> And the shadows longer creep,
> Say for me before I go,
> Now I lay me down to sleep.
>
> I am at the journey's end,
> Nothing more to give or keep,
> Nothing more to make or mend,
> Now I lay me down to sleep.

Both my parents, from their own accounts and all the supporting evidence I can muster, had extremely happy childhoods, which doesn't qualify as a coincidence when you consider how well-off both families were and how comfortable and propitious American affluence was in the last years of the nineteenth century. Family ties remained very close, Ring's with his closest siblings, Rex and Anne, and Ellis's with all four sisters and three brothers. The Abbotts communicated with each other for several decades by means of a round-robin letter to which each added his or her separate news for the benefit of all. The seven-bedroom summer home their parents had established at Lake Wawasee continued to be a collective vacation resort, especially for the branches of the family that lived in Chicago, Detroit, Indianapolis and Goshen. On the occasion of my maternal grandmother's seventieth birthday in 1923, more than thirty of us from the two succeeding generations assembled there—six, not counting our nurse, in the Lardner delegation alone, and we came all the way from Great Neck. All the grandsons slept in the hayloft above the stables.

Jeannette Hascall Abbott as a
young woman in the 1880s

"Do you know the Abbott
children?" (Ellis, second
from right)

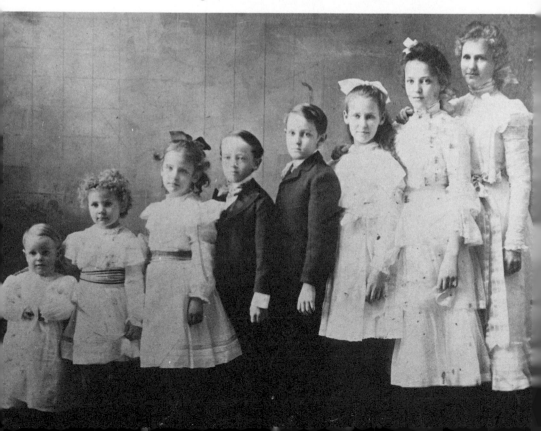

Ellis, second oldest of the Abbott children who survived to maturity, was a notably pretty and popular girl with the easy self-assurance that those qualities bring. She was valued in her family for her ability to keep the younger children entertained and for her equable disposition. Schoolwork came easily to her, especially mathematics and science, her only academic failing being an inability to spell—a weakness that lasted all her life and created a bond between her and Scott Fitzgerald when the two couples were friends in Great Neck. Like Scott, Ellis was an omnivorous reader, but in both cases constant exposure to even quite simple words on the printed page failed to correct the way they saw those words when they came to write them out. For my mother, the block resulted in the phenomenon that while she was extraordinarily good at solving puzzles, including verbal ones like crosswords, with or without diagrams, double crostics, cryptograms and letter divisions, all of which required a combination of vocabulary and intuitive perception, she would often abandon one in frustration after having done 95 percent of the work in record time. In almost every case it would turn out she couldn't complete her solution because at some earlier point in the process she had misspelled an ordinary word.

From childhood on everyone felt she was very bright but not really an intellectual; in her priorities, right after basic moral principles and consideration for others came getting as much fun as possible out of living. Her father's teaching that money and social prestige didn't make her better than anyone else had its effect, but there was nothing directly contradictory in devoting most of your attention to parties, clothes and how you were doing in the "beau" department.

More serious-minded people often came away with the feeling that there was greater potential depth behind her beauty than she allowed herself to presume. After Maxwell Perkins of Scribner's came to dinner in Great Neck for the first time, he wrote my father, with whom he was then planning the first volume of Ring's short stories, a letter that appears in a collection of their one-sided (five from Max to every one from Ring) correspondence edited by Clifford Caruthers and published in 1973 under the title *Ring Around Max*. The published version of that letter was drawn like the rest of his from the carbon copies in the files at Scribner's, but I recently came across the original, which contains this handwritten postscript:

> Ask Mrs. Lardner to read in War & Peace, Part XIV, chaps 3, 4, 5, 6, 7, 8, 9, 10 & 11. She can easily do it in an hour. It's a separate episode & though it does not reveal the ideas of the book, to speak of, it does show its quality.

Perkins was trying to break down a resistance she, like many others who have found it formidable to contemplate, had expressed to reading the book. He had learned how much she loved to read but that she was haphazard about it, and he wanted to broaden her horizons. It was an impulse she often provoked in the (usually masculine) erudite.

After Ellis's third year at Goshen High, the Abbotts sent her along with her older sister, Ruby, to Rogers Hall, a girls' school in Lowell, Massachusetts, a few miles from the old family homestead in Andover. Ruby decided the only higher education that interested her was of a musical sort, but Ellis, who did very well at Rogers Hall, reporting a grade of 98 in geometry, went on to Smith College in the fall of 1905, where she was succeeded by two of her sisters, an unusual record at that stage of higher education for women.

She had a successful four years there, socially and academically, graduating in 1909 as "one of the honor scholars of the whole class," to quote a friend's letter of congratulation. Then she found herself in the anomaly that faced women graduates in general and contributed in her case to the uncertainty of her response to Ring's pursuit. Despite the degree the pressure was still there to assume the conventional female role in society; when Ellis did finally announce her engagement (after starting the teaching job at Culver), a classmate perched on the horns of the same dilemma wrote:

. . . Now that your future is settled we hope you will do something for your more unfortunate co-mates. Life is very, very gay here at present though nothing doing in the matrimonial line. Dear Ellis, I fear in a few years you will be blushing for your number of old girl friends. You must be delightfully happy. I can imagine nothing more inspiring than having found out that you are really in love. You are particularly fortunate to have had considerable experience with men. [The phrase as used here might be applied to a junior high school student today.] Mr. "Ringlets" (I never knew his legal title) may consider himself a most fortunate individual (he no doubt does.) And Ellis, be thankful you are procuring someone with *brains* besides his other attractions. We poor women who are carrying around a college education in St. Louis are having the devil of a time with men, they are such ignorant and prejudiced creatures. . . . What kind of a job have you? Do you think it could be handed down to me? I just can't hang around here next year and I haven't the price for Europe. . . .

Ellis and Ring were introduced to each other in July, 1907, at one Billy Beeson's house on the St. Joseph River in Niles by Wilma Johnson, who had been a close friend of Ellis in Goshen before moving with her parents to Niles, where she became a close friend of Ring and the other young Lardners. Wilma, known to Ellis as "Johnny" and to Ring as "Ginnie" from "Ginseng," a corruption of "Johnson," was also the girl to whom Ring wrote the letters I heard of for the first time in 1972. There is evidence besides that he wrote a number of letters in the same period to Helen Hawks of Goshen, Ruby Abbott's closest friend. The letters to Wilma contain much the same sort of verse and nonsense as the ones to Ellis, but not the occasional lapses into romantic entreaty; in fact, his pursuit of Ellis is a frequent topic.

Without any further facts or insight into my father's feelings at the time, I can only submit the opinion of the only surviving eyewitness, Ruby (Abbott) Hendry, who became ninety in 1975, that each of the others, Wilma and Helen, privately hoped Ring's affections would turn to her. And it's possible that he was consciously or unconsciously preparing for such an eventuality. In any case the way he put it to Ellis was:

> The first time that I cast my eyes upon young Ellis fair,
> I thought: "It's my affinity who's seated over there."

They exchanged few words at that first meeting, but the following weekend Ellis, Ruby and Helen Hawks all came to Niles to visit Wilma, and Ring saw Ellis twice, though not without competition. There was another weekend at Wilma's a few weeks later, and then just before Ellis left for Northampton and her junior year, a picnic at the dam in Goshen.

Apparently he found he could make her laugh and capitalized on that talent. He called her "Rabbit" or "Rabbits," using the two interchangeably in his letters, the first couple of which were simply elaborate puns he had thought up since he saw her. The very first words he wrote her, to Northampton, were:

Esteemed Rabbit;
    I used to know a man named Master and we called him Massa for short. One day we all went into the shop and I ordered some cinnamon gum. The girl said "You don't want it for yourself, do you?" I said "No, but Massachusetts."

She answered, in a postcard addressed to Ringling's Circus in care of him in Niles: "May the Rabbit perform in your circus?" and he responded to that with another pun and: "The rabbit well knows that Ringling has an option and that she must join his circus whenever he wants her." His third communication was a long poem about their acquaintanceship to date, from which I have quoted the "my affinity" couplet.

From the start and for the first year and a half they were writing each other, Ellis seems to have been both flattered and disturbed by the intensity of his emotional commitment. She expressed her appreciation of that first poem while pointing out that "it's very difficult to carry on a correspondence with such a clever person when one isn't born clever," and in a later letter, "You may have a fertile enough brain to think of a wonderful new poem each time but believe me, mine is not fertile enought to coin a new adjective to fit each new one so don't expect it.''

A month after that she failed emphatically to see the point of a joke he devised with Wilma, whom he had seen at Lake Forest, Illinois, where she was going to college and he was covering the Carlisle Indians in training for a football game with the University of Chicago. The two of them separately, on the same day, sent Ellis the same poem, written by Ring, about their afternoon together, and thereby offended Ellis so much she told him, ''Don't do it again and if you write me any more poetry I'm going to rebel and never answer your letters as long as I live.'' But she had begun the letter with ''You are the sixth this evening —so don't be overcome by anything I may happen to write as I am unaccountable'' and continued it in a quite friendly fashion to ''Ever sincerely yours, Ellis.''

He answered on December 5:

Dear Rabbits,

In the happy past, I often boasted to myself thus:

However harshly I may be used by others, the Rabbit is incapable of a deliberate attempt to hurt my much-abused feelings.

Vain boast—the Rabbit, with premeditated malice, ridicules my poetry to my very face and requests that I burden her with it no longer. All right, Rabbit; if you should ask me on bended knee to ship you more of my inimitable verses, I will refuse you with a curse in my throat and sneer in my ear.

To Wilma he confided: ''What the Rabbit handed you was a ripe tangerine compared to the things she heaved at me.''

Ellis apologized for hurting ''your poor abused feelings. I won't *ask* you to write any more poetry but if you should I will read it—really I will, and gladly.'' She went on to say, ''Wilma wrote me about your gay and happy meeting in Lake Forest. I envy you both. And was that not prettily said?''

Ten days later, in mid-December, he received an invitation to a Christmas holiday dance in Goshen, of which she was one of the hostesses, but he didn't go. He was not a dancer and always

35

avoided competing in that area. He sent her a box of candy for Christmas, and she said: "It was kind of you to remember me though I am just the least little, *just the least little* afraid that you thought—well, that you thought—that's all." To which he replied: "I will admit that I did think and still do think you were and are a little—a little—my innate shyness prevents me from telling you what."

They did see each other at least once during that vacation, and she referred to the occasion and, apparently, another Christmas present before she went back to Smith. It was the first letter with the salutation "Dear Ring" and she said: "I tried to thank you for my Christmas present but found it difficult. You know that I think it was lovely and I do appreciate it, don't you, but you shouldn't have given it to me, really."

From Northampton she reversed her earlier stand entirely: "Won't you please write some poetry? It was only in a fit of rashness that I asked you not to and I really pine and yearn for more—really, truly I do. I did not mean at all that I would not write you because I would, you know I would. . . ."

Instead of recognizing that for the considerable progress it was, he was soon offering her an out: "We will now play truth. Didn't you wish just a little that I had written more awful poetry when you told me not to so you really could carry out your threat?" And he went on to speculate that "one Ellis Rabbit was weary of her bargain." Her reaction was: "Now I wonder—if a man takes me to a dance and asks me if I am tired and want to go home, I always have a lurking suspicion that he wants to go home himself. I never do."

Once that was cleared away she was full of admiration for the new verses he sent her, speaking of his "genius" and his reaching "the giddy pinnacle of fame." Despite her admiration for Browning, she wrote, he "put Pippa on the shelf." And then, in a complete switch from all her protestations of inferiority, she took him on in direct competition. He had sent her "a Guide for his genial Correspondents (With Carbon Copies)" under the title "The Route of Ringlets," giving the addresses where he could be reached as he traveled with the White Sox during their preseason schedule. It began:

> On March 18 young Lardner'll go
> Down to the city of N. O.
> New Orleans is the city's name,
> A city not unknown to fame.

Ellis came back with "The Run of the Rabbit":

> The Rabbit thanks the Ringlets kind
> For thus enlightening her mind,
> And she would like to do the same
> For one who's long been known to fame
> The twenty-fifth of March, dear sir,
> Northampton sees the last of her. . . .

"Ringlets" was the name signed to all his letters to Ellis and to Wilma during this period. The name "Ring" has a tendency to make people improvise variations. My father addressed a verse to me in his column on my first birthday:

> When you are nicknamed Ringworm by the humorists and wits;
> When people pun about you till they drive you into fits;
> When funny folk say "Ring, ring off," until they make you ill;
> Remember that your poor old dad tried hard to name you Bill.

I think he used "Ringlets" because it had an ironic quality in view of the fact that he started to lose his hair early—to a considerable extent by the time of his marriage at twenty-six. His outstanding physical feature, however, was his height, which was a shade over six feet two, but that, like most statistics of the era, has to be adjusted to current standards.

Money, for instance. When Ring was born in 1885, his father was worth something over two hundred thousand dollars, which made him an indisputably rich man. When Ring died in 1933, Ellis was left with approximately the same sum in life insurance; it was still, in the midst of the Depression, a substantial amount; she lived comfortably on the income while her holdings actually increased in value. If I were to leave two hundred thousand

37

dollars in the 1970s to be shared by five children, they could pay the taxes, take their families on a round-the-world cruise and return to the status quo.

Even a person's age is a variable statistic. On the occasion of my oldest son's thirty-fifth birthday in 1973, I read aloud my father's "Symptoms of Being 35," and even after we had discounted the exaggerations for comic effect, it was clear that Ring Lardner in 1920 and Peter Lardner, after having lived the same number of years a half-century later, were not really at the same stage of life.

So it is with the figure "six feet two." You even see women that height nowadays, but they were such a rarity when I was a boy that after a visit from one to our house in East Hampton, my father's reaction was: "First time I ever saw a woman's nostrils." In his baseball days he traveled with either the White Sox or the Cubs for five consecutive seasons and enjoyed most of his waking hours, but sleeping in the confines of a Pullman berth was more often wish than reality. The players didn't have that problem because, with rare exceptions, they were shorter men. Most of the men on a baseball team today, however, would have Ring's trouble with a Pullman berth; for our basketball or even football teams, they would have to design completely new cars.

So to see Ring as people looked at him then, you have to think of him as about six feet five—a lean six feet five for most of his adult life. His hair was black, his eyes dark brown, gentle and unusually large, with heavy dark brows, his nose so impressively aquiline that when Bob Davis, a well-known columnist and photographer of the twenties, did a portrait of him, he captioned it "The look of eagles." Most descriptions of him emphasize that he was never seen to laugh; what is literally true is that he never laughed at his own jokes and he applied high standards to other people's comedy. But he did laugh at people who amused him: his sister Anne pre-eminently, his children most of the time, and some of the professionals he appreciated like Ed Wynn, W. C. Fields, Bobby Clark and Joe Cook.

Ellis was a full foot shorter, small-waisted, wide-hipped, medium-breasted. Her hair was brown, her eyes blue, her complexion light. She had a small, straight nose and a full mouth. Her hands were small, her feet even smaller, and by about the time I was born, even people outside the family could observe that she had well-turned ankles. Ten years later, when hemlines had risen a startling twelve inches, it became public knowledge that she had shapely legs and liked to display them in black silk stockings. She laughed easily and her voice had a vibrant quality that added interest to whatever she said. Intended or not, she had a smile and a way of walking that men found provocative. She preferred living with her nearsightedness to wearing her glasses.

A letter she wrote Mrs. Abbott in May, 1908, is worth quoting in full because it gives a sense of the person she was a month after her twenty-first birthday and of what it was like at a college for young ladies:

Dearest Mother—

Now the Prom is all over and I will begin at the beginning and tell you all about it. In the first place my dress came all right Monday and was *perfectly beautiful.* I can't conceive anything lovelier and it fits like a dream. I was so happy about it and liked it even better than Julia's which is saying a great deal. All my things have been so satisfactory this spring.

I don't remember whether I told that I had invited Loring Hoover or not. Well, I did and he accepted with alacrity. He is at Yale now and turned out to be so much older and more self-possessed and nicer all around than he used to be that I was very pleased with him.

Julia had a man from Boston Tech whom I have met several times and like very well; Helen Gibson had a man from West Newton whom I knew and liked, and Ruth Magee (a cousin of Monk Magee's at Wawasee) had Helen's brother who is at Dartmouth. The eight of us played together all the time and it was very nice for me as I knew all of the men as well as the girls.

They all came Wednesday noon but didn't come up to the house till about two thirty. First we all went down to the Vaudette for a little excitement and all joined in the chorus of the illustrated song. Then we went over to the reception in the orchard. I wore my new white suit and hat (with Florence's blue plume). The apple blossoms were all out and the girls looked so beautiful in their bright fluffy clothes and the men in their white flannels.

All the other classes go to the orchard tea too tho' only the juniors have men. The other girls all carry kodaks and nearly drive you crazy trying to take pictures of you with the men. After the tea we came back and had supper on the porch. The freshmen served us and the porch was all beautifully fixed for the occasion. The freshmen are so nice. All during the Prom time they help you dress, and make your beds and put away your things for you.

Then after supper we all went up and dressed for the Prom. Of course it was wonderful and we had a beautiful time. They lay canvas all down through the trees and around that part of the campus with a row of Japanese lanterns on each side where we can walk between dances and not spoil our dresses.

Thursday we had planned to drive all day and have a picnic—(the juniors have a Holiday that day)—Well, you can imagine how distraught we were when we woke up and found it a cold, rainy day. We decided we would not be disappointed, however, and so we found a place where we could eat our lunch (at a friend of one of the girls) and drove out in the rain. We all wore sweaters with rubber coats and hats over them and had more fun than as if it hadn't rained. Julia and Mr. Sloss and Loring and I went in one double carriage and the other two couples in single carriages. On the way home Loring was driving and Julia discovered a funny little mountain road. So they decided we should go that way tho' they hadn't any idea where it went. It was a road that would have delighted father's heart only a little more so. We went around one hill seven times I do believe and through a million deep puddles. However we did reach home in time to go down to Boydens for dinner. After dinner we went to see the Amherst dramatic club give "The Taming of the Shrew" which was lots of fun. We expected the men to go that night but in the middle of the performance they decided to stay over till the next morning—all but Helen's man who had to go at 11:20 that night. So they came up the next morning and we went canoeing till twelve when we sent the men down town while we went to a class. Julia's man went at 12:02 but in the meantime Loring had decided to stay till 8:00 with Stewart Gibson, though as he said "it took a lot of nerve to stay when he wasn't urged."

40

In the afternoon we went over to Amherst to the Amherst, Princeton baseball game which was very close and exciting. Amherst beat which was very unexpected so they had a grand bonfire and celebration in the evening. Stewart went at eight but Loring decided once more not to go till 11:30 so we went over to Amherst to the celebration. I think he went that night at last as I have not seen him since. He really was very nice though and I was glad to have him stay.

This has been a long letter all about the Prom and I must write some others. If I have forgotten anything I'll write tomorrow—Ruby comes at five tomorrow and I can scarcely wait to see her—

> Love to all the family
> Ellis

Her account of the same event to Ring was in its entirety: "Last week we had our wonderful Junior Prom and we're all still in the process of recovering."

He was working for the Chicago *Examiner* now, covering the league-leading White Sox both at home and on the road, but he somehow learned more details of the prom weekend from another source and made frantic efforts to arrange a meeting at the railroad station in Goshen, which was a stop on the New York Central. But his plan was foiled the one time it looked feasible before she went off to Lake Wawasee, which was less accessible. So he wrote about what he had heard, first in prose, as a sort of casual afterthought to a letter:

> Oh, yes, I was told by a small bug that you came home from Northampton minus a vital organ to wit, your heart; so I will know what's the matter if you haven't the heart to write me any more. But I wish you would relate every detail of the romance to me. Talk to me as you would to your attorney. I can advise you.

Given a choice between breaking off the correspondence or confiding in him, Ellis accepted neither: "You must live in a dreadfully buggy place but don't trust those bugs—they are not safe. You see, my heart is a much-traveled organ and I think it is now in Chicago."

Instead of interpreting the Chicago reference as favorable to him and leaving it at that, he renewed the attack in verse:

What, Rabbits have come home to roost?
Is this what you would tell us?
A full-fledged senior now is she,
But still heart-whole and fancy free,
This girl entitled Ellis?

Why, no, she brought her trunk back home,
Its each and every part.
Then what was it she left behind?
Her fertile brain, her brilliant mind?
No, just her Goshen heart.

Far East of here she left her heart;
Is that what you would tell us?
Ah, rather had she left her shoes,
Her powder rag, the gum she chews,
This most forgetful Ellis.

What will she do without her heart?
Why that no one can tell us.
And least of all young Ringlets tall,
Why, no, he cannot tell at all,
So peeved is he and jealous.

We've lived full twenty years and more
And nothing e'er befell us
That stung so much as this same news
That she her Goshen heart did lose;
Is't true? Come, tell us, Ellis.

Though eight months went by that year without their seeing each other and he failed to reach her on the telephone the one time she was in Goshen during the summer (there presumably was no phone at the Wawasee house), he finally accepted her reassurances and wrote in August from the team's New York hotel:

Dear Rabbit;

You shall have all the prose (meaning blank`verse) you want. This, however, is merely a date-maker. Will 1:30 P.M., Friday, September 4th, at entrance to Marshall Field's on State Street, nearest Washington Street, do? If not, please respond with a querulous explanation.

Ringlets

As always, the personal contact advanced their relationship considerably. He took her to a White Sox game and a theater, and she wrote afterward, "Even if you are a bold, wicked man you were very, very nice to me in Chicago." Which prompted him to begin his answer:

> Cheered in spirit by your missive, cute and kind,
> And by the picture which accomp'nied it . . .

And he began one letter "Love of my Life," then reverted in the next to the conventional "Dear Rabbit."

He cared about the White Sox, among whom he was known as "Old Owl Eyes," and was distressed when the team lost the pennant on the last day of the season. But there were two other events at the beginning of autumn that pleased him besides the improvement of his standing with Ellis. One was his move from the *Examiner* to the *Tribune,* the other Anne's marriage to a colleague, Richard G. Tobin. Tobin and Ring had roomed together when they both worked for the *Inter-Ocean,* and Ring had brought his friend home to Niles to meet his sister. So he happily served as best man at the wedding. Tobin acquired two other Lardners along with his bride: Ring and Rex became part of a *ménage à quatre* that lasted two years.

Back at Smith, Ellis wrote in November:

> I just came from a class where we were requested to give a list of the six great contemporary authors and tell why we ranked them as great. I included in my list among others such as George Meredith, Henry James, Kipling, etc., Ring Lardner, but when it came to

telling why I thought he was a classic, I didn't know. Do you suppose you can help me out?

Ring, unpublished except as a sports reporter, had no comment on this fantasy. Instead, he wrote in his next letter: "And remember, Rabbit, leap year is drawing to a close. Remember, I am as shy as a kitten but ready and eager to jump at an opportunity when it is presented in the right spirit." To which Ellis replied: "I am deeply indebted to you for your suggestion or rather caution concerning leap year. Perhaps if you would tell me what the right spirit is I might see that someone presented you with the required opportunity."

His besetting frustration continued to be the difficulty of getting together with her. His change of employers lost him the Christmas vacation he had been counting on to coincide with hers from college. But he still made arrangements to get to Niles on the one evening Wilma was having a party to which Ellis was also invited. When he phoned, however, to verify the date, he found it had been advanced to the previous night and Ellis was already on her way back to Goshen, a fatal twenty-five miles farther away from Chicago. And then just before she returned to Northampton an elaborate plan to combine a visit to Goshen with a mission to Cincinnati for the paper collapsed at the last minute. Without such a contrivance the mechanics of conforming a two-hundred-mile round trip to a railroad timetable on one day off a week were just about unmanageable.

They both remarked on how often they had expected or hoped to meet and been thwarted, and Ellis wrote in April, 1909: "But you know you can't expect to keep up a very exciting correspondence on one conversation a year—and *that* over the telephone." He had said before joining the Cubs for spring training, "Some time before June I probably shall see Bosting and if I do —no, I'll say no more as me hoodoo already is preparing to laugh at me." Then he learned she had come home unexpectedly for spring vacation and that a letter advising him of this had not been forwarded to him in time. And when she tried to console him by saying it didn't matter very much, he was appalled and described, in verse, her letter as "the most disturbing I ever did get." She answered:

> I cannot recall what I wrote in my letter,
> But whatever it was, I know it were better
> Not written at all, for it is a habit,
> I'm forced to admit, that belongs to the Rabbit
> To always be sorry for what she has said,
> For she says the first thing that comes into her head.

Despite his misgivings the Northampton visit did come off in May shortly before her graduation. He devised an elaborate rerouting for himself between a Saturday game in Boston and a Monday one in Brooklyn, earning by many hours' extra train travel a few Sunday ones spent in

> . . . rabbit hunting
> In the valleys of Mass'chusetts.

Again he exploited his hard-won time to the fullest, declaring his love and asking her to marry him. Her answer must have been equivocal because he sent her a contract to sign, pointing out that all baseball players must receive one by May 27 and had till June 1 to agree on terms or be subject to a fine or to suspension and blacklisting for five years. She answered that after careful consideration she had decided not to sign it. "I know a girl who is engaged to two men. She says she is not engaged to them but they are engaged to her. I think the idea is a splendid one."

After reading an autobiographical piece by Robert Louis Stevenson, she wrote: "I was so comforted to find that there was someone else in the world who couldn't spell. . . . Reading Stevenson makes me think of you. There is some curious similarity—I suppose it is genius."

Her misspellings, which I am not reproducing in the quotations, almost always involved vowel sounds that could just as logically be rendered her way as the proper one: "bargin, probible, cheif, deamon, devine, moovies, medecin, smoaking, tem-

The fellow traveler

perment, carnaval, measels, Santa Clause," etc. All these occur in her letters, but she was just as likely to produce other variations, even the correct ones.

From Marblehead, Massachusetts, where she visited her best friend, Helen Gibson, after graduation, she demanded, "Why haven't you sent me a beautiful picture postal card? I might have been dead for all you know. And that is not very attentive for a fiancé even if he is an unaccepted one." He responded, "And please cease reminding me that I am an unaccepted suitor for your hand—I keep remembering it all the time and will keep on suing you until you accept me in sheer desperation or kill me with a cruel look." His letter ended with his schedule for the immediate future:

> July 7—Fort Pitt Hotel, Pittsburgh
> July 8–12—Majestic Hotel, Philadelphia
> July 13–16—Copley Square Hotel, Boston
> July 17–24—Colonial Hotel, New York
> July 24–28—Doubtful
> July 29–31—Washington, Arlington Hotel
> July 31–Aug. 5—Majestic Hotel, Philadelphia
> Aug. 6–Aug. 10—Copley Square Hotel, Boston
> Aug. 11–Aug. 14—Somerset Hotel, New York
> Aug. 15–Aug. 19—Cadillac Hotel, Detroit
> Aug. 21—Home if still alive.

And a pathetic postscript:

> I saw Goshen at 4:30 this morning.

In this new phase of their relationship he started, after Northampton, addressing her by her first name, and her reaction was: "I'm so glad I have been promoted to Ellis—it sounds as if I were somebody rather than something." And she signed the letter "Ellis Nott Rabbit." When he lapsed back to "Dear Rabbit," she insisted on her due, provoking three consecutive salutations from him: "Dear Elsie (I'll call you anything I want to)," "Dear E——e (You can't tell what I'm calling you now)" and

"Dear Ellis (I'll never call you no blanks again)."

Helen Gibson wrote her: "I am simply popping on the Ring question—don't you want him now he's to be had?" Instead, Ellis enrolled in a teaching course at a college in the Goshen area.

At the end of August she announced a visit to Chicago and a desire to be taken to a ball game. They saw each other twice during her stay and he introduced her to the Tobin-Lardner household, writing her afterward that his three housemates had earnestly requested him to marry her forthwith.

In October they visited each other's families for the first time. Ring had arranged a long weekend after the World Series in Detroit and Pittsburgh, and called from Niles to ask if he could come over on the interurban. He came after the evening meal and remained from seven to nine-thirty. Then Anne Tobin invited Ellis to come to Niles of an afternoon, stay for dinner and be escorted home by Ring. Ellis reported the visit to her sister Florence: "Their house is a great big, tumble-down, old-fashioned one. . . . I'm crazy about the whole family. Mrs. Lardner is enormous and queer but very bright and a great talker. Mr. Lardner is an old dear." Ring played the piano for an hour; it was the first time she had heard him and she was impressed.

He got her home to Goshen at eleven-forty and spent the night at the principal hotel, named the Hascall after Mrs. Abbott's family. Next morning Mr. Abbott took them for a drive in his car and Ring caught a streetcar to Elkhart and then a train to Chicago.

Anne Tobin, who was actively promoting the match, invited Ellis to visit them at the apartment the following month, and then to return to Niles during the Christmas holidays, when Ring was finally able to take some accumulated vacation time. The Abbotts were giving a large dance at the Knights of Pythias Hall, and though Ellis begged Ring to come he declined for the third straight year. But for the first time they were able to see each other almost daily over a stretch of time. As it turned out, it was the last such opportunity until they were married a year and a half later.

On one of their Goshen days he renewed his proposal impressively enough so that in my mother's recollection this was the one that counted. The event took place on a sleigh ride—one of the few means at their disposal to achieve the necessary privacy. The problem at the Abbott house, especially during vacations, was that they had five daughters and only three parlors. Ruby says she and her husband-to-be, Robin Hendry, were forced outdoors to get away from her teenage sister Jeannette, who was also smitten with Robin. They paused in front of a livery stable to plight their troth, but when they tried to kiss goodbye back at the house, they were thwarted by the youngest of her three brothers. Florence, the next sister after Ellis, received her proposal from Paull Torrence in a rowboat on Lake Wawasee, and immediately created a problem for him by fainting.

Ring had to return to work sometime in January before a further vacation period in February. Once more Ellis came for a visit; he took her to the theater one evening and the next afternoon, and then, as he recalled it on the first anniversary of the event:

> A year ago tonight, you and I sat on the sofa at Anne's house and I read to you and Anne went out and while she was gone, something happened that made me happier than anyone who ever lived. I kissed you and, after awhile, you kissed me and told me you cared. And Anne came back, but we staid up after she had gone to bed. And we talked and our conversation was the most interesting—to me— I ever took part in.

3

Their letters, when they begin again on February 11, 1910, have changed in mood, style, length and frequency. Both of them tried to maintain a schedule of writing every other day. When they did and he was writing from Chicago, Detroit, Cincinnati, Cleveland, Pittsburgh or St. Louis, each letter was an answer to one mailed by the other the day before. In those days you had to be as far away as the East or Gulf Coast for a letter to be two full days in transit to the Middle West. But no matter how often and how fully each of them wrote, the other reproachfully demanded more.

His letters especially are much longer now. They contain little verse and very few light touches to relieve the theme of his incredible good fortune and his fear that it won't last. On the latter score he had a full-fledged crisis to face almost at once. Within two weeks of her acceptance, after a farewell meeting in Goshen before his departure with the Cubs to spring training at West Baden Springs in southern Indiana, she called for an agonizing reappraisal: "But, honestly, Ring, you know there is something the matter with us . . . neither of us feels very much at ease when we are together. . . . I never can say anything I want to or be the least bit natural. I don't know whether it is because you don't really love me or because I don't love you."

Two days later she had a letter releasing her from her obligation and urging her to reconsider in her own true interest, even

50

though "I feel as if I were writing my own death sentence." He realized, he said, that he was not a "good catch" but a "bad muff"; he believed people get out of life just what they earn; and he knew he had not earned anything as fine as life with her would be. "And never reproach yourself . . . you have given me a taste of more happiness than I ever thought of."

While awaiting her reply during "two long days of hell," Ring effortlessly persuaded rightfielder Frank Schulte, his best friend on the team, to suspend their agreement to be "decent" (sober) during the season, and as a result, "I'm afraid he is one athlete who hasn't profited much by his 'training trip' to West Baden." Then Ellis's decision, when she was faced with the actual prospect of losing him, that "I can't give you up" catapulted Ring right back into decency, the docile Schulte along with him. "It's heaven again now. . . . After your dear letter came this afternoon, I told him the agreement was on again."

The spirit of reform remained very strong in him. On April 12 he made a deal with Artie Hofman, the centerfielder, to give up cigarettes, the one who weakened before New Year's Day to pay a forfeit of a hundred dollars. "We will have to be college boys and have pipes instead." The following night after a poker game "Mr. Tinker, Mr. Evers and I made an agreement not to play poker again this season. Any of us violating the agreement must give fifty dollars to each of the other two." The same evening Hofman and he were each presented with a pipe by Frank Chance, the Cubs' playing manager and end man of the game's most famous double-play combination.

Ellis commented that his reforms seemed to be very wide but she wondered how deep and lasting they were. "I have a suspicion you may not be the one who will get the fifty." He wrote back: "You haven't much faith in my swearing off ability, have you, honey? I will fool you and the rest of them who think it will be up to me to pay the fines. No, dear, the cigarette question was not one of health. A pipe or a cigar is just as bad the way I smoke it. It was entirely a question of money."

He was subject to constant temptation to return to his bad

habits. On April 21: "It develops that Mr. Hofman did not smoke a cigarette. The three people who told me he did were trying to lead me astray, but I refused to fall." And on a rainy May 4 in Pittsburgh: "Mr. Tinker and Mr. Evers tried to get me to call off the poker bet after the game had been called off, but I was firm as an old rock." And at the end of the summer back in Chicago:

A co-worker came up last night and offered to take me out and satiate me with drinks at his expense. That was a rash offer because I have a reputation—an unfortunate one—for infinite capacity. But I was very good—good to him, too—and declined with thanks. I *think,* after the world's series is over, I'll quit altogether, but it's a horribly hard thing to do on this job, especially when one is about to join some celebrating champions.

The Cubs won the pennant but lost the Series, to the Athletics.

I don't know who if anyone paid off the smoking and poker bets. There are obvious gaps in the letters she saved—one of nearly six weeks when he was clearly sustaining his pace of better than one every other day. The only reference to smoking that remains is on October 26, when he reports that Ruby Abbott and he "partook of two ice cream sodas and I smoked two ciga-rettes." A week later he writes:

Sweetheart,—
You mustn't say a word ever about my giving up anything for you. The things I have given up were bad for me, so there was no hardship about it. If you hadn't come into my existence so forcibly and insistently, I might have been dead by now, so you are a big, big help, even if you are a small, small child. Even if I had given up anything worth while, your love would repay me many times over. But it does worry me to think what you are going to sacrifice for me. All I can give you in return is my whole heart, and I don't believe it would bring much in any market. . . .

Among the topics they discussed was religion. Ellis reported that spring that she was teaching a Sunday school class, "and I'm such a little heathen myself that I'm scared to death for fear I'll shatter some of their most particular beliefs." "Even if you are a heathen," he replied, "I think you would be shocked by some of my beliefs, or unbeliefs, so I won't tell you what they are." And then went right ahead and gave her one sample shocker: "I do think, though, the people that wrote the bible never intended to be taken as literally as they have been."

She also revealed that her Sunday school lesson one week was a temperance one and that she had told her little children it took more strength to be a moderate than a total abstainer.

When Ruby's music teacher found and played some music of Ring's and expressed the opinion that he could make a great success as a popular composer, Ellis was impressed and her query brought this answer from Ring:

> About songs—I'm not at all confident of my ability to fool any publisher with one, but I have two or three "in preparation" which I'm going to try to do something with in New York. That's the only place to try anything like that in. The first thing I must do is get some musical comedy actor or actress to say he or she will sing it or them. How am I going to bluff any he or she into saying that?

He went on writing them, though, all his life, sometimes both words and music, sometimes collaborating on the music part, sometimes functioning as lyricist only. During the engagement period he wrote and published three with G. Harris (Doc) White, a pitcher for the White Sox. The titles were "Little Puff of Smoke, Good-Night," "Gee! It's a Wonderful Game" (about baseball) and "My Alpine Rose."

On an overnight visit to the Abbotts' once, he presented Ellis's mother at breakfast with a family song he had written after going upstairs the previous evening. The words and simple melody were neatly set down on his own improvised staff paper:

> Do you know the Abbott children?
> Eight of them there be.
> At least I think there's eight of them,
> That's all I ever see.

Ruby Abbott, Florence Abbott, Frank Abbott, John Abbott,
Ellis Abbott, William Abbott, also Dorothy.
And then again there's Miss Jeannette,
Whom you may think I did forget;
Ah, no, but I'm not certain yet
About the spelling of Jeannette. . . .

Ellis seems to have stipulated, at least in her own mind, that they should wait a full year from the time she agreed to marry him. But when she made some reference to this not long after, he asked: "Dear, will you satisfy my curiosity on one thing? I can't hope to have you before 'the year' is up, I know, but why do you set that time limit?"

She answered:

> I think we both need at least a year to try to learn to know each other a little better. Do you realize how little we really do know each other and how very, very seldom we can see each other in that year? Then, too, haven't you heard that it always takes a girl some time to get ready to be married and you know that I cannot even start until I tell Mother, and we are both going to take time to be as absolutely sure as we think we are now. Is that or are those reasons enough?

Her mother was not a problem at all, but her father was a major reason why they had to wait a good deal longer than a year. There wasn't anything personal about it; Mr. Abbott just didn't want to relinquish Ellis or any of his daughters. Although she was already twenty-three years old, it was considered proper that Ring should put in a formal request for her hand. He did so in writing the first week in July, apologizing for his inability to get time off at the height of the baseball season and make his plea in person.

He said he did not flatter himself that he could be worthy of such a girl and his only justification for asking was that she cared for him in return. He acknowledged that he was not well-off and that it would be better to wait till he had done some more saving. He said his present job took him away from home too much and he intended to have another arrangement after this season. He knew what a sacrifice he was asking from the family but he cared for her so much that he couldn't help asking anyway. He was going to be in Cleveland for one night and then in New York and would appreciate an answer at the Somerset Hotel there.

It didn't come. At first Ellis pleaded her father's health and Ring responded gallantly, "I don't suppose my letter did him any good." But after four weeks, during which Mr. Abbott was well enough to travel on business, she wrote from Wawasee:

> As for Father you know as much about it as I do. He has not said a word to me about us since I came home. He was in the South all last week and when he came home he stayed in Goshen so I've only seen him two or three times myself. I think he doesn't know what to say and so doesn't say anything. I'll try and make him write to you very soon though. You know Father hasn't been well for two or three years and you must be forgiving and not think he is being intentionally unkind. Mother said she knew that he liked you but first needed time to adjust himself to things.

After another few weeks of silence Mrs. Abbott wrote to apologize for her husband and to invite Ring to Goshen at his earliest opportunity. Ring replied hastily that it had never occurred to him to imagine that he was being unjustly treated and that even if Mr. Abbott were not sick, he wouldn't blame him for delaying his answer and that he was *"too* grateful over the prospect of having her at all to want to take her from you before you are ready to let her go."

A week after that Ellis took her father off the hook by accepting the job of teaching the elementary school at Culver for the year beginning in September. That meant more delay and also made it harder for them to see each other because she could get back to Goshen on weekends only, which were Ring's busiest time. He did go to Culver once and complained to Ruby that he had to watch five "cross-eyed" and "generally homely" children aged three to twelve crawl over Ellis and kick her while she murmured, "Aren't they just too sweet to live?"

For Ellis the job was not an alternative to marriage but something she felt she had to experience before marriage. She predicted before she started: "I'm going to be very enthusiastic about teaching those children. It will be *doing* something worthwhile and my brains are getting dreadfully rusty." The work lived up to her expectation, but she promised Ring that since she couldn't get anywhere with her father, she would secure her mother's agreement on a wedding date. By the end of September she told him it would be June.

But there was still the ritual of Mr. Abbott's formal consent. Now this is a scene described to me many years ago by one or both of my parents, and I checked it with two aunts and an uncle before I started this book. Their recollections were substantially the same as what I remembered hearing. Ellis complained to her mother that her father still hadn't answered Ring's letter, and Mrs. Abbott agreed to intercede for her, with the result that Ring was invited to pay a call on Mr. Abbott. Ellis was away at Culver, but some of her siblings and her mother were waiting outside the double doors when the two men emerged from their conference. Mrs. Abbott said she hoped Mr. Lardner could stay for supper, and Mr. Abbott said, "Supper! He's staying all night," and everyone knew the meeting had been a great success.

All of it true, my parents' letters to each other tell me, but lacking one significant detail. The meeting took place on Tuesday, October 25, and the previous Saturday Ellis had been home at a formal luncheon for her girl friends, announcing to them and the press her engagement and June wedding. There was no permission left for her father to grant.

Ring had written her on Friday before what turned out to be the deciding game of the World Series. On the train back from Philadelphia, he told Ellis, a colleague had stated that the life of all newspapermen's wives was hard and that of a baseball writer's wife particularly so. "I realize he is right and I feel sorry for poor little Ellis but perhaps some day I will be something different, although it doesn't look as if I could." If that was meant to discourage her, it was too late. It reached her the day of the announcement. Tuesday morning, having read the engagement story in the *Examiner* and "glad the dark secret is out because it makes it more real," he wrote he was taking the 1:40 P.M. for Goshen "to become better acquainted with members of your family and to see if I approve of them."

If he hadn't been so personally involved, I think Ring would have found it funny that the ritual of consent had to be played out after the public announcement. But perhaps not. Both he and my Grandfather Abbott were conservatives (and Republicans) and may have felt an obligation to perform their roles in a ceremony that was already becoming old-fashioned.

The best testimony on what went on below the surface of relationships should come from those closest to the principals. Florence Abbott, then a senior at Smith, reacted to word of the engagement party with: "Won't you *please* write me more about it? What girls were there Saturday, how did they take it, were they surprised, especially Helen Hawks—When did Wilma hear it and what did she say and what does Father say if anything?"

Ellis was rapturous in her expressions of love during the succeeding weeks. They contrived a few opportunities to see each other and that always intensified her feelings. The only issue between them was the Christmas dance, which Ring was trying to duck for the fourth time. Now, Ellis insisted, even if he didn't dance at all, he had to put in an appearance and be introduced to Goshen society.

He won that argument the only way he could have—by taking a job in St. Louis. Actually, the only aspects of the change that bothered him were not being able to see Ellis at all and losing his accumulated time off. "I wish they had waited till after my vacation to offer me this wonderful job," he wrote.

There were two wonderful things about it. From a baseball reporter he was to become *the* editor of a newspaper, the *Sporting News,* one of a chain of specialized weeklies. And his salary went from thirty-five to fifty dollars a week.

These figures have no meaning for wage-earners in the present inflation. But I was taken aback when I read them to find he was earning that much. When I went to work for a New York newspaper in 1935, my salary was twenty-five dollars despite a 40 percent rise in the cost of living in the intervening quarter of a century.

His bosses on the *Tribune* promised to hold his job open for two months and his colleagues gave him a send-off which he used much later in the play *June Moon:*

> I'm glad you didn't hear my speech at the "banquet" last night. They gave me a traveling bag and I had to thank them for it. It was awful. But I was all swelled up on myself because their efforts failed to knock me off the water wagon.

Ellis said in reply, "I think if you stood the rest of that banquet —I've read the menu—you must be strapped to your seat on the wagon." But her reaction to his statement "I intend to retire at 9:30 every night, and arise at 6:45" was skeptical and additionally disconcerting because it was blended with a glimpse of her social life at Culver:

> My sweetheart, I must hurry and write this now because Captain Willhite is coming over in a little while to show me his new books. I haven't seen him since Sunday. You wouldn't know Culver. I went to another party this afternoon, the fourth in nine days. . . . I would like to make a bet with you on how long you'd spend your evenings alone and go to bed at 9:30.

After his first working day in St. Louis he wrote:

> . . . please promise you will try to love me even if I can't hold this job. It's a lot heavier than I was led to believe and I started wrong today by heartily hating my employers at first sight. . . . What was it I told you about my hours? The real ones are from eight to five-thirty except on Sunday, when there is only about an hour's work.

Shortly he was more reassuring in a letter to her mother:

The first two weeks here, I was a little doubtful of my ability to hold the job. I always forget that a new job is lots easier than it looks at first. I guess I'm all right now, and I'm beginning to be glad I made the move, and will be even more glad after June. That was my reason —so I wouldn't have to travel or work nights.

Throughout the month of December, his first in St. Louis, he gave Ellis various details of his monastic life at his boarding house:

I came home to dinner and played the family's accompaniments for awhile. I pretended I was a good sight reader and got away with it because none of them knew the difference. . . .

Tomorrow my trunk is coming with its set of Balzac and from tomorrow night on, I'm going to divide my time—evenings—between him and you, with the piano once in awhile. . . .

At lunchtime I did a very extravagant thing—I ordered a full set of Mark Twain. Cost $25. It will be our first piece of furniture. . . .

A prettier sister of the pretty Southern girl and a young lady named Miss Marshmallow came to supper and I had to play accompaniments for three hours straight. . . .

Everybody has gone out and I've been playing for myself—things I really wanted to play. . . .

If only you can love me almost as much as I love you, life after June will be a million times nicer than I ever thought it could be.

For her part Ellis told him what was going on at the school with remarkable candor or coquettish provocation or perhaps a mixture of the two:

Captain Willhite came over yesterday afternoon and we went for a little walk. Then he came over again in the evening at 7:45 P.M. and stayed until 11:15 P.M. Why he wanted to stay three hours and a half is more than I know unless he wanted a good listener. I was so sleepy I couldn't talk. More than that he offered to go to South Bend with me if I went Friday night and re-check my trunk for me.

But I am not going Friday night. Perhaps that is enough of Captain Willhite.

It was more than enough for Ring, who wrote, "I guessed him right and if he keeps it up I'm going to quit my job and make a quick trip to Indiana." She wrote back:

I guess I'll have to let you win one argument anyway, the one about Captain Willhite. He came over again last night and stayed until 11:45. He brought me a beautiful little book as a "Christmas gift." We had lots of fun until just before he went. I think he forgot for a few minutes and said things he didn't mean to say. I'm awfully sorry about it because we had good times. But don't you think for a minute that I can't manage my own affairs. You stay right where you are. I'm not telling you this because I think I ought to but because I want to and trust you. And besides a pretty girl is much more dangerous than any man and I am jealous.

On December 21 Ring announced a resolution: "Beginning New Year's Day, I'm never going to lie again. I haven't lied to you and I don't intend to, so this pertains only to people in general." And at the end of a very lonesome, trying month, particularly in his relations with his new employers: "Today is the 28th and I've been riding the wagon two calendar months. That's the longest for five years." He reached a climax of virtue on New Year's Eve:

There were thirty-one days in this month, and during it I have written you thirty-one letters, *one every day.* . . . I have not gone outside the door of my boarding house once after supper. . . . I claim this as a world's record for a single gent, in good health, between the ages of twenty and thirty. . . . Tomorrow I will write you a beautiful New Year's poem if I remember it.

He did not remember it. Apparently he went out that night to mail the letter and forgot to come back in. Whatever happened, all three records fell at once. And all he would say to Ellis on January 3 about not having written for two days was:

I won't tell you why my beautiful record was spoiled for a minute or two, because of my New Year's resolution not to lie, and I don't want to tell you the truth. A piece of the truth is that I had been a little too good and something had to break. But everything's all right again now, and I'll try to keep it so.

Far from satisfied, Ellis wrote:

I'm sorry that anything happened but not surprised. One can't begin all over again and succeed—at first. But I think you had better tell me the truth about it. The truth is always better than an imagination let loose, and don't you think perhaps I'll have to know some time? . . . Has it occurred to you that if anything—that could have been helped—can keep you from writing to me for two days *now*, that there is a strong probability of similar events in the future?

To which he said:

The answer is, "No, it hasn't," for there isn't a strong probability nor a bare possibility of similar events in the future. . . . You don't understand, Ellis dear. When I have you I will have *everything I want.* . . . I give you my word, dear, that you'll never, never have occasion to worry about anything like that.

The extent to which Ring's life is a tragedy rests, I believe, on the fact that he believed implicitly in those words. He subscribed to all the moral principles he had grown up by, including the proposition that the love of a good woman could effect a fundamental change in a man. At his family home in Niles, each day began with a religious service and there were two on Sunday, and although Ring gradually withdrew from religious observance, he had a sense of guilt about it: "This was another Sunday morning which didn't find me at church. Bedtime was four o'clock so I guess the Lord will forgive me." Or: "I'm not going to church today because I have been for three Sundays straight. Isn't that a good reason?" Or:

The young man got up early and went to church this morning in order to uphold his record of never having missed a Palm Sunday.

Then he wrote and told his mother about his good deed and sent her a program as evidence.

Eventually he gave up formal adherence entirely. Neither of our parents ever took any of us to a church or Sunday school, and the extent of Ring's religious conviction in my memory is expressed in a piece of paternal counsel to John: "Don't ever kill yourself. You don't know why you've been put here but there's probably a reason and you should fulfill it."

But at twenty-five we have a man whose upbringing was as devout as it was indulgent; who prided himself in his teens that he looked old enough to fool saloonkeepers; without any ambition, fixed or general; drawn to theater, sports and popular music; drifting into the newspaper business when it was still working up to the degree of refinement Hecht and MacArthur portrayed in *The Front Page;* a young man in his fourth season of traveling as much as eight months a year (with spring training and World Series) in solidly masculine and conspicuously uncultured company; a young man, finally, who has never, in his own words, "refrained from doing anything I couldn't afford to do if I wanted to do it. I have been associated with a lot of people who had all the money they needed and spent it crazily, and I, who didn't have any, spent mine just as crazily."

What is expected of this young man—what he expects of himself—is that he will shed all his bad habits, shun all social contact outside his work, and concentrate on strengthening his character for the role of ideal husband. And this during a prolonged period of acute sexual frustration.

A sexual frustration, incidentally, that he will scarcely admit to himself. For the extraordinary fact about Ring is that he has come through all his associations with his extreme prudishness intact. He will not listen to a dirty story and frowns upon off-color language and almost any kind of reference to sex in conversation, literature or song lyrics. And though he will live beyond the sexual revolution and new candor of the 1920s, he will be unaffected by them. My brother Jim and I, about nine and eight years old at the time, had a month's allowance confiscated for introducing the following sidesplitter at the dinner table:

Q: What was the longest slide in the Bible?
A: When Joshua went from Jericho to Jerusalem on his ass.

The allowance was only a dollar apiece, but it covered four or five movies and various other luxuries, and was sorely missed. We were so indoctrinated ourselves, however, that we felt we had been fairly, if a bit severely, treated.

In his obituary piece on Ring for *The New Republic,* Scott Fitzgerald referred to "his odd little crusade in the *New Yorker* against pornographic songs." Those columns were written in 1932, the year before he died, and the oddest thing about them, when you look at the lyrics he was trying to have banished from the airwaves, is that they aren't pornographic at all, even by majority standards of the time. The objectionable feature in every one of them is the same: the countenancing of intimate physical love between persons not licensed by church or state to enjoy such pleasures.

The proposition could be indirect ("Love me tonight," "It would really be a sin not to hold you in my arms") or more overt ("And So to Bed," "Forbidden Love")—they were all denounced as "risqué," "questionable" or "suggestive." Even after a song from a Broadway show, "Let's Put Out the Lights and Go to Bed," was altered to make it acceptable for radio by changing the last word of the title to "Sleep," Ring branded it as "just on the border."

An extreme offender was Allie Wrubel's "As You Desire Me." Ring reprinted the entire refrain in his column to illustrate how far the bounds of decency were being transgressed:

As you desire me,
So shall I come to you,
Howe'er you want me, so shall I be.
Be it forever or be it just a day,
As you desire me, let come what may.
I doubt not but you will do what you will with me;

63

I give myself to you, for you're my Destiny,
And now, come take me, my very soul is yours,
As you desire me, I come to you.

"You can't apply 'suggestive' to this sort of lyric," he wrote, "if you do, you probably call '[Mourning Becomes] Electra' an amusing skit."

The same lyric violated his standards of taste in a whole other respect. " 'I doubt not but' is a phrase I dasn't criticize because a descendant of mine used it in an essay contest at Andover and won $15.00. Of course, he might have been first but for the but."

I was that descendant and it's true I had come in second, but not because of my unthinking use of the common barbarism "There is no doubt but that . . ." That error had eluded a whole committee of English teachers.

"You're saying exactly the opposite of what you mean," my father had explained. "You're saying 'that' is the only thing concerning which there is a doubt." For him the solecism seemed to outweigh whatever merit the rest of my essay might have had. It was one of the few other areas he could be stern about.

His campaign to clean up radio was undertaken more as a matter of conscience, an obligation he could not bypass, than out of any real hope of accomplishing anything. For in his judgment, and it was one that saddened him: "Not more than 2.75% of the Invisible Audience can be morally or mentally hurt by the vulgarities and obscenities they have to listen to, if they listen at all. You can't teach the Red Sox new methods of hitting into double plays."

Edmund Wilson has been quoted as believing that Ring became a prude because of a skirmish with venereal disease as a youth. Conceivably there may have been such an episode; if so, about the only person he might have confided it to was Fitzgerald, who might have passed it on to Wilson. But I strongly doubt it. In any case, Ring's puritanical, almost antisexual attitudes were more deeply rooted than that. For one thing, with some differences in degree, his brothers and sisters shared them.

And so to a large extent did the community they came from. Queen Victoria had no more loyal subjects, morally speaking, than in the proper households of the American Midwest. Episcopalians, Presbyterians, Methodists—whatever their differences, they shared the doctrine that sex outside the framework of marriage was an abomination. Ring's standards were just a more literal and rigid version of the prevailing view.

What, then, about other writers from the same general background who managed to liberate themselves from it? Why didn't Ring do that? The answer has to start with the fact that he didn't want to. He felt no impulse to rebel against existing standards; he liked things the way they were. He was conservative about everything; he didn't see much future for the radio or the talking pictures when they were invented. Hemingway and Fitzgerald were enough younger to be part of the war that produced the lost generation and the jazz age, but by the time America started moving toward intervention in Europe, Ring was a settled family man with three children, more devoted than ever to the status quo.

But there was another difference, perhaps more significant. The two younger writers had ideas about life to sell; they had themselves to sell; they were determined at an early age to make their marks in American literature. Their self-interest lay in change, in the new, in the novel. (I set down this last word with deliberate ambiguity, even before consciously recalling Ring's line: "Mr. Fitzgerald is a novelist; Mrs. Fitzgerald is a novelty.")

Ring on the other hand was a twenty-eight-year-old professional man when he sold his first short story, and it was years after that before he could think of fiction-writing as his main occupation. In the first months of 1911, before his twenty-sixth birthday, when he was in a panic over the possibility of losing Ellis, it seemed more plausible to sell himself as a businessman than as a writer.

He had disliked Charles Spink and his son, publishers of the *Sporting News,* from the start, but determined nevertheless to stick it out there. He began looking for a place to live in after he was married, and when the Chicago *Tribune* reminded him his job there was being held open:

I burned my bridges . . . after the craziest change of mind I ever suffered. . . . I sat down to write and say I would come if certain concessions were made, and, instead, I said there wasn't a chance for me to leave here and it might as well go ahead and get a successor.

Disaster struck a few weeks later, on February 1:

I think I would rather be kicked downstairs than write this letter. . . . It didn't take me all this time to discover Mr. Spink was dishonest. I knew it before I'd been here a month, but I decided to swallow it "for the good of the cause." He did something about a month ago without my knowledge that was against all newspaper rules, but I explained my innocence to the offended person and was believed. Day before yesterday he tried to put over something else, but he told me about it and I kicked. I told him I'd quit if he did it, and he was afraid to have me quit because Ban Johnson, the president of the American League, which is responsible for his paper's success, recommended me. But we had some warm words and I told him I would just as soon work for Jesse James and that I was going to leave very shortly.

He went on to tell her that the following day and again the day after that, he had lunch with Billy Grayson, owner of the Louisville baseball club in the American Association but a resident of St. Louis. Grayson offered him the job of business manager of the ball club and dangled the prospect that they would start a newspaper of their own the following year with Grayson's capital and Ring in full control. The first day Ring declined for the same reason (besides pride) he was reluctant to go back to the *Tribune:* he didn't want to have to travel after his marriage. Grayson came back with an offer of only one trip after June; the club secretary would do the rest of the traveling with the team.

Ring accepted, he told Ellis, subject to her acquiescence. Ellis, who had already adjusted to setting up housekeeping in St. Louis instead of Chicago, switched her sights to Louisville and wired him that anything he did was all right with her. Then she told her father what had happened and wrote a follow-up letter:

On the other hand, Dad thinks a "sporting man" is a "sporting man" and can't change his spots, and that his daughters are delicate and rare things, and that they must not come in contact with that "damned sporting crowd." He is in fact quite strenuously opposed to the Louisville idea.

Ring, who had meanwhile concluded his arrangement with Grayson, was driven to such desperation by this that he positively degraded himself in the argument he addressed directly to Mr. Abbott:

It is a much different thing, in respect to my relation to the ballplayers, from my former job with the *Tribune.* Then it was up to me to mingle with them so that I might know what was going on. In the Louisville proposition, it will be to my interest and the interest of the owner to keep away from everyone but the manager, who, in this case, is one of the most decent men I ever met. You can depend on it, Ellis won't ever have to see a ballplayer or a ball game. She can go to a game when she wants to, but I'm just as much opposed to her being "mixed up" in it as you are. . . . My chief duty is to see that none of his employees, such as his ticket sellers and privilege men, are stealing from him, to oversee things in general, and have his books in such shape that he will know always how he stands.

Ring's image of himself as a bookkeeper was preposterous to anyone who knew him then or later, but it was the only one he had to offer. After dropping the information that Grayson was a fellow lumberman as well as a baseball owner, he wound up his long letter by returning to the main theme: "You needn't be a bit afraid that she will be forced to meet an 'athlete.' I won't let her, but I guess she won't be so anxious that I'll have to 'forbid' it."

I don't know exactly how the problem was resolved because there are no letters during a two-week period in which they were seeing each other. Neither of my parents ever spoke of the crisis in my hearing, it is not mentioned at all in the Elder biography, and I had no knowledge of the whole episode till I read the letters after Mother died. What I do know is that Ring went from St. Louis to Chicago, where he consulted with Rex and Anne, the two members of his family that mattered most to him, and then to Culver, where he picked up Ellis and proceeded to Goshen for the showdown. At some point in that fortnight Hugh Fullerton passed on a job offer he couldn't accept himself to cover baseball for Hearst's Boston *American;* the paper welcomed his recommendation of Ring instead, offering him a salary of forty-five dollars, and Ring somehow sold that to Mr. Abbott as an acceptable compromise.

How did he get around the fact that it was the *Tribune* job all over again, having just argued that that had involved a deplorable degree of contact with the athletes? Was it because everything in Boston, including the ballplayers, seemed more refined to the Abbotts of Andover? Or did the ten dollars a week more than his last reporting job indicate that he was on his way up in the profession?

All I can say is that by the last week in February he was at work on the *American* and writing Ellis daily about his efforts to find a suitable place at a suitable price for them to live come, if it ever would, June 28. His eventual choice was Brookline, which "can't be so horribly swell and exclusive, for four or five employees of the *American* live there. It's a dry town, that's one reason I like it."

Another letter shows how seriously he regarded the recent crisis:

There were times in St. Louis when I felt almost sure I was going to lose you. It wasn't a nice feeling either. There was one night, part of a night, in Goshen, too—you remember—when everything looked hopeless.

His appeals for sympathy because of his sacrifices and because life without her was such "hell" for him brought only this:

I should think you would become so used to hell that you would be cold anywhere else. You seem to be on the most familiar terms with it. Moreover, I have my doubts about poker. If you haven't played yet, you will soon. That is a prophecy.

She continued to write him about the attentions paid her by Willhite and other unmarried officers at Culver, and about the young men she saw on her occasional weekends at home in Goshen, and she admitted that she got a lot of satisfaction from their interest. He came up with a couple of counterploys that were not as directly provocative as hers. From spring training in Augusta, Georgia:

This town is full of pretty girls. I'll take back all I ever said about there being no Southern beauties. I've finally discovered them when I am proof against them.

That spring she raised, hesitantly yet almost as if it were her right to know the answer, a question that was clearly giving her some concern:

It is a very delicate subject but I wish that sometime when you feel very confidential and practical you'd tell me *about*—you needn't be exact if you don't want to—how much our monthly income is going to be. You see, when I'm learning to cook and to sew, etc., I'd like to know what sort of things we can afford to cook, etc. And then of course I'm just naturally curious.

He answered:

Dear, I never feel practical and never confidential while I'm on the water wagon. We'll not wait for one of those moods, because you really have a right to know things. So I'll discuss the "delicate subject" briefly. . . . It's $45 now and still it isn't, and that's the delicate part. My family used to be "well off," but got over it. My father is kept busy paying for insurance and taxes, and he and my mother and Lena have to have something to live on . . . so you see it's up to Rex and me. [Henry Lardner ran for city clerk of Niles about this time but was badly beaten by the Democratic candidate.] Each of us ships home $10. Balance for me—$35. . . . Lena would rather die than ask us (Rex and me) for anything and I guess she thinks I'm going to "stop" when I'm married. But I'm not. R. W. Lardner and company, which is you, now possess about $800. About $200 of this will go for the Goshen furniture and probably $150 or $200 for the furniture we are still to get. Another $200 for my typewriter (which I must have) and for my trousseau etc., and we'll be lucky to have $200 left when June comes. . . . There'll be a pay-day on "Little Puff of Smoke" in July and perhaps something from other things some time. These can be used in helping to pay for a piano.

"Gee! It's a Wonderful Game" was also published during this period by the Remick Company, and one of the letters reports that a quartet sang it in the ball park in Chicago before a game. The indispensability of a typewriter of his own came from his plan, once he was married, to go home after baseball games, write his stories there and have them picked up by a boy at eight o'clock and delivered to the *American* office. There was still no suggestion that he might do any different sort of writing from what he was doing, not one mention even of thinking about an idea for a short story.

Toward the end of March she wrote him:

Another boy has scarlet fever and there is a new case of measles or mumps every day but I've escaped so far and feel just like the spring weather.

We saw pussy willows when we were driving Sunday, and the air is like May. I do wish something would happen about the middle of next month to close school for I have spring fever if I haven't scarlet fever. This is the twenty-first of March—the first day of spring—and next summer—just next summer—I'll be a married woman. I hate to say goodbye to my girlhood—we've had nice times together and when she has gone she can never,

never come back. But I'm going to have a new friend and I know she is going to be even nicer—though I am just a little afraid of her.

It's after school now and time to go.
Your own girl

Before she mailed that she received a letter from him in Augusta, brief and formal, and obviously provoked by the style and content of her last previous one:

Dear Miss Abbott:

I sincerely hope you will enjoy yourself at Captain Stewart's party. There are flirtations that are harmless, but I don't advise you to go very far with a married man.

I was glad to hear from you and to know you were still having good times at Culver. As for me, I don't recall that I ever spent so pleasant a winter. The weather down here is ideal, my friends are most congenial, and the Southern girls are really charming.

I hope you will find time to drop me another line soon.

Sincerely,
Ring W. Lardner

Ellis added a postscript to hers:

Your Sunday letter just came. I wouldn't send this at all if I had time to write another. Perhaps you think you're funny but you're not. If you are going to make fun of my letters I won't write at all. I can find other ways to occupy my time.

Ellis

That was the only sour note struck during these final months of separation. Ellis got her wish: her school was closed in April for the rest of the term because of the epidemics. Ring signed a lease for their future home, sending her a painstakingly neat and precise floor plan with all the dimensions required for rugs and drapes. He acknowledged ambiguously the success of her effort in converting him from made-to-order cigarettes to her own brand, Fatimas; it had saved him money, he said, but "got me in the habit again and I haven't been able to stop it." He also admitted to playing low-stake poker.

At one point he expressed the wish that she would "cease tiring yourself in your wild career around Indiana." The use of that noun in that unfamiliar and completely accurate sense is evidence of Ring's self-education in the language. His fastidious precision in vocabulary, rhetoric, grammar and spelling was part of his preparation for creative writing at a time when he had no thought of undertaking it.

Beginning his last eight weeks of celibacy, he wrote:

On the 23d of May and the first of June, I can buy a drink or two —my last—for the Cubs will be here on the former date and the White Sox on the latter. These occasions will be sort of bachelor luncheons for me, with the advantage that my guests will do part of the buying.

And after the first of these events:

The Cubs have gone and I'm glad of it even if I do like them. It will take me about a week to recover my right mind, but I'm pretty sure that they succeeded in permanently curing my thirst.

His only report of the second one was that "We had a concert down at the White Sox' hotel last night. It was my first pianisting since March, but, believe me, I'm just as good as ever."

Ellis's reaction was mild:

Dear, I'm sorry you were so lonesome—but I'm *not* sorry that you love me more. You know you weren't lonesome while the Cubs were there and I'll bet you didn't even think of me for hours.

On June 21, a couple of days before he started the trip to Goshen, Niles and then Goshen again for the wedding, he wrote his penultimate letter to Ellis Abbott, signing it, with no special emphasis for himself except first billing: "Ringgold Lardner, Horace Nordyke, Irvin Copper, Stewart Gibson, Loring Hoover, Dean Taylor, Ray Lindsay, Fred Hurtz, Harold Fonda, Hugh Newell, Jerry ———, and Old Cap Willhite." It was the total list of her beaus and/or suitors known to him.

The wedding took place at the Abbotts' in Goshen and was reported at length in the Niles *Daily Star:*

The bride was gowned in Japanese hand-embroidered silk, trimmed with real lace, with tulle veil caught with orange blossoms. She carried a bouquet of bride's roses and lilies of the valley, and wore a cameo in antique setting, the gift of the groom.

The bridesmaid [Ruby Abbott] wore pink marquisette over pink satin and carried pink roses.

The ceremony, which was witnessed by 175 guests, was performed in front of a beautiful screen of elderberry blossoms. Roses and hydrangeas were also used effectively.

The color scheme in the dining room was pink and green, where a three-course collation was served by caterers from Toledo.

Beautiful gowns were worn by the guests and the affair was one of the most elaborate ever given in Goshen.

The gifts were numberless and very beautiful, among them being a solid silver vegetable dish from "Doc" White, the noted Sox pitcher, who is a particular friend of the groom; from the Cubs, a 200-piece Haviland set of dishes; from Ban Johnson, Pres. of the American League, a cut glass dish; Chicago *Tribune,* of which the groom was formerly sporting editor [an exaggeration], electric lamp; from Jimmie Callahan, another celebrated baseball man, set of glass-cut tumblers and pitcher.

4

"You never, Ellis, will be happier than the first year you're married. It's all too good to be true." A college classmate, already married, wrote that to her two days before the wedding. It doesn't matter much whether it was what the young woman really felt on the basis of her own experience or just what she thought was the right thing to say. It was a standard expression of the romantic attitude toward marriage, which in the Lardners' case seems to have been fulfilled. Circumstances often separated them during the first year and a half, and the letters they wrote, along with other evidence, indicate an even greater intensity of feeling than during the courtship. My impression is that for many years at least the satisfactions outweighed any disappointments.

I have no revelations to impart about my parents' sex life. It was an unlikely subject of conversation for either of them, especially with their sons. I have to assume that anyone as prudish as my father suffered from repression and guilt about his sexuality, and that that would have made for a problem in the marriage bed, but how serious or long-lasting a one, I have no idea.

My Aunt Ruby says she wondered aloud to Ellis and Ring, after they were engaged, how they could be sure they loved each other when they never kissed, and they obliged her by retiring to a corner and, she was left to presume, kissing each other out of her sight.

Ellis went on living for more than twenty-five years after he died, which brought her into a whole new stage of the liberation of the arts from censorship and of personal behavior from Victorian artificiality. Her standards, not as rigid as Ring's to begin with, broadened but never fast enough to keep up. Her mind and her dignity drew respect from the people around her; her grandchildren restrained their language in her hearing, but they didn't have to be afraid of expressing their ideas, because she was quite ready to discuss what she couldn't bring herself to accept. She exercised her privilege not to finish reading the more explicit of the postwar writers and once she called my attention to a particular book as an example of how sex could be written about without violating her sense of good taste.

The book, a very short one, was *Leave Cancelled* by Nicholas Monsarrat. It deals with a recently married couple trying to make the most of the one night they have left together in wartime London and there is a lot of sex in it without any words that couldn't have been used by Louisa May Alcott; the most graphic bit of dialogue is the bride's: "Glad to have you aboard, sir!" But the most significant thing about it is that it's a paean to married sex, to love-making as one of several binding forces in an exclusive and enduring intimacy.

The only other clue I have in this area is my mother's firm advocacy of twin beds as opposed to a double one, and, in her own case, of separate sleeping rooms for spouses. I am not aware of any scientific study of the question, but my own impression, based on random observation of middle-class homes, is that twin beds came into vogue in the twenties as a symbol of sexual liberation. My generation in the thirties, more concerned with the sensual than the symbolic, rediscovered the pleasures of proximity in the broader confines of queen- and king-size mattresses, which have become increasingly popular since.

I favor bed-sharing myself, for the physical contact and impromptu spirit, but I am also a light sleeper and having been awakened many times by the night noises of a loved one, I long ago conceived the slogan "The same bed but separate rooms." I have yet to find an architect to realize that vision.

Mother was known for her taste in furnishing and decoration, and it was natural for her sons and daughters-in-law to seek her help in the initial stages of homemaking. She invariably recommended single beds and in at least one instance bestowed a pair on the newlyweds without prior consultation. In the three houses she furnished for herself within my memory, averaging more than eight bedrooms apiece including servants' quarters, the only double bed in each establishment was the one in which she slept alone. When in 1952 the pressures of the Hollywood blacklist transformed my present wife Frances and me from Southern California homeowners to nonpaying guests in her Connecticut house, and we moved our twin beds together into a single unit, my mother avoided the view into our room because it was no longer as she had designed it.

The facts of human biology are more slowly absorbed in a family where all the children are the same sex, and the process may have been further retarded for my brothers and me by the fact that we were never aware of our parents' sharing a room, much less a bed. I say "we" and "never" without knowing for sure how much perception John, the oldest, had of the different state of affairs that existed until he was five. Ellis confided to Frances once that she instituted the separate bedrooms in their newly rented house in Evanston, Illinois, while Ring was in France on a brief assignment to cover the war. The impression she left was that it was Ring's drinking habits that led her to make the change.

The apartment Ring had found in Brookline was their home for only four months. Practically as a wedding present he was elevated to sports editor of the *American,* and he welcomed the promotion not only because of the increased prestige and pay, but also because it meant the freedom from travel he had promised Ellis and Mr. Abbott. Although his job in St. Louis had had the grander-sounding title of managing editor, his inherited staff there consisted solely of a typist and a file clerk. In Boston he was supposed to have real executive authority, and he immediately put it to use by importing Rex and another sports reporter, Frank Smith, from Chicago.

Addressing Mrs. Abbott as "Dear Mother II," Ring wrote that he was having the best time of his life, though he worried privately that he was still not making enough money, especially in view of the need for help in Niles. Ellis, who took only a month to become pregnant, applied herself to the new tasks of cooking and cleaning, though neither activity became such an ingrained habit that she couldn't easily abandon it as soon as Ring's income permitted.

That fall he went to New York and Philadelphia to cover the World Series, the one traveling assignment still required of him. After he left town the Hearst management, in a typically abrupt retrenchment, observed the end of the baseball season by firing Rex and Smith. Ring responded to this clear repudiation of his authority by resigning as sports editor but, probably because he needed the week's salary, continuing to cover the Series. In New York, he tried to promote his songs and evidently found some encouragement, for Ellis wrote on October 19:

My Dearest Boy,

I have all my things packed and my ticket bought for New York. Honey, you know that one place is the same as another to me as long as you are there, so you are to do just as you want without thinking whether I'll like it or not, because I'll like it whatever it is. . . . I bought a paper this afternoon and found there was no game. However I saw your name so I know you are still on the paper.

The next day she wrote: "My heart broke when I bought a paper on the way home and found that there was no game today. Is the World Series ever going to end? It looks hopeless." That was after the third consecutive day of rain; there were three more to follow so that an entire week elapsed between the third and fourth games, enabling Christy Mathewson to pitch, and lose, two in a row for the Giants.

In the end Ring couldn't find a job in New York to keep them going while he launched his career as a songwriter. He returned to Boston briefly and, with nothing saved and no other job in prospect, quit the *American,* borrowing money impartially from both Boston baseball clubs to take him and Ellis back to Chicago. (Rex went to a Cleveland paper for a short period.)

The Lardners moved in with the Tobins, who had a son approaching two to support on Dick's thirty-two fifty a week. Unpaid bills from Boston pursued the Lardners, and Anne later recalled that the most dastardly act she ever knew her baby brother to commit was to write "Address unknown" on some of them. The best Ring could do for a job was copyreader on the Chicago *American.* After a couple of months of this, he became a sports reporter for the *Examiner* once again, and was soon back in the old routine of traveling to spring training with the White Sox, this time in Waco, Texas. It was more than a year before he rose again to the salary or the prestige he had had in St. Louis and Boston.

They soon found a small apartment within a block of the Tobins, and so shortly did Rex and his bride, Dora McCarley of Nashville. Ring returned from the road for the new season in April and the birth, at home, of John Abbott Lardner on May 4, 1912. He continued to cover baseball, traveling back and forth across the Northeastern quarter of the United States, and in the fall, football, forming friendships with the outstanding coaches in that sport because he understood the game on a specialist's level close to their own.

While he was away that summer Ellis made her first postmotherhood public appearance at Wilma Johnson's July 7 wedding to Walter Ostrander. She wrote Ring:

> There is so much to tell about Wilma's wedding that I don't know what to leave out. There is one thing I'd like to omit but I'll be good and tell it. There were just a few at the ceremony, which was very short and simple. Wilma looked awfully pretty and Walter awfully scared. . . . Evan was best man and two fraternity brothers of Walter's from Toledo. One of them was the part I'd like to omit because I spent most of the evening with him and we had lots of fun together. You see, it was the first time I had been really dressed up and at a

real function in so long that I couldn't resist the temptation to see if I still could keep anyone interested a few minutes. I wore my wedding dress and I looked very nice and if I were Dora I'd say, "My hair looked beautiful," but I *did* look well for my hair. . . . I love you very much and you don't mind if I flirted just a little, do you, if I tell you about it?

Ring began to attract attention by the individuality of his baseball coverage. With a daily by-line and a tolerant editor, his stories were as apt to be funny as factual; he frequently kidded the home-town players within the terms of an unwritten license they granted him. Even his daily stories often came out in a crude verse form, and on Sundays he had free rein to parody popular songs or fashion primitive couplets about the players:

> A is for Archer, whose first name is Jim.
> An A No. 1 first-class catcher is him;
> As first baseman also this gent has made good;
> He's strong with the bat, which they build out of wood.

That winter, the only one of their first four that Ellis wasn't pregnant, she went with Ring to the White Sox training camp in California, leaving John with her family. While they were gone, Hugh E. Keogh, a friend of Ring's and long-time conductor of a daily column in the sports section of the *Tribune,* died, and Ring was invited to take over the feature, called "In the Wake of the News." Keogh, who filled it mainly with humor and light verse, had a strong following, and Ring was nervously unsure of his ability to hold the readership.

His decision to try it, the effort he put in, and the confidence that grew in him when he found he could do it to his own and his readers' satisfaction—these are some of the known factors at work in the year that changed the direction and style of his whole life and the lives of his family. Between that spring of 1913 and the following one, a sports reporter became a writer and in his belated realization of his talent produced an astonishing amount of creative work.

Ring on the Chicago *Tribune*

He was twenty-eight when he took over the "Wake," twenty-nine when his first story appeared in a magazine—a late start for both the main facets of his career. At twenty-seven John Lardner was doing a national feature for a newspaper syndicate and his own page, "Sport Week," for *Newsweek*. I had won an Academy Award for a screenplay at the same age. My brother David was doing three different departments for *The New Yorker* before he was twenty-four: the movie reviews, sports and the nightclubs. Jim had the maturity at twenty-four to perceive the limitations of most newspaper work and risk his life in the struggle to head off World War II.

It could be argued that these comparisons are unfair to the father of the family because it was his reputation that made it easier for the sons to get started. The point is valid as far as getting that first job was concerned, especially for John and Jim and me, who were hired by newspapers during the grimmest four years in the history of American employment statistics. Once hired, however, you couldn't ride very far on a name alone, not with dozens of applicants waiting for every job opening.

More important, I think, to the start of our careers than the influence of the Lardner name on our employers was the informal guidance he gave us in newspaper work and the use of the English language in general. We had that sense of being professionals at an age when the nearest thing to a goal in Ring's life was his mother's image of him in a pulpit.

But these two factors together don't quite explain the contrast I'm talking about, and I have suggested that a third one can be found in the phenomenon of varying rates of maturation. Jim and David died too young for us to have any idea what they might have accomplished, but it's certainly clear that neither John's best writing achievements nor mine approach the level of our father's, yet I think we were more advanced in our different branches of the craft by, say, twenty-five than he was. Besides the environmental influence, in which my mother also played an important part, there must have been a difference between his inheritance and what we got as a result of the new Abbott-Lardner combination. By blending one strain with another, geneticists produce early-maturing grains that may be better or worse than the ones that develop more slowly, and there's no reason the same shouldn't go for random mixes of humanity.

It is my contention that Ring Lardner's professional life was shaped by accidental circumstances to a much greater extent than by conscious intention. In this whole decade from the end of the courtship correspondence to my own early memories, I have to operate more on speculation than direct testimony, but it's informed speculation and I offer it without diffidence. Before his marriage Ring seems to have felt no responsibilities beyond supporting himself and giving some help to his parents. But as his own family expanded so did his view of his obligations, and his guiding motive was always to increase his income and provide more luxuries.

The "Wake" made it necessary for him to experiment with various kinds of writing and learn, with the help of his readers' reactions, what he could do best. Besides his verse, which he frequently attributed to Frank Schulte and other ballplayers, he developed the two main variations of English in which almost all his work was written until about 1925. Although they contain enough identical or similar locutions to justify bracketing them together as a single Lardner idiom, I think the differences in the illustrations below are worth noting.

Semiliterate American (As Written):

Well Al it is all O. K. with me because I cant help not feeling sorry for Allen because I dont beleive he will be in the league next year and I feel sorry for Marie to because it must be pretty tough on her to see how well her sister done and what a misstake she made when she went and fell for a left hander that could not fool a blind man with his curve ball and if he was to hit a man in the head with his fast ball they would think there nose iched.

Semiliterate American (As Spoken):

They even got a barber and a valet, but you can't get a shave wile he's pressing your clothes, so it's pretty near impossible for a man to look their best at the same time.

"Wile" in the second quotation (from *The Big Town*) is not a misspelling as such but the written form of a mispronunciation. In the first one (from *You Know Me Al*) the easier words, those the writer thinks he knows, are more apt to be misspelled than ones like "because" and "league" and "tough," which he would be less sure of and accordingly more likely to ask about or look up. Ring didn't invent this distinction; he learned it from reading ballplayers' efforts at prose composition, just as he learned the oral idiom from listening to their speech with an ear tuned to the subtlest distinctions. H. L. Mencken in his monumental *The American Language* quotes him on one of the more mysterious of such distinctions:

A player, returning to the bench after batting would be asked, "Has he got *anything* in there? ("He . . . in there" always means the pitcher.) The answer would be "He's got *everything*." On the other hand, the player might return and (usually after striking out) say, "He ain't got *nothin'*." And the manager: "Looks like he must have *somethin'*."

In another context Ring amplified the point: "There appears to be somethin' about the 'y' near the middle of both these words [anything and everything] that impels us to acknowledge the 'g' on the end of them."

It should make a present-day columnist shudder to learn that in Ring's case for the first four years he wrote it, a daily column meant seven days a week. But as a special concession he was given less space to fill on Mondays and the suggestion from the sports editor that he send in just a verse or two so the paper would never appear without his by-line. An early, and soon almost the only, topic for the Monday spot was his first-born son, and the stuff of his verses was what all new fathers discover afresh:

Breathes there a parent of masculine gender,
One whose young hopeful is seven or less,
Who never has cursed the designer or vendor
Of juvenile-out-of-doors-winter-time dress?

* * *

I've sat and watched you a long, long while,
And not since I came have you ceased to smile,
So it strikes me as wrong to arouse you, boy,
From sleep that's so plainly a sleep of joy. . . .

Orders are orders and I'm afraid
It's trouble for me if they're disobeyed,
But I'll bet if the boss could see you, son,
She'd put off the duty, as I have done.

* * *

An instant after some unlucky stumble
Has floored him and induced a howl of pain.
He's clean forgotten all about his tumble
And violently sets out to romp again.

But if, when I leave home, I say that maybe
I'll get him something nice while I'm away,
It's very safe to bet that Mr. Baby
Will not forget, though I be gone all day.

Ah, would I might lose sight of things unpleasant:
The bills I owe; the work I haven't done,
And only think of future joys and present,
Like the approaching payday, and my son.

The character of Jack Keefe, also known as "the Busher,"
narrator and central figure of *You Know Me Al,* had roots in
Ring's first season in the big leagues. There was a player on the
White Sox of 1908 who could neither read nor write but was so
determined to conceal the failing he would pretend to go
through a newspaper column by column or "insist on seeing the
bill of fare in hotels or diners and, after a long and careful study,
order steak and baked potato, or ham and eggs, or both."

Ring suddenly contracted the habit of reading menus and baseball news out loud, and the player, whom he gave the name "Jack Gibbs" in his reminiscences, attached himself to him. Once Gibbs came to the hotel room where Ring was working on a typewriter, said he had a letter from his wife and had figured out what a great joke it would be if she got a typed answer. He gave Ring the letter with the suggestion he read it out loud so they would both be fresh on what needed answering. Ring found it short and to the point, something like: "How can you expect me to meet you in Chicago unless you send me some money? I don't intend to make the trip out there on a freight, and I don't want to get my feet all blisters from walking."

As Ring recalled it later, the dictation went about this way:

"Dear Myrt." And then tell her she knows damn well I don't get no pay till the last of April, and nothing then because I already drawed ahead. Tell her to borrow off Edith von Driska, and she can pay her back the first of May. Tell her I never felt better in my life and looks like I will have a great year, if they's nothing to worry me like worrying about money. . . . Oh, you know what to tell her. You know what they like to hear.

In one respect only, Jack Gibbs and Jack Keefe were about as different as they could be. Gibbs couldn't write at all and Keefe found it hard to put his pen down once he got launched on his favorite topic. But they shared a general outlook on life.

During his first year with the "Wake" Ring made experiments in style that put him on the road to both variations of the Lardner idiom. The first was a "novel" about baseball in ten chapters attributed to "the Copy Boy." Full of spelling and grammar mistakes, it was a parody of the sports fiction of the day, which invariably made the athlete heroes glamorous and quite unbelievable. Then ten days before the World Series of 1913 he ran what was represented as an account of the first game with the by-line "By a Athlete*" (the footnote read: "*Unassisted"):

We ought to of trimmed 'em. When Egan, the big shot, said I was out at second he musta been full o' hops, the big boob. I like t' known where he was at las' night, the big bum. Some o' them umps oughta be on the chain gang, the big boobs.

This, of course, is the spoken tongue, transcribed to convey the way it sounds, but it's closer to Keefe than the "novel" because it has the vital ingredient of character revelation through first-person narration. It is crude compared to what he conceived only two months later, but this and subsequent columns in the same vein attracted a lot of attention and the Sunday editor of the *Tribune* offered Ring fifty dollars if he could come up with a short story good enough for the feature section. The proposal came when Ellis was pregnant again and they were acquiring a house in suburban Riverside with a small inheritance that had come to her on Mr. Abbott's death a few months before.

With the success of the column, Ring's salary had been raised to a hundred dollars a week, which meant, according to Ellis, a life of considerable comfort in those days. Except, she added, that they always spent a hundred and five.

The form he chose for the first sustained piece of fiction he ever wrote was a series of letters from a rookie pitcher with the White Sox to his best pal back in their home town in rural Indiana. It told the simple, funny, sad story of his high hopes and failure to make good in big-time ball. There is no reason to think Ring had sequels in mind, but it is different from the non–Jack Keefe baseball stories he proceeded to write in the next few months in that it had the potential for sequels, indeed for a book that fulfilled all the specifications of a novel except the author's acknowledgment that it was one. The other stories, all told in Semiliterate American As Spoken, depended on plot, on some unusual situation applied to the medium of baseball, and came to a definitive conclusion that precluded any further extension of the narrative.

"A Busher's Letters Home" contains misspellings and other writing errors as opposed to speaking ones, but grotesque spelling is not used for comedy as it was in the works of Josh Billings and Petroleum V. Nasby. Mistakes are deliberately kept to a minimum and their main function is to remind the reader that these are letters, directed to one trusted intimate and dealing with the most private events as well as public ones. It was an extraordinarily happy matching of form and content, and popular response was so enthusiastic that he did ten more episodes in the next fifteen months, and then, after a three-year gap, another fifteen.

Before that first one reached the public, however, the Sunday editor decided the prose was too unorthodox for his readers, and Ring sent it to the *Saturday Evening Post* in Philadelphia instead. The story has been told in a number of places, including the Elder biography, that it came back so fast Ring claimed it must have been intercepted in Cleveland. Then, according to the legend, he showed it to a writer named Charles Van Loan, who called it directly to the attention of the *Post* editor, George Horace Lorimer.

What is true is that he did discuss the idea with Van Loan, who liked it. Van Loan wrote for the *Post* and probably told Lorimer to be on the lookout for Ring's story. In any case, Lorimer accepted it immediately with a check for two hundred and fifty dollars.

Another frequently repeated myth is that a subordinate editor carefully corrected all the grammar and spelling mistakes into acceptable English prose. But the fact is Ring didn't run into that kind of minor obstacle either. Before the year was over and while he continued to do the "Wake" every day, he had written and published in the *Post* all six of the Busher episodes that became the book *You Know Me Al,* plus three unrelated baseball stories in the spoken idiom. In November still another story, the first of many, appeared in the monthly magazine *Redbook.*

From then on it was just a question of what he wanted to write when, and except for a few forays into songwriting and the theater, the controlling consideration was usually the amount of money offered. The *Post,* meeting the competition, raised his price per story over the next seven years in jumps of two hundred and fifty dollars each to its top of twelve hundred and fifty.

Almost everything he wrote was in one of the two variations of the idiom. Even after something impelled him in 1916 to do his first two third-person stories, "Champion" and "The Facts," he decided for himself he couldn't handle the form and didn't attempt it again for nine years.

I don't quarrel with my brother John's statement, five months before his death, in an introduction to a reissue of *You Know Me Al* that Ring "had the world's best ear" since "best" is not necessarily perfect. But Mencken goes too far:

> His ear for the minor peculiarities of vulgar American was extraordinarily keen. Once, sitting with him, I used the word *feller*. "Where and when," he demanded, "did you ever hear anyone say *feller?*" I had to admit, on reflection, that the true form was *fella*, though it is almost always written *feller* by authors. But never by Lardner. So far as I can make out, there is not a single error in the whole canon of his writings.

The impressiveness of this tribute, and of Mencken's scholarship, is diminished somewhat when one finds that in three of those 1914 stories, "Sick 'Em," "My Roomy" and "Horseshoes," Ring himself used "feller," nor did he bother to change it in later years when two of the stories were reprinted in collections—probably because he didn't reread them. But by the last story of his first year, "Back to Baltimore" in *Redbook,* he had switched to "fella."

My own guesswork on this is that he was intimidated at first by the very fact that "feller" was so firmly established; he felt he would be drawing too much attention to himself by revising it. (This diffidence didn't apply to other locutions of his because they hadn't even been approximated before: "acrost the state line," "oncet in a while," "offen my chest," "ast me a question.") But by the time he got to "Back to Baltimore," he was feeling more confidence. Also, it was a different magazine and a different copy editor.

In any case the idiom, both versions, with slight variations according to the educational level of the particular speaker and writer, did evolve over the years, in my judgment for the better, and continued to be his main form of expression in both fiction and nonfiction. It reached its final and most readable stage when he broke away from the early pattern of drawing comedy from the narrator's malapropisms and unconscious character revelations, and devised the character of the "wise boob," investing him with conscious humor:

"Personaly, the only horse who I ever set on their back throwed me off on their bosom before I had road him 20 ft. and did the horse wait to see if I was hurt, no."

The approaching birth of Jim led to the purchase of the house in Riverside, and that called for an increase in income beyond the *Tribune* salary, and the way Ring found to supply it was writing fiction. Six months after Jim was born, our mother was pregnant with me and there was that much more pressure for magazine money. The death of Ring's father in 1914 also increased the need for help to be sent to Niles.

I still have to rely on the "Wake" for information about our home life during those early years. Since my parents concentrated their hopes after John on a female child, they were at a loss for a name each time when they found themselves with another boy. After Jim's birth he wrote:

If you were Barbara, I know
You'd cost your dad a lot more dough.
And when you married, it would be
Like last night's second round—on me.

And after mine:

I love you, New Arrival;
I love you, No. 3
That's why I won't allow them
To name you after me.

And a year later (for "Bill" in all intrafamily references, read "Ring, Jr."):

"Bill can say 'Daddy,' " I was told.
"Just think of that for a 1 year old!"
And, seeming skeptical, I was led
To where, unwilling, he lay in bed.

"Bill, say 'Daddy,' " his coach implored.
Bill looked up at us, plainly bored.
"Blah," said he, and his champion smiled.
"There! How's that for your year-old child!"

Jim was under three years old when his father wrote:

They said he resembled an angel
Ere he got all these bruises and knocks.
And now? Well, he looks like a boxer
Who never did learn how to box.

The "Wake" also ran "Riverside Locals" that must have fascinated huge segments of the *Tribune* circulation. Selected samples:

J. P. Lardner has a host of mosquito bites.

J. A. Lardner expects to go to Niles, Mich., next week for a sociable visit.

B. Lardner has learned to wave his hand to indicate hail or farewell.

J. P. and B. Lardner will be guests of honor at an adenoid and tonsil party on Chicago Avenue this A.M.

"I know who the Americans are fighting against," said J. A. Lardner on his return from kindergarten Monday. "It's the Germans and the Turks and the Christians."

During those years in which Europe went to war and America moved ever nearer to involvement in it, the "Wake" and the Midwest generally seem to have been much more disturbed by our extended conflict with Mexico. In April, 1914, Ring ran a verse called "My Alibi," in which he said that, while of course he'd love to go off to war and be shot at by "greasers," he had to stay home with John—"And so I prize my little kid/More highly than I ever did."

More than two years later another outbreak was so imminent that an account of a tennis tournament in Cleveland that ran alongside the "Wake" told how "the match was interrupted three times when troop trains carrying the national guard from various eastern states passed within a short distance of the courts. The fans in the stands stood up and cheered wildly as the soldiers passed en route to the Mexican border." This renewal of crisis resulted in the only instance I know of when Ring fell prey to one of the haunting hazards of column-writing and repeated himself shamefully. His verse this time was addressed to all of us and wound up: "You're my three excuses for/Not competing in this war." The reason I'm sure the repetition was accidental rather than deliberate was that he used almost the same title: "Daddy's Alibi."

Finally, after four years of the Monday verses on top of six full columns a week, Ring rebelled, typically making a public matter of his private problem and sparing himself most of the effort of writing a column by devoting the space to this open letter:

TO THE SPORTING EDITOR:
It is a known fact that one day off per week is allowed everybody on this floor except the comical cartoonists, who have five or six, and the undersigned, who has none. . . . It was the original understanding that he was to have something in the paper every morning but one. Then came your honorable request that the seventh morning, Monday, also show some product of his creative genius. "Not a great deal," you said, "but perhaps a little verse or two in order that your name may be never out of the paper."

I now say that if it is necessary that the undersigned's name be never out of the paper, why not print merely the undersigned's name on Monday mornings, adding perhaps some phrase such as "who did not work yesterday. . . ."

It is from no lack of ideas that this request is made. The subjects of the little verses have been most generous about furnishing same. But they have now progressed so far beyond average males of five years and under that certain readers find their present pranks and conversations impossible of belief. And one hates to be regarded as a malicious falsifier when one has always regarded truth as one of the two great essentials, the other being one day off a week.

In conclusion let me say that inadvertently the little verse or two, as well as the undersigned's name, stayed out of the paper last Monday morning; in spite of the fact, Max tells me, many papers were sold and several were even read.

A personal reply would be appreciated.

Ring W. Lardner

There were very few verses about the boys after that, but we continued to occupy a good deal of space in the column, mostly in prose now—our own prose as recorded and edited by our father. There were a number of stories dictated by John, and later on by Jim and me, and a series of family dialogues, usually at the breakfast table.

The column as a whole was supposed to center on sports, but Ring wrote about practically anything that entered his head and I have encountered a number of old "Wake" readers (not many lately; actuarial tables are catching up to them) who had little interest in sports. A lot of older people who react to the name, incidentally, remember Ring Lardner solely or primarily as a newspaper writer, either from the *Tribune* column or the weekly syndicated one he wrote in the 1920s.

An indication of the extent of his following came one Thanksgiving when he wrote a wishful column about an imaginary Michigan-Chicago football game that was supposed to take place that afternoon, complete with a "probable line-up" of stars who had been in retirement for a decade or two. The two universities had severed relations many years before and Thanksgiving Day games had not been played in the Middle West for even longer than that. But more than five hundred people showed up at the University of Chicago football field that day, and a high percentage of them phoned the *Tribune* indignantly when they found there was no game.

His younger followers included James T. Farrell and Ernest Hemingway, both of whom imitated the Lardner style in their high school newspapers. Hemingway, out in suburban Oak Park, signed his pieces "Ring Lardner, Jr." until his principal persuaded him it was not a good idea.

Free competition, the lifeblood of our economy, sometimes flows too sluggishly to maintain perfect equilibrium. Ring didn't discover how underpaid he was until Illinois liquor interests, haunted by the Prohibitionist threat, entered Chicago journalism with their own paper, the *Record-Herald.* Disdaining a "gentlemen's agreement" among the other publishers not to raid each other's staffs, they offered a substantial raise to Ring along with others, and the *Tribune* responded with a three-year contract at twice the hundred a week he was getting under the code of chivalry.

By 1916, when that occurred, he was selling enough stories to magazines to almost double his new newspaper income. One series of them (later a book, *Own Your Own Home*), which had run in the *Post* the previous year, was based on the Lardners' own experience in Riverside with the problems of home-building and suburban living. But the characters of the narrator, a small-minded Chicago detective, and his social-climbing wife, were superimposed for comedy purposes on that experience. That pattern of using autobiographical details with fictional principals to satirize middle-class values was continued in two more books, *Gullible's Travels* and *The Big Town,* and a number of short stories.

In the spring of 1917 America entered the war and the Lardners sold their house in Riverside. Ellis and we boys spent the summer in St. Joseph, Michigan, a lake resort, and Ring went to Europe as a war correspondent. He cabled back columns that were run in the *Tribune* under the name "In the Wake of the War," and wrote a series of articles for *Collier's Magazine* that were later collected in a book called *My Four Weeks in France* (after *My Four Years in Germany* by Ambassador James W. Gerard). Actually the whole trip, with waits in New York and London and long Atlantic crossings, took eleven weeks. It was not a happy experience for either Ring or his readers. The book is the least readable of all his published work.

What is basically lacking is an attitude toward his material. He didn't even have a clear-cut point of view on the war, not sharing the jingoism rampant in some parts of the country or the *Tribune*'s long-standing isolationism or Ellis's unobtrusive pacifism. His feelings about one aspect of it were reflected in a column after America was in it and before his trip abroad, that had the Wilson cabinet calling for hissing ballplayers with German names and changing the Chicago street names Goethe and Schiller to [Robert W.] Chambers and [Elinor] Glyn. But when he got near the actual conflict, he couldn't decide on proper targets for his humor, and it came out lame and ineffectual.

Two other inferior books resulted from the same ambiguity of attitude. Early in 1918 he returned to the Busher character after a lapse of three years, and for the next two published almost no other fiction. The first of these magazine stories, "Call for Mr. Keefe," is a funny account, as good as the best of *You Know Me Al*, of Jack's losing battle to stay out of the army while professing militant patriotism. The next nine episodes deal with his army life, in this country and in France, and again there is the same strained uncertainty about what is a proper subject of fun. Then came five distinctly superior stories of Jack returned to baseball in the immediate postwar era, including "Along Came Ruth," in which he is pitted against the Babe while the latter was still a pitcher.

The wartime stories, with the significant exception of "Call for Mr. Keefe," were collected into the books *Treat 'Em Rough* and *The Real Dope.* None of the other, better ones had ever been reprinted until the 1976 collection, *Some Champions* edited by Matthew J. Bruccoli and Richard Layman, in which both "Call for Mr. Keefe" and "Along Came Ruth" appear in a book for the first time.

The last of those final Busher stories appeared in the *Saturday*

Evening Post of October 13, 1919. On or about the day that issue hit the stands, Jack Keefe's team, and Ring's, the Chicago White Sox, finished throwing the World Series to the Cincinnati Reds in baseball's biggest scandal ever. It was eight years before Ring published another story about the game.

On his way to the war, Ring saw the *Ziegfeld Follies of 1917* in New York and reported to his mother: "Contrary to my previous information, the song Bert Williams is singing is one to which I wrote both words and music. . . . He expects to put it on a record this fall." The song was called "Home, Sweet Home (That's Where the Real War Is)." On his way back he saw the musical *Chu Chin Chow* in London and returned with the score, which he pronounced "the best since *The Merry Widow.*"

His arrival home was notable for the welcome from his three-year-old:

> Home from the war, my son I spied.
> "Jim, did you miss me much?" said I.
> Spurning my arms, he thus replied:
> "I eat my brekkus, you old guy."

On his return the family moved into a rented house in Evanston, and the following year, after another summer in St. Joseph, to an apartment on Buena Avenue in the city. Ring and Ellis had already decided to move east but delayed their departure until after the birth of my brother David in March, 1919, and the expiration of Ring's *Tribune* contract in June.

He was not ready yet to cut himself off entirely from the newspaper world and a regular payroll. Capitalizing on the fact that his magazine stories had won him a national instead of just a Chicago audience, he talked in New York to John N. Wheeler, a former sportswriter and old friend, whose Bell Syndicate sold features to a hundred and fifty newspapers. They discussed Ring's doing a weekly column for Bell when he was through with the *Tribune*. Some time later Wheeler, hearing a rival syndicate was after Ring, proposed to come to Chicago to work out a contract with him. Ring wired back: "If you knew anything about contracts you would realize we made one in the Waldorf bar before five witnesses, three of whom were sober." Their deal lasted six years without any other written confirmation.

His first work for Wheeler was covering the heavyweight championship fight between Jess Willard and Jack Dempsey at Toledo on July 4. Ring had a bet of six hundred to five hundred dollars on Willard; he never felt his own gambling on sports events interfered with his function as a reporter, nor were his bets ever for token amounts. In this case he believed the champion's sixty-pound weight advantage would count more than his thirty-six years against the challenger's twenty-four. The day after Dempsey's knockout victory in the third round, Ring wrote that his support of Willard "was just a kind of practical joke on my part and to make it all the stronger I went and bet a little money on him, so pretty nearly everybody thought I was really in earnest."

That holiday weekend in Toledo was Ring's first encounter with Prohibition. The Eighteenth Amendment had been ratified the previous January, to go into effect a year later, but Ohio was one of the states that put the reform in effect ahead of time. Although Ring had on one occasion expressed the hope that outlawing liquor might help him stop drinking, he joined Grantland Rice, Rube Goldberg and other friends in their initial bout with illegal alcohol, which turned out to have much the same influence as the regular kind. Ring composed a song for the group:

> I guess I've got those there Toledo Blues;
> About this fight I simply can't enthuse.
> I do not care if Dempsey win or lose,
> Owing to the fact I've got Toledo Blues.

More professional—in fact, most successful of all the songs for which he did both words and music—was "Prohibition Blues," which he wrote for Nora Bayes as star and producer of a musical farce about the feminist movement called *Ladies First.* It was the hit song of a successful show and Ring received an advance of two hundred and fifty dollars. But he was listed as lyricist only, Miss Bayes taking over composer credit for herself, thus participating in the royalties in exchange for introducing the number. This was a common custom in the days when sheet music sales were the main source of revenue for a song. The words to the mournful refrain were:

> I've had news that's bad news
>   about my best pal.
> His name is Old Man Alcohol
>   but I call him Al.
> The doctors say he's dyin'
> As sure as sure can be
> And if that's so
> Then oh oh oh,
> The difference to me.
> There won't be no sunshine
> No stars, no moon,
> No laughter, no music
> 'Cept this one sad tune.
> Goodbye forever to my old friend "Booze."
> Doggone, I've got the Prohibition Blues.

I am still writing about a time before my own earliest recollections, and the only source I have for what our home life was like in those last months in Chicago are the family dialogues recorded in the "Wake." One thing they reveal is that as I approached the age of four, with one brother already seven, another five, and the youngest an infant, I had a strong compulsion to assert myself and compensate in words for the physical inadequacy I must have felt. In dialogues involving the full family, the characters are listed as "Le Père; La Mère; John, the eldest son; Jim, the middle-sized son; and Bill, the son-of-a-gun," but in some of these excerpts one or two members of the cast are absent or not participating:

BILL: I'm all through my breakus.
LA MÈRE: Have you got a kiss for me?

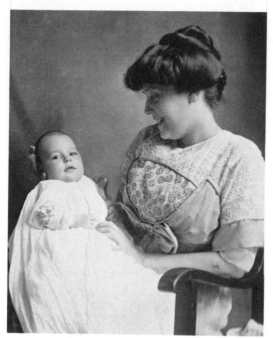

Ellis with John in his third month

Ring, Jr. (the author) at two

Father and sons, before there was a David

BILL:	I can't be kissing peoples every day. Just Wednesday.
LA MÈRE:	But this is Wednesday.
BILL:	Just afternoons.
JOHN:	I've rhymed a valentine for you, Daddy.
LE PÈRE:	Go ahead.
JOHN:	This valentine's for Mr. Ring
	From his son John to the black-haired king.
LE PÈRE:	Oh, thank you.
BILL:	I can see all over the world.
JIM:	Daddy, are you shaving?
LE PÈRE:	Yes.
JIM:	What for?
LE PÈRE:	To remove whiskers.
BILL:	Everybody shaves.
JIM:	Oh, everybody yourself! Little boys don't shave.
BILL:	I shave, I think.
JIM:	Oh, shave yourself! Just big mens shave.
BILL:	Giants shave.
JIM:	Giants do not. Giants keep their whiskers.
BILL:	I am a giant and I don't keep my whiskers.
JIM:	You ain't a giant and you don't shave.
BILL:	I shall shave, I think.
JIM:	When you're a big mens.
BILL:	No, I shall shave now, I think.
JIM:	Daddy won't let you shave.
BILL:	If Daddy don't let me shave I shall kill him.
JIM:	Will you let him shave, Daddy?
LE PÈRE:	Not for a few years. Little boys don't shave.
BILL:	Gods shave. I shall shave.
JIM:	Gods have whiskers.
BILL:	I don't. I shall shave right now.
JIM:	Just fathers shave.
BILL:	I am everybody's father. I am the father of the whole world. I shall shave.
JIM:	You're not my father.
BILL:	I'm the whole world's father. I shall shave.
JIM:	Just fathers shave; fathers and gods.

BILL:	I am God's father and I shall shave, Mr. Jimmie.
JIM:	Oh, Mr. Jimmie yourself!
BILL:	If you say one more word to me, I'll kill you, Mr. Jimmie. And Mr. John and Mr. Daddy and Mr. baby brother.
JIM:	Oh, nobody could kill baby brother bees [because] he's too little.
BILL:	I'll kill him because I'll bake him in the oven and kill him; that's what I think I'll do.
JIM:	Oh, you don't bake baby brothers in the oven or big mens either; just pie.
BILL:	I bake them all, Mr. Jimmie; big mens and babies and boys and mothers and everybody; that's who I bake.
JIM:	Oh, bake yourself!
JOHN:	(Giggles.)
BILL:	I think I'll bake you, Mr. Jimmie. And when you're baked, I'll eat you up. And then kick you in the face. That's what I'll do.
A PARENT:	You mustn't talk so roughly.
BILL:	That's the way I talk.

Although she doesn't appear in the dialogues, a new member had joined the household along with David. A trained nurse, she came home with Ellis and the baby from the hospital to stay, at the rate of seven dollars a day, for as much time as she was needed, which turned out to be more than ten of the next twelve years. She had come to this country from her native Berlin before the outbreak of the war in Europe and her name was Gusti Feldman. (There had been two *n*'s in the name to begin with, but she had severed one of them to give it a less Germanic flavor during the war. In the 1930s, belatedly realizing how many Jewish Feldmans had done the same thing, she put the missing letter back and restored the name to its Prussian purity.)

Miss Feldman, which was the only name by which anyone ever addressed her, was in her thirtieth year when she went to work for my parents in 1919. After she left us in 1930 she went back to being a trained nurse and worked out of Doctors Hospital in New York for the next forty years. She died in 1971, unmarried and almost certainly a virgin.

Shortly after the Toledo fight, Ring and Ellis went to New York and found a house to rent in Greenwich, Connecticut, forty minutes from the city. At the start of the school year we all moved there. It was Ring's account of that journey that contained one of his most quoted bits of dialogue:

> Are you lost daddy I arsked tenderly.
> Shut up he explained.

The book was *The Young Immigrunts* and it was factually based on the automobile trip Ring and Ellis took with John, aged seven, while we three younger boys traveled by train with Miss Feldman. But Ring, wanting to tell the story from a child's standpoint and still have the sales value of his own name on the book, transferred me to the car and John to the train so the work could be credited to "Ring W. Lardner, Jr.—With a Preface by the Father." The fact that I was only four also served to broaden his parody of a current book, *The Young Visiters,* that was attributed to a nine-year-old English girl, Daisy Ashford, with an introduction by J. M. Barrie. Ring obviously felt that Barrie or some other adult writer had contributed more than editorial supervision.

The Young Immigrunts is a skillful parody that also stands up by itself, and though most of its admirers have been aware it was making fun of another book, few have found it necessary to read the original. When you do, two interesting things emerge. One is the thoroughness of the parody: Ring adopted Miss Ashford's style in considerable detail with mild exaggerations. A sample from each book will illustrate the technique:

> They went upstairs and entered number 9 a very fine compartment with a large douny bed and white doors with glass handles leading into number 10 an equally dainty room but a trifle smaller.
> Which will you have Ethel asked Bernard.

Oh well I would rarther you settled it said Ethel. I am willing to abide by your choice.

The best shall be yours then said Bernard bowing gallantly and pointing to the biggest room.

Ethel blushed at his speaking look. I shall be quite lost in that huge bed she added to hide her embarrassment.

Yes I expect you will said Bernard and now what about a little table d'ote followed by a theater.

(The Young Visiters)

Myself and father hoped out of the lordly moter and helped the bulk of the family off the train and I aloud our nurse and my 3 brothers to kiss me tho David left me rarther moist.

Did you have a hard trip my father arsked to our nurse shyly.

Why no she replid with a slite stager.

She did too said my mother they all acted like little devils.

Did you get Davids milk she said turning on my father.

Why no does he like milk my father replid with a gastly smirk.

We got lost mudder I said brokenly.

We did not screened my father and accidently cracked me in the shins with a stray foot.

(The Young Immigrunts)

The other revelation to the Lardner fan is how risqué for its time Miss Ashford's book is. Its humor, quite unconscious if you accept it (and I do) as the work of a preadolescent, depends a good deal on the author's innocence concerning the sexual matters she deals with, and I believe this slightly salacious flavor offended Ring's prudishness and made him overly suspicious of how such a deplorable effect had been achieved.

I formed this opinion and indeed wrote the above paragraph before I first saw a letter Ring wrote in 1925 to an editor who had asked him to review a similar book. Ring replied:

. . . I think it had better be reviewed by someone less skeptical than I. I didn't, and don't believe Daisy Ashford in spite of Swinnerton's testimony and that of other "witnesses," and this new book is, to me, palpably conscious humor written by somebody much older than they say the author is. . . . I don't mean to say the Stokes people are trying to put something over, but that they have been deceived. (Though some of the lines and paragraphs in the book are so "raw" that it is hard to know how they could fool anybody.)

A stereotype of the Midwesterner moving on to the sophisticated East at the end of America's first involvement on the European continent would include a measure of old-fashioned morality along with a roughly equal portion of naïve credulity. The Ring Lardner who moved to the New York area in the fall of 1919 had more than a normal share of the former and almost none left of the latter. He was a strait-laced cynic.

Part Two

1923 *(left to right):* Ring, Jr., Jim, Ring, Sr., David and John

5

My own first recollections begin with Greenwich and the Garden City Hotel on Long Island, where we moved to be nearer the remodeling of the large house Ring and Ellis had bought on East Shore Road in Great Neck. But these are the vague kind of recollections that are hard to distinguish from what you were told later by other people, and it isn't till after my fifth birthday in Great Neck that there are images I can securely call my own. I realize that many people go much further back in their memories (the claims extend right into the womb), but I don't feel my limitation is a serious one in this sort of chronicle. The early reminiscences of a writer whose recall went all the way back to the age of two might have their own special interest and even some literary value, but as autobiography not be up to what he derived from secondary sources, simply because they were circumscribed by a too infantile perception. I don't think I was capable of much perception before the age of eight at least, and by that time there are plenty of images to recapture.

One of these is sharp because it is the only occasion I can recall when I was ashamed of my father. Some organization in the nearby community of Bayside put on a benefit baseball game between a team of writers and one of "artists," a loose term including "actors," a loose term including the former world heavyweight champion, James J. Corbett, who made personal appearances. Dad wore his white flannels, which was in keeping with the unwritten understanding that there would be no sliding or other overly vigorous play. When he came to bat and managed to hit a slow grounder in the pitcher's direction, he started running, to my utter shock and humiliation, not toward first base but down the other base line toward third, where, to confuse matters further, there was already a base runner. The pitcher, fielding the ball on the eighth bounce, was bewildered as some of his teammates urged him to throw to first and others favored home plate, where the man on third was headed, passing Ring en route. The runner from third scored before he could make up his mind, so the pitcher threw the ball to the first baseman, who touched the bag and then, in order to satisfy all schools of thought, threw to the third baseman, who tagged Ring, who looked at him with the contempt reserved for people who thought they could put a man out when he had one foot planted firmly on the base.

The disgrace of having a father who didn't know one base line from another was aggravated by the fact that everyone was laughing at his ignorance. Then I noticed that John was laughing, too, and that Jim's expression was changing from initial uncertainty to amusement at our father's joke, and suddenly everything was set to rights. Except the ball game, which never recovered.

The three-story house in Great Neck was situated on two acres of steeply sloping land above the narrow part of Manhasset Bay and just inside what became in 1924 the Incorporated Village of Kings Point. On one side in front was a driveway with a formidable upgrade leading to a parking area alongside the house and a garage-and-stables farther up the hill. Directly in front of the house the slope rising to it from the road was divided into three terraces that served a basically decorative function. The hill behind the house, quite undeveloped when we moved in, was broken over the next couple of years into four staggered level areas. Nearest the house was a more or less formal garden with a circular lawn and goldfish pool surrounded by shrubs and flower beds. At one point Ellis had part of this area transformed into a rock garden, which Ring, commenting in his weekly column as he did on so many domestic events, pronounced a startling reversal since "In all the other estates I ever lived on we used to hire men to pick up all the rocks out of our garden and throw them over in the neighbor's yard."

The large garage building and a vegetable garden took up the next level along with a few fruit trees. Then came a tennis court, which on a few choice winter nights could be flooded and converted to a hockey rink. Just above that, farthest from the house and largest of the level areas, was the playground, in one corner of which were gymnastic equipment and home plate for a baseball diamond big enough to contain a Little League triple.

The top floor of the house was occupied by servants, generally three of them, of whom Miss Feldman, as she frequently made clear, was not one. The six bedrooms on the second floor should have made for a reasonable distribution among seven people, but the way they were actually allocated, Ring, Ellis and Miss Feldman each had one, and two were set aside as guest rooms. That left one for the four of us and it didn't even have a bed in it; we used it as a dressing room. Where we (the three older boys, and David when he graduated to a regular bed) spent our nights, including the ones we froze the tennis court, was a screened porch with awnings that could be lowered against anticipated precipitation. The unanticipated kind made its way with considerable freedom through the screens, and I can recall lying awake while an inch of snow accumulated on the floor and each of us waited in silence for another, more enterprising one to get out of bed and let down the awnings.

This Spartan practice was part of a comprehensive code of health and diet regulations more suited to an athletic training camp than a nursery. Devised and enforced by Miss Feldman, it began on her return from an absence that lasted from the summer of 1920, when we moved into the house, till the following spring. And it was because of that interregnum that the rules which governed the three younger boys were to apply much less rigidly to John.

I don't know the circumstances of her departure or her return; it may have been simply that she had a prior obligation to a couple who were having a baby at that time, and yielded first to their pressure to remain in their employ and then to my parents' to come back to us. I have a hazy recollection of a succession of substitutes while she was gone and some documentary evidence that she was missed. Ellis wrote in a round robin to her family in October, 1920, while Ring was off covering the World Series between the Cleveland Indians and the Brooklyn Dodgers: "We have been without a nurse for over a month and you know what that means for me. Julia had to go back to her school the 11th of September. . . . [She] has been out every weekend or I would be dead by now." And again on March 21, 1921: "We have been having a wild time lately with the latest nurse, who, I hope, leaves tomorrow. . . . Ring can't stand to be in the same room with her."

Anyway, by the time Miss Feldman returned John was nine years old and had gained too much independence to fall back under her sway. Her authority extended to him when Ring and Ellis were away, which was a significant fraction of the time, but he managed to separate himself from much of the discipline applied to his siblings. This removal was enhanced by the fact that he went to a different school, Greenvale in the community of Glen Head (deriving its name from the Reverend Joseph Phillips's adjoining Glen Cove) nearly ten miles away. He was driven there and picked up daily by the current chauffeur-gardener in one car while Jim and I, and eventually David, were transported by Miss Feldman, relentlessly dressed in white starched uniform and white starched nurse's cap, in the other. Ellis, who had driven during the first two years of her marriage, never took the wheel again after an accident when John was a baby. The car, a Chandler with the standard soft top of the day, overturned on a trip from St. Joseph on Lake Michigan to Niles. She was slightly hurt herself by the impact of the steering wheel, but the shock of John's being thrown out of the car unhurt was even more traumatic. It was by Ring's request that she gave up driving and even after he died she never summoned the initiative to start all over again.

Between John, with his seniority, and David, with little voice in his or anyone's affairs, was a unit referred to impartially as "Jim-and-Bill" or "Bill-and-Jim." Not only was there the smallest gap—fifteen months—between us, but Jim's inclination to identify himself with John instead was thwarted by the fact that from about age four-and-three I was always heavier and generally taller than he was.

These divisions and our differing contacts with Miss Feldman explain, I believe, why John was able in later years to relate to her more easily than David or I. She took care of his children in infancy and of John himself when he was sick in his last years. I didn't have to face the issue because all my children were born in California, but David did, and he and his wife chose other nurses for their two. Neither of us would have been able to do what John did, which was to take over Ring's formal, detached and uncommunicative role with Miss Feldman.

Though that lack of communication between our father and our nurse was almost total, the kind of life we led as children was shaped by a strange collaboration between his Puritanism and her Prussianism. They both felt character could be molded by tight discipline (Ring attributed his own weaknesses to the permissiveness of his upbringing) and good health by sound eating and exercise habits. They were also inclined to believe that a little suffering was necessary to the formation of a responsible adult. And unquestionably they shared the delusion that Miss Feldman by her very training would know what was good for children.

Ellis, more sensitive to Miss Feldman's limitations, sought to mitigate the influence by maintaining her maternal role in direct daily contacts with her boys, particularly in relation to their school work and entertainment. But Miss Feldman did not believe in sharing authority, upward or downward, and she was such a total glutton for responsibility that she moved inexorably

III

into any vacuum that developed. Her takeover of such areas as meal-planning, shopping, supervision of the servants and car-driving was the harder for Ellis to resist because she was thus freed to fulfill two strong drives of her own.

One was social—the expression of her impulse to be with other people, to entertain and be entertained, to keep abreast of trends in style, books and theater, and to fill her guest bedrooms with as many Abbotts, Lardners and even nonconsanguineous visitors as she could coax into them. The other, often in conflict with the first, was to be the most helpful wife she could to an increasingly famous man, taking on the added roles of social secretary, business agent and protector against his admirers and his compulsion to do favors for other people. These duties ex-panded steadily with the decline in his resistance to alcohol and the general deterioration of his health.

An added element in all this, which I became aware of when I was about eleven, was that Miss Feldman was in love with Ring and desperately jealous of Ellis. She managed to keep these emotions under control at tremendous cost to herself and quite a bit to us, for she was given, but never within sight or earshot of our parents, to terrible rages which even we could tell were beyond the borders of normality. In what is still my strongest image of her she is stretched supine on the floor and banging the back of her head against it, bemoaning her fate at having to put up with David's inability or unwillingness to swallow a mouthful of food within what she considered a reasonable time.

Miss Feldman naturally retained her own individual view of her role in those years. When she was close to seventy, she taxed me with my coolness toward her, and I ventured, for the very first time and quite foolishly, to say I disagreed with part of her approach to child-rearing. I tried to soften the blow, but she was deeply wounded and chose to respond to my limited criticism as if it were a total indictment of everything she stood for. After a lengthy oral defense of herself she went home and restated her position in writing:

Having been in your family for twelve years, which was the best time of my life and all the years thereafter with all the trouble and heartbreaks, I do not deserve to be maligned.

Have loved all of you boys with all my heart and no stranger ever sacrificed more for other people's children.

I may have been harsh at times; but I hoped that you would understand my position as you got older.

You had an ill father who had to be protected and could not give his sons more time and the influence of your mother was not too profound. Due to that I have tried to make he-men out of you boys.

The only reason of staying so long with you was the pleading of your father and my love for you. It certainly did not help my profession. . . .

I have taken care of your health, manners and principles, and many times it would be much easier to let you all do as you wanted. All that you have done after the death of your father and many mistakes have been made. . . .

Your father had T.B. but was never told how not to spread the disease and I was petrified for all you children, especially you since you had pneumonia twice in one year when I was not with you [before she came, when I was two].

The other reason for my wanting you outdoors was that when your father drank too much I did not want his children to see him —And your mother was not much around the house to help.

I thought of your father a lot; in fact he was the only one that thought I was all right and I wanted you children to love and respect him. I never even wanted you to shake hands, because of spreading germs.

Could I tell children [the reason] for seeming hard on them when in fact it was harder on me to act the way I did? As I told you before, your father meant a lot to me; but my heart was with you children.

More than once I would not let Albert [the chauffeur with the longest tenure] meet your father at the station as he fell all over himself and I had to see that you were not around until I had him in his room. . . .

When Jim and David went don't think for one minute that I did not suffer most. I brought them up and felt they were my children.

No mother ever did more for children than I did—taking com-

East Shore Road, Great Neck

Our first new car in Great Neck

David, John, "Peter," Jim and "Bill"

Miss Feldman, David, Jim, John and "Bill," Great Neck, 1922

plete care of four children, helping them all around; being part maid and part cook as I insisted you should have the best. Unless I did the shopping and planning it was not so.

I want to let you know, nobody did that much for a family with so little gratitude!

I don't want to be bitter; but sometimes it is hard.

You do not have to react to this note, you can destroy it as soon as you have read it.

I never have nor wanted to be close to children again—I had more than my share.

My best to you and your family
Gusti Feldmann

Although my mother was still alive at the time of that letter, I felt no impulse to show or quote it to her. In the twenty-five years since Ring's death, Miss Feldman had expressed her devotion to Ellis by visiting as often as Ellis would have her, either by the hour in a New York apartment or for days at a time in Connecticut when she was between cases. For her true emotions to emerge after so long a period of loyal attendance would have been like the fifth act of *Cyrano de Bergerac,* with a twist.

The remaining years of her life saw no abatement of her masochistic drive. By working hard for good wages and not spending any of it, she had accumulated more than two hundred thousand dollars, but she refused to quit until the hospital forced the issue when she was seventy-nine, and would not permit herself a television set or an air conditioner or any other frill in the hot little one-room apartment she occupied twelve months a year. But she gave away substantial sums to people she cared about, including me and John's children. (I had become reconciled with her by the simple device of conceding she was totally right.)

Before she went to bed the night she died in her sleep, she wrote out a draft of a new will, in which I was to be the executor and main heir, with bequests to all eight of Ring's and Ellis's grandchildren. It was never validated by witnesses and her savings went, in accordance with a previous one, to the niece in Germany whom she had decided to disinherit.

Some of the principles by which we were raised have been exposed as fallacies only recently. Others didn't sound very convincing even then, but we soon found logic was of no avail. We got further applying the same effort to evasive action.

Fresh air was a major obsession. Having spent the night outdoors and entered the house to dress and have breakfast, we were regularly dispatched up to the playground until it was time to leave for school. Even at lunchtime we might find ourselves with ten minutes to "play," but it was a tight squeeze. Other children had lunch at our select and expensive private school, but Miss Feldman drove up in her white uniform and starched cap more days than not to whisk us off to the superior fare she provided at home. The school day usually wound up with athletics, outdoors whenever weather allowed (the colder the winter day, the better for hockey on the school pond), but we still went to the playground when we got home. And for roughly the same duration as Daylight Savings Time, we returned there after supper till darkness impended. On a rainless day in summer I doubt if we averaged as much as two hours indoors out of twenty-four.

Our parents thought this was all to the good, and Ring especially went to great lengths to provide us with the best equipment for a variety of sports. In 1921 he wrote the essay on "Sport and Play" for a symposium called *Civilization in the United States,* displaying a thorough disillusion with spectator sports and even some skepticism about the value of the participatory kind. But in practice he was a strong believer in the interdependence of the healthy mind and the healthy body. The tennis court was a major enterprise that somehow took two years to build and then had to be done over the following summer. Ring had expected to use it himself but rarely did; by the time it was finally finished he was confining himself mainly to golf. We played on it, however, though not as much some summer weekends as the adult players drifting over from the Herbert Swopes' next door. Occasionally Ring would ascend to the playground to join or supervise the baseball games we played along with visiting cousins and school-mates. As always in anything involving physical grace, I, with my surplus poundage, was the one whose ego needed protection, though it took a mother's instinct to discern it. Once, after I had displayed my ineptitude with both grounders and flies as well as at the plate, she said hopefully, "Couldn't Bill be a catcher?" Ring's scorn was directed at her, but I got some of the fallout: "How many left-handed catchers did you ever hear of?"

The start of one of our games was briefly delayed when a visiting player noticed an unusual design on the ball and found on closer examination that it was autographed by the entire Yankee team, including Babe Ruth and Lou Gehrig. We had to assure him that we almost always played with autographed balls, replenishing our supply whenever we visited a ball park with our father and the players came over beneath our seats to greet him. It was the one piece of equipment he didn't have to buy.

One summer Ring hired an All-American end from Vander-bilt University named Lynn Bomar to teach us and our playmates basic football skills, and we devoted something like two days a week to it for a month or so without it steering any of us into the most rudimentary gridiron career. Jim, the only one with the essential speed and agility, remained too light for football, never reaching a hundred and fifty pounds in weight. The rest of us were simply not the stuff of which athletes are made, and in this respect I was outstanding. We liked tennis and eventually there came a time when Jim and I against John and David made a close doubles contest, but none of us ever got to be a good player. Swimming was everyone's favorite sport and the only one of our activities that also had Miss Feldman's wholehearted approval. Our first couple of years in Great Neck, we could swim right down the road in Manhasset Bay, but pollution ended that and we had to be driven around to a beach club in Sands Point, at the outer end of the bay on the opposite shore.

As far as protecting us from our father is concerned, the tuber-culosis didn't start until after we had lived six years on East Shore Road, by which time Jim and I were beginning to slip out of Miss

Feldman's clutches anyway. It's true there were occasions when Ring didn't arrive home from New York until morning, and I know from other sources that he would sometimes delay his return until we had left for school. I remember one time right after breakfast when Miss Feldman suddenly yelled at us to go up to the playground immediately, provoking our curiosity about the taxi struggling up the steep driveway. We retreated to the nearest observation post affording some concealment and watched Ring in dinner clothes emerge from the taxi and walk to the house on Miss Feldman's arm. Another time we spotted him before she did and were having a fine time when she broke the gathering up. Actually, he was known for his remarkable equilibrium when drunk, and I think "fell all over himself" was an exaggeration. What stays in my memory is that he was gayer and more communicative than usual, and we probably would have benefited from more of such contacts.

Another sight we were supposed to be spared was the bootlegger's delivery, but I have a distinct recollection—and I think I saw it more than once—of a man lifting a burlap sack out of a car and dragging it to the front door, instead of where other deliveries were made at the rear.

With all the facilities provided us by our parents and all the opportunity to use them provided by Miss Feldman's outdoor policy, the reader might assume we spent a good deal of time in exercise of one sort or another. But the fact is we didn't. You can banish a child to a playground but you can't make him exert himself. The majority of all those outdoor hours were spent reading. We were all horizontal readers by preference, perhaps because we inherited the nearsightedness of the Abbotts rather than the farsightedness of the Lardners, and there were generally two or three of us stretched out on the ground with a book. And for days when the ground was too damp or too cold there was a swing with two facing seats and a capacity of four.

I have never found a better test of an author's hold on my attention than reading in that swing on a really cold winter day. Dumas was dangerous, especially *The Count of Monte Cristo* and

The Vicomte de Bragelonne. (Who decided one name should be translated, the other not?) I could get so engrossed I'd forget to stamp my feet occasionally to ward off frostbite.

Another outdoor activity was slightly better suited to cold weather because it kept us on our feet and even included sporadic bursts of motion. It started with John telling stories to Jim and me and, when he grew old enough, David. They might be wholly original or based on something he had read. One set of characters that endured for a long time came from a series of stories in the *Saturday Evening Post.* I never read them, so I didn't know then and still don't how freely he adapted them. Gradually each of us became a character in the story and, when the narration came to a dialogue scene involving him, would improvise his own lines. I think it was after John went away to boarding school when he was thirteen and I took over the function of narrator, that we began to play out certain key parts of the action, too, such as a sword fight or an escape from a dungeon. By this time it was the same never-ending historical drama in which each of the three of us played one main character and a few subordinate ones. It was called "our game" by this time, and none of us to my knowledge ever spoke of it to anyone else, adult or child. For some reason or other we had such a feeling of privacy about this activity and it had departed so far from what he had started that when John was home weekends (his first boarding school was across Long Island Sound in Greenwich) or vacations, we wouldn't play the game within even his hearing.

When any of the cousins who came to visit in Great Neck recalled in later years their stays with us, the most memorable aspect was always the dietary laws. The visitors were not actually bound by them, but they were under a good deal of social pressure to conform. In Miss Feldman's view of life, if something was good for you, the more of it you consumed the healthier you became—a theory that caused enormous quantities of cholesterol to be introduced into our bloodstreams, for milk, eggs and red meat were considered, along with fruits and vegetables, to be the main building blocks of strong bodies. Commercial milk wasn't rich enough, and at her prodding Ellis and Ring kept a cow for most of our eight years on East Shore Road. Flossie, and, when she became in Ring's words "just an ornament," Blackie, produced two and a half to three gallons daily ten months out of twelve, and Miss Feldman strove mightily to see that as little as possible went to waste. What we didn't drink found its way to the same destination in the form of butter, cream, cottage cheese, custard and, when somebody had the time and energy to crank the freezer, ice cream.

From some source or other she had absorbed the message that vegetables and eggs were more beneficial when eaten raw. Experiments with various uncooked vegetables established that our resistance was weakest to lettuce with sugar and vinegar sprinkled on it, and this unique dish was the main ingredient of our evening meal for years, accompanied by milk and eggs so scantily boiled they couldn't qualify as solid food. Only when these essentials were totally consumed could we taste such embellishments as jelly sandwiches and dessert.

It was one of the principles of this regime that it was healthier to eat one's main meal in the middle of the day so as not to overwork the gastric juices during sleeping hours. This gave added weight to the argument for bringing us home from school at noon, and since both Ring and Ellis had been raised in a tradition of meat and potatoes twice a day, it worked out that this was the one meal the whole family ate together.

When at the age of thirty-five I put in nine months at the Federal Correctional Institution, Danbury, Connecticut, for contempt of Congress, it was a strict mess hall rule that whatever you chose to accept on the chow line you had to finish eating. Some of my fellow inmates, finding intolerable to the palate what had seemed innocuous to the eye, had to foist their surplus upon hardier eaters or suffer the penalty imposed by the custodial staff. The rule didn't seem as burdensome to me as to these colleagues because it was far less stringent than Miss Feldman's. In her domain you had to clean your plate even though you had had no voice in determining what was put on it in the first place.

Along with millions of other people, then and since, she believed firmly that a daily bowel movement at a fixed time was essential to perfect health. But for her, to believe was to act: she didn't just favor regular movements, she required them. And since it was too important a matter to be governed by mere trust, she conducted inspections every morning of what the three younger children had produced in order to determine what, if any, laxative dose was called for.

Among the areas she deemed under her jurisdiction, despite her lack of personal experience in the field, was our education in the basic facts of mammalian sex. Accordingly, when our cow (I think it was Flossie) was about to calve, she announced that we would all witness the event even if it cost us some of our otherwise highly valued sleep. Ring must have been skeptical about this project because he expressed a high degree of amusement to friends when both she and we boys slept right through the birth noises.

He also revealed, in one of his syndicated pieces, that there were risks attached to even the primary function of maintaining a cow.

> It seems that on some parts of the estate they's quite a growth of what they call wild garlic which no cow could possibly enjoy eating it, but Blackie eats it to get even and I will say she gets even. Sometimes you can shut your eyes wile imbibeing the oatmeal and pretend you are enjoying the $1.00 table de hote at Madame Galli's.

Ellis didn't subscribe to all the Prussian theories, but neither did she see any significant harm in them. In any case she knew Miss Feldman's alternatives, quite unnegotiable, were complete control or resignation. And she had learned from experience that among less dedicated governess candidates, a family of four boys was not considered a choice berth. Most telling of all was the certainty of Miss Feldman's devotion to duty and to her charges personally. Ellis and Ring spent a month or two every winter in Florida, the Bahamas or California, and they traveled on other occasions, too, for diversion or for Ring to cover a sporting event or a political convention. With Miss Feldman at the helm, calamities would be met with unfailing efficiency, if not actual relish.

6

Out of our inheritance and environment, we four brothers had certain qualities in common, and observers of us, both as children and as adults, were likely to comment more on the similarities than on the differences. The most striking of these were acquired from our father: intellectual curiosity with a distinctly verbal orientation, taciturnity, a lack of emotional display, an appreciation of the ridiculous. It was a matter of course that you mastered the fundamentals of reading and writing at the age of four, and by six reading books was practically a full-time occupation. (We all began to wear glasses in our teens.) When I was in the first grade, I was detached from my peers for reading purposes only and assigned to the third instead. Later on we each skipped a grade at some point, though David required some special tutoring for the purpose the summer he was eight. His instructors, at ten cents an hour, were Jim and I.

If any significant part of the reading and writing we did at home had been devoted to school work, we would have been prize students, but homework had a very low priority. The general pattern for the family was high marks in English and one or two other subjects we liked, and just getting by in the rest. The lowest rating on any of our report cards was apt to be for effort. Jim was the only one who had Ellis's facility at mathematics, and this along with his English skills kept his average above the family norm until his first year at Harvard, which he dedicated to songwriting.

The only serious setback to any of us was to David the spring he became fifteen and failed in two subjects at the end of his second year at Andover. He had to switch to the Taft School in Watertown, Connecticut, from which two years later he graduated cum laude with honors in Latin and English and the school medal for French composition, and rejoined half his Andover classmates in the freshman year at Yale.

Besides his distinction as the oldest, John was further set apart from the rest of us by the fact that he was at all times the tallest for his age, eventually matching Ring at about six two. His leadership was unquestioned, and in view of his later reputation for oral uncommunicativeness, it's surprising how much he did talk within the family, not only telling us marathon stories but passing on to us vast stores of the information he had a superlative talent for accumulating. As a boy and as a man he was the most like Ring in manner, style of speaking and wit. He assumed without challenge the role of poet laureate of the Lardner menage, dashing off an appropriate verse whenever so moved by a local phenomenon or family event. A few of them, written when he was ten or eleven, have stayed in my memory:

> We have a tennis court in back
> Being built by Crampton.
> And every other day his men
> Are working in Southampton.

> A tugboat passes every day
> Along the smooth Manhasset Bay
> And when we hear its chug, chug, chug,
> We always say "There goes the tug."

> Two Chandlers and three Cadillacs,
> A Ford and then a Dodge.
> If we had all those cars at once,
> We'd have a full garage.

As for events it was part of his self-assigned duty to observe birthdays, holidays and other special occasions. A sample, of which I recall only the opening lines:

> A few choice lines of sentiment
> On Mother's anniversary,
> Commemorating this event
> In manner somewhat cursory,
> Should not seem out of place when sent
> From this, the Lardner nursery. . . .

But his juvenile masterpiece, written at fourteen, was an American version of *H.M.S. Pinafore* called *U.S.S. Skinafore,* keeping the Sullivan score intact but substituting fresh words for Gilbert's, which would have been quite a piece of presumption for even the most professional lyricist. John took it on with serene confidence, and his work ended up justifying itself by the fact that his lyrics are a reflection of the American twenties as seen by a precocious teenager in much the same way the master's are of the English 1870s.

They, and the dialogue scenes as well, were also written for the peculiar limitations of production and cast at his disposal. Performed in the Lardner living room for an audience of six or eight adults, the show had to be conceived for the available pool of talent, comprised of the four boys and our thirteen-year-old cousin, Anne Tobin. It was not too much of a problem for Toby, as she was known, to play the two female roles, but in order for John to undertake both the captain and the Secretary of the Navy (First Lord of the Admiralty in the original), he had to devise a plot situation in which one owed the other money and therefore ducked offstage whenever he saw him coming. That enabled John to change hats in the wings. Jim was the young hero, and I the villain, leaving only David to play the rest of the crew.

The opening chorus left the spectators in no doubt about the transfer of location:

> We sail the ocean blue
> And you ought to see us skim it;
> We're sober men and true,
> Inside the three-mile limit. . . .

Jim sang of his unrequited love to the tune of "A Maiden Fair to See":

> The captain of this boat has a fur-lined overcoat
> And gold and jewels too many;
> But if I had my wish, I'd let the lazy fish
> Keep ev'ry single penny.
> I'd like his daughter though, so we could undergo
> The marriage ceremony;
> And he could have his dough, except a cent or so
> In case of alimony.
> A minister I'd buy to legalize the tie
> And hallow the connection;
> But the lady in the case won't look me in the face,
> Or glance in my direction.

The swift rise to power in "When I Was a Lad" reached its climax with:

> A bunch of crooks selected me
> For governor up in Albany,
> And such renown I there did get
> That Calvin picked me out for his cabinet.
> He chose his cabinet so carefully
> That now I am the U.S. Naval Secratree.

As the only member of the family who couldn't carry a tune at all, I was a problem that John overcame by making my one solo bit a recitatif, with himself and David coming in on the melodic part. This song, to the tune "Kind Captain, I've Important Information," had little to do with the plot but concerned the great excitement that summer of 1926 over exploring the North Pole by air. I told of meeting "an emigrating polar bear" whose "eyes were red with weeping and deploring" and who "fixed me with an ultra-arctic stare."

"The reason why I'm dreary is Amundsen and Peary,
Commander Byrd and Wilkins," said the polar bear.
And when at last I reached the arctic regions,
The sight that met me filled me with despair:
Dirigibles and aeroplanes in legions
Were floating through the ultra-arctic air.

The casting of Jim as the romantic lead in this or any of our other, lesser theatricals was doubly automatic because of his qualifications and the lack of them in the rest of us. John was shooting up from moderate plumpness to outright ungainliness, and could only be cast in comic roles till the rest of him caught up with his height. I ranged at various ages from merely over-weight to seriously fat, and moved with an unheroic awkwardness. David had the abiding handicap of juniority. But Jim, with the slighter stature and fairer complexion of the Abbotts, as well as the most regular features and best-proportioned physique, was clearly the handsome-hero type.

His parents tended to think of him as frail and in need of protection, which was pretty laughable from my point of view since he would check his condition every now and then by testing how few seconds it took him to pin my shoulders to the ground. Ring, who in those Great Neck days seemed interested in raising an athlete, never quite realized he had done so, simply because Jim didn't show much interest in the usual major sports. He knew Jim played rugby and lacrosse at Harvard, but they were unfamiliar games and he didn't realize how vigorous they both are. And it wasn't till the winter after Ring died that Jim became New England intercollegiate wrestling champion in the one-hundred-and-forty-five-pound class and incidentally mastered the technique of tearing a Manhattan phone book in half.

Nor did they have to worry about his getting on in the intellectual world. Not only did he have the best school record in the family after Ellis, but both his teachers and his peers recognized the unusually detached precision of his thought processes; people came to know they could count on a truly objective opinion from a mind that seemed to operate on logic alone. He never lost his outward serenity; I was the closest person to him till the last two years of his life and I never saw him, as a boy or as a man, display anger or more than the mildest sort of enthusiasm toward anyone or anything.

And yet there was a vulnerable, appealing quality to prompt that special feeling his parents had about him. Ring revealed an aspect of it to his readers when Jim was ten:

> We been haveing quite a orgy of birthdays and generally always when they's one in sight we ask the hero of same what he would like for presents and most always the reply is a pony or a sail boat or a parrot or something else that they ain't no chance of him getting.
>
> But the 2nd boy is different and a week before his birthday we asked him what he would like and he says he would like something to clean the rust off his bicycle. That is the way he has always been and will always be the same way not wanting nothing and nothing will probably be what he will always get.

Those words have an added significance because of the fact that they were published one week after Jim's birthday and therefore written either just before or just after Ring and Ellis decided his present that year was to be a parrot. Which led to another Sunday piece in which we were the collective target of our father's irony:

> Well I told you a few weeks ago how we got hold of a milch cow that was jet black and we leaved it to the kiddies to give her a name and after they had only thought a part of one day they all of a sudden hit on Blackie just like they was inspired. Well we give our little boy Jimmie a parrot for his birthday and the bird could not have been in the house more than 2 hrs. and a 1/2 when all 4 kiddies was calling her Polly.

I was regarded as the difficult one in the family and got myself into the most trouble, usually out of a general sort of undirected rebelliousness. Perhaps some of my self-assertion was a defensive reaction to having brothers one and three years older. Perhaps those two bouts with pneumonia in my second winter of life made me cling more to what seemed a precarious place in the world. Anyway, the nurses who filled in for Miss Feldman our first year in Great Neck tended to emphasize me in their valedictory remarks.

If I felt put upon, and I did, it was further compounded by the forces that united, in kindergarten and at home, to correct my natural left-handedness by instructing me to write and eat with my right one. At a minimum this caused me to grow up with a scrawl instead of a respectable handwriting. It probably also produced a stutter that plagued me intermittently until I deliberately went in for public speaking at boarding school and worked it down to a mere speech hesitation.

There are fat kids who are overweight-athletic and others who are, as I was, overweight-sedentary. One of the substitute nurses used to take the younger three of us for walks along East Shore Road. Although David was only two, it was my estimate of my range that determined the length of these expeditions. When I decided we were far enough from home, I simply sat down in the street and refused to rise again until our direction was reversed.

My son Joe advanced from a tricycle to a bicycle before he was five. I was nine before I could make it on two wheels, and Ring recorded the event as follows:

> My little boy Bill (and when I say my little boy Bill I am comparing him with Firpo) well anyway my little boy Bill had a birthday and what he wanted was a he-man bicycle as he had got on the board of one of his brother's bicycles a couple of days before and had found out that he could ride it without falling off very often. . . . I forget the original cost but when it is added to what he done to the yard by falling off why it will mount up to something ridiculous.

Many a boy has known the solace of having a big brother come to his rescue in a losing battle with one or more tormentors. The twist in my case was having a *smaller* brother rescue me and I sometimes taunted a bully on purpose just for the surprise dramatic effect. Since Jim himself was not at all pugnacious, but was usually quite concerned for my safety, it was the best way to get to see him in action.

He could of course have applied his strength and agility against me, not just when he felt the need for a workout but in order to impose his will on mine. But I was saved from such a fate by his mild disposition, and when that failed, by the judicious use of poison ivy, to which he was very allergic and I immune. Fortunately, it grew in abundance throughout the unlandscaped areas of the property, and it was easy for me to arm myself for defensive purposes.

Mostly though, despite our differences in physique and temperament, Jim and I found ourselves in splendid accord. We liked the same books, games, movies, radio programs and people. We had an appreciation of and a sensitivity to each other's minds that enabled us to divine in most situations what the other was thinking. This literally paid off for us years later when we won money as bridge partners.

The gap of three and a half years between me and David was just enough to make him too removed, too small and delicate to be a fair target for anyone's aggression. And this image was enhanced by his being kept in unshorn curls and homemade middy-blouse suits (velvet overalls for dress-up occasions) till he was about six. Even his brothers collaborated in the effort to prolong his infancy and showed him off proudly as a thing of fragile beauty. Ellis and Ring were so determined to preserve that cherubic look they hired a portrait painter to record him life-size on canvas. The painter, complete with a wife whose jabber drove Ring into taking all his meals on a tray, was with us more than a week, taking over the large guest room and a downstairs room for a studio.

There must have been a reaction to this treatment seething within David, because when finally, on his entrance to first grade, he was permitted to look like a normal boy, he asserted his maleness with a vengeance. In a relatively short time his manner and even his appearance took on a toughness beyond his age, and in a year or two people were commenting on his resemblance to one of the great sports heroes of the decade, Mickey Walker, middleweight boxing champion and prime example of rough, freckle-faced, stub-nosed Irish good looks. Once under way, the process continued: each year for the next twenty, which is all he had left, David seemed to me more mature (as opposed to precocious) than any of his brothers at the same age.

Ring told his readers about the new David in September, 1925:

> It ain't no secret by this time that I am the father of 4 boys and I have made it a rule that as soon as each of them got to be 7 yrs. old I would cease from kissing him good-night as boys of such advanced age don't relish being kissed by parents of their own sex. Well 3 of them has been over the age limit for some time and I only had one left on who to vent my osculatory affection namely David who was 6 yrs. old in March. Lately I noticed that he did not return my caress with any warmth and one night he held out his hand to shake like the other boys and then run upstairs and told his brothers gloatingly that he had escaped daddy's good-night kiss. Naturally this remark was repeated to me and naturally it meant the end as far as I am conserned being a man of great pride and I suppose in time the wound will heal but mean wile hardly a evening passes when I don't kind of wish down in my heart that one of them had been a daughter.

There are various and conflicting theories about what your place in the family unit does to you psychologically. Whether it was from being the youngest or something else entirely, David had more social assurance than the rest of us. In the face of new situations and new people, John and Jim tended to clam up. I felt the same self-consciousness, but my way of revealing it was just as apt to be showing off. David's manner was comparatively natural no matter what the circumstances. He ventured boldly into such areas as dancing and dating at an age when his brothers dealt with these matters in fantasy only.

Intermittently in the mid-twenties a weekly magazine under John's editorship was distributed to our parents and a few close friends. Typically each issue contained at least one article, story

132

or poem by each of the four of us. The only outside contributor I can remember was a cousin, George Paull Torrence, Jr., who was "our Indianapolis correspondent" for a few issues following a summer visit with us. The publication was always expiring and then being revived again, mainly because of John's absences at school and returns home for vacation, and it went through a number of titles. As *The Weekly Post* it combined verse and fiction with baseball predictions and family news items. We produced only a single copy of each issue, written in penciled block capitals on both sides of a sheet of newspaper copy paper broken up by horizontal and vertical lines to present a diverting layout. Ring commented in his Sunday piece:

> Their writings seems to be largely mystery stories though one by Jimmie was a character study of a hypochondriac. In the first paragraph it said that Mr. Jones the hero "married young so he would have somebody to complain to." It was taken from this that the author had been observing family life outside his own house.

The *Post* expired in the spring of 1926 and was succeeded in August of that year by a new publication that announced itself in the first issue:

> The Lardner brothers (four) present
> A son, a literary scion;
> 'Tis called in harmless merriment
> *The Lardner Literary Lion.* . . .
>
> Our hearts and souls are with the Muse:
> Its destiny we live or die on,
> So put it mild when you abuse
> *The Lardner Literary Lion.*

The *Lion* was done on a typewriter and, as indicated by its name, was all literature and no journalism. The first issue, which has been preserved, is marked by flagrant race prejudice in a verse about a "colored crook" named Snowdrop with a mother named Snowdrift, and by arrant misogyny:

> A man once tried to kill himself
> For he was tired of life;
> He couldn't stand its tortures
> Especially his wife.

Other selections ranged from fourteen-year-old John's

> The Bay's at rest,
> Its shores asleep,
> And on its breast
> The ripples creep.

. . . to seven-year-old David's

> I do not know what to write, but I must write some thing;
> A poem or a story or a song if I can sing.

Occasionally Ring would submit a sample of his sons' work to his public. Many preadolescent authors would have welcomed the circulation jump to eight million readers, but Jim and I, aged nine and eight, had mixed feelings when he reprinted a lyric we had adapted from the current song hit "Yes, We Have No Bananas":

> Yes, we have no pajamas,
>   we have no pajamas tonight.
> We've got some night dresses,
> We've got some mattresses
> And sheets that are snowy white;
> And there's a blanket so yellow
> For each little fellow,
> But yes, we have no pajamas,
>   we have no pajamas tonight.

Our professional identification was already so acute that we saw a clear distinction between publication for free and for a paid circulation. If he had filled nine lines of copy with our stuff, we asserted at the midday meal, he owed the two of us nine times whatever it was he got per line. Recognizing the future potential of such a precedent, our father squelched us decisively by pointing out that we were already cutting into his income for a higher percentage than that. Who, he asked, did we think paid for the forkfuls we were raising to our mouths at that very moment? It was a point we had somehow not taken into account.

We were exposed to a remarkable number of periodicals in those days. The main emphasis was on newspapers, of which a minimum of six a day were delivered, but there were also a great many weeklies and monthlies, almost all of which no longer exist, and the founding of entirely new magazines like *Time* and *The New Yorker* were important cultural events.

Ring still considered himself primarily a newspaperman; short stories didn't become a major activity until 1925. Before that most of his magazine stuff was nonfiction of a topical nature, and for more than two years, starting in the fall of 1922, he was doing a daily comic strip based on *You Know Me Al* for the syndicate besides his Sunday piece. Newspapers were a dominant factor in his environment and accordingly in ours.

You couldn't keep up in that environment by just reading one paper in the morning and another in the afternoon. Important stories and ones that had a special interest for you, you read in several different papers to compare their coverage. We all became part of this process quite early, exchanging opinions about how the *World* or the *Times* or the *Herald Tribune* or the *Sun* had handled some story. Ring, who was such a purist about the exact ways in which semiliterates abused the language, was equally fastidious about the proper use of it by those who claimed literacy. We learned to react with the same scorn he had for, say, an infinitive that suggested deliberate intention where none existed: "The Prince of Wales dropped into the Broadhurst Theatre last night to create a near riot among the assembled spectators."

The New York *World* held a special place among newspapers not only because of its superiority in so many respects but because we knew so many people connected with it. The summer after we moved to Great Neck, the Swopes rented the house next door and it continued to be their country residence for eight years. Herbert Bayard Swope was executive editor of the *World* from 1920 to 1929, and his commanding presence was felt on East Shore Road as it was on Park Row. His house was a week-end gathering place for the famous, some of whom crossed the vacant lot between it and the Lardners'. His children, Jane and Herbert, Jr., were our age and our friends. *World* writers with whom Ellis and Ring had more than a casual acquaintance included F.P.A. (Franklin P. Adams), Deems Taylor, Quinn Martin, Heywood Broun, Dorothy Parker, Alexander Woollcott and H. L. Mencken.

Besides training yourself in the craft, the purpose of reading the papers was to increase your general information, and we devised an unending series of games and contests to test each other's store of facts while showing off our own. I remember a typical one because I was able to stump my father with it even though he clouded the issue by claiming a foul.

I had read a feature story somewhere about the ten living people who could expect the greatest obituary space in the world press, and I challenged Ring and one or two of my brothers, none of whom had seen the list yet, to name the ten. I don't remember now what year it was or the precise ten listed; Gandhi, Chaplin, Ford, Mussolini and Shaw were among them; anyway, after I had rejected two or three wrong guesses and dropped a few clues, they got the list up to nine of the specified ten. Then, when they were clearly stuck, I offered the hint that the missing man's initials were "A.R." Now the silence was really painful and the pain clearly visible, Ring's especially, as they struggled with those initials. When he finally gave up, I told him the tenth man was Achille Ratti, also known as Pope Pius XI.

It didn't occur to me that I might be making myself unpopular with tactics of this sort. At some point, which must have been while John was still too young to care about such things, Ellis decided to shave two years off her age, so that within our memory she was officially four years younger than Ring, rather than the actual two. But either she herself or her mother or one of her sisters told some family story when I was about eleven involving the fact that Ellis had been born on Easter Sunday. I repaired to an almanac at the first opportunity, established that Easter had occurred on April 10, her freely admitted birthday, in 1887 but not, obviously, in 1889, and confronted my mother with the discrepancy. Her reaction was even surlier than my father's to the revelation about "A.R." and I was quickly persuaded to the view that her age was whatever she said it was.

For all our interest in newspapers and magazines, the main leisure-time activity of our family was reading books. There were evenings when all six of us would be sitting, or lying on the floor, in the same living room, each with a book. Movies were never more than a once-a-week proposition, and though we acquired a radio quite early—Christmas, 1923—it was rarely used when the novelty had worn off. After we moved to East Hampton in 1928, the music we listened to most often, when Ring wasn't playing the piano himself, came from the same instrument, an Ampico grand that was also a player piano, with a drawer beneath the keyboard into which you inserted the recorded rolls. The sound was superior to any other method of reproducing piano music at that time.

Both our parents encouraged us to read certain books in a casual, soft-sell kind of way. Ellis pushed the familiar nineteenth-century English novels, Dickens, Jane Austen, Thackeray and one of her particular favorites, George Meredith, though she herself read rather indiscriminately—mysteries and a lot of current fiction, not necessarily the best. Ring kept up with contemporary writing but was much less tolerant of it. He had a preference for Russian literature, Dostoyevsky above all: *The Brothers Karamazov* was so much his favorite novel that he read it over again every few years. The last few years of his life, he almost gave up reading fiction at all in favor of historical writing, especially about the American Civil War.

Jim and I went through a spell of reading Louisa May Alcott when we were about ten and nine, and once at lunch we talked about our respective preferences among the sisters in *Little Women.* "I liked Beth best," my father said, "because she died."

I was jolted at the time by what seemed pretty close to sacrilege, but he revealed a familiarity with the book which, I figured out later, meant he had once been just as captivated by it as I was. John recalled in later years that he was rebuked for being discovered in secret possession of a "risqué" book called *The Plastic Age,* but that Ring was even more concerned about his reading one called *Won in the Ninth,* which presented a false image of baseball.

None of the four of us was ever enrolled in a public educational institution at any level. The private school Jim and I attended most of our Great Neck years and in which David began his schooling was newly founded and comprised only the early grades to begin with. Jim's class was always the highest one; as it advanced each year the school expanded by one grade until it went up to the eighth and final one. That was why John had to go to another school under the same management in nearby Glen Head. When he graduated from the eighth grade there, and when Jim and then I graduated from our school, the only two possibilities were Great Neck High and boarding school, and the first possibility was never seriously considered. I didn't question this policy at the time and thoroughly enjoyed my four years at Andover. By the time my own children were ready for high school, however, I had developed a strong bias in favor of public education that happily coincided with a sharp drop in my income. Part of that bias sprang from a recollection of an American history class in the Great Neck Preparatory School, as it was called. My classmates, of whom there were never more than seven or eight, were children of investment bankers, corporation presidents and the similarly situated. Adapting herself splendidly to her audience, our teacher presented to us the heroic struggle of Theodore Roosevelt against the temptations of wealth and indolence. It was easy enough, she maintained, to work hard and make a name for yourself when you were born in a log cabin and the only choice open to you was hard work. But when the heir to a proud name and secure fortune gave himself to public service, it was pure altruism all the way.

7

For my parents what turned out to be the last thirteen years of Ring's life were divided roughly into a period of growing success, enjoyment of life and development of his creative powers, and a period of decline in health, in happiness and in both the impulse and the ability to create. There were spells of gloom and frustration in the first period, involving bouts with alcohol and the fact that the work he cared least to do brought the most money; and it was during the second period that they built a more congenial home in East Hampton and Ring scored the success that mattered most to him with the play *June Moon;* but in general and with some overlapping in the middle years, the contrast is quite distinct and the main event dividing the two periods is the diagnosis of tuberculosis in 1926.

The move east had been a good one for both Ring and Ellis. They found New York and Great Neck a good deal more stimulating than Chicago and its suburbs. Two men Ring had grown up with, his brother Rex and Arthur Jacks, moved to Great Neck with their families about the same time he did. People they had already known became in proximity best friends: Grantland and Kate Rice, John and "Tee" Wheeler, James and May Wilson Preston, Frank and Esther Adams, Rube and Irma Goldberg, Percy and Florence Hammond. An added attraction for Ring in the Great Neck area was the number of successful people in the entertainment world: Ed Wynn, Eddie Cantor, W. C. Fields,

Ellis and Ring on vacation in the early 1920s

Fanny Brice, Groucho Marx, John Golden, Gene Buck, George M. Cohan, Laurette Taylor, Jane Cowl, Thomas Meighan, Richard Barthelmess and Blanche Ring. All of these became friends or acquaintances, but Ring and Ellis's closest ties, during the year and a half they lived a couple of miles away, were with the much younger Scott and Zelda Fitzgerald.

For several decades Frank Adams as F.P.A. ran a feature in his column called "The Diary of Our Own Samuel Pepys," and a few excerpts from it provide a glimpse of the life the Lardners led in the twenties (the first item quoted is from the column of January 25, 1920; the last one, September 10, 1927):

R. Lardner played upon his saxophone, very sweetly, too, a gift I envy him; and Mistress Ellis, his wife, hath a pretty voice, and a fair spoke manner, and four fine boys.

. . . and thereafter, with my wife and Mistress Ellis Lardner and Neysa and Sally and Rosina and R. Lardner and J. Hutchinson and H. Harrison, to the circus, and Neysa and Ellis rode upon the elephants, and looked more royal than any queens ever I saw. [Neysa McMein, the artist, was the glamour girl of the North Shore celebrity set.]

Thence to the city, and stopped by for Mistress Neysa, and with her to Great Neck, to Mistress Ellis Lardner's, and her son John shewed me the weekly paper he edits, and writes the most of . . . and it was the most readable Sunday newspaper I ever had seen.

At four arrived in the city, and so to Great Neck, and went to call upon R. Lardner and Ellis, and we hard at the Cross Word Puzzle, the hardest in a long time, nor could we get the word for Class of Bivalves, which later we found to be Veneracea.

. . . and thence to Ring's for dinner. . . . And we played a variety of guessing games, and Mrs. Tobin of Niles, Mich., the most amusing lady ever I met and very sweet, too.

[In a game of charades that night, our Aunt Anne appeared in a jacket of Ring's and announced that she represented two French cities, which turned out to be Toulouse and Toulon. We boys enthusiastically shared F.P.A.'s judgment of her.]

So met with Mistress Ellis Lardner, and begged her for a lodging, so I and my wife to R. Lardner's, and had a pleasant time talking of this and that, and R. tells me that his four sons and his little niece, Miss Anne Tobin, are writing a libretto called "Skinafore," which they will play Friday, and the musick will be good, being written by Sir Arthur Sullivan himself.

Up by times and with my wife and R. Lardner and P. Palmer to Germantown, and saw the French players win the Davis Cup. . . . So home by train, and saw on a hoarding a sign that said, "Lillian Gish in 'Annie Laurie,' " which R. Lardner and I sang at the top of our voices, the top being very high.

Traveling to sports events and other occasions in those years, Ring played a dual role as reporter and celebrity. He and Ellis went to Washington for the inauguration of President Harding in 1921, and Ellis reported in the Abbott family round robin: "I was very favorably impressed with Mr. Harding. He is a good speaker and very forceful and dignified looking. Even Mrs. H. is better looking than I expected." A month later Ring was back in Washington with Grantland Rice for a golf foursome with the President and Under Secretary of State Henry Fletcher. He, too, was favorably disposed to Mrs. Harding because she gave him three large cups of coffee with lunch.

On the course a drive of Ring's broke off a tree branch which fell on Harding. "I did all I could to make Coolidge President," Ring told him. When Harding wanted to know if there was anything he could do for him, Ring said he'd like to be made ambassador to Greece. Asked why, his only explanation was "My wife doesn't like Great Neck." Writing to her family about the President, Ellis reported that "Ring thinks he is a little too much of a good fellow."

Ellis and her friend from Smith, Helen Jacks (she and her husband, Ring's friend Arthur, had met at the Lardner wedding), had birthdays on successive days in April, and that same year Ring gave them matinee tickets to John Drinkwater's *Mary Stuart* as a present. When they returned from Manhattan by

Leaving the White House for a round of golf, 1921: President Harding,
Grantland Rice, Ring Lardner and Under Secretary of State Henry R. Fletcher

train, the current chauffeur, Lawrence, drove them to the golf club, where Ring, Rex, Arthur Jacks, the Wheelers and Helen's brother, Jimmy Gibson, were gathered for a surprise dinner. Afterward they went to the Lardners', where the living room was arranged as a theater with a sheet for the curtain. The play, written by Ring, took place in their Smith dormitory, with Ring as Ellis Abbott, Jimmy as Helen Gibson, Arthur as a third girl and Rex as Loring Hoover, Ellis's guest at the Junior Prom.

The second winter in Great Neck they began an annual practice of going on a winter vacation with the Rices, staying some or all of the time at a Florida resort called Belleair so Ring and Granny Rice could get in some golf. In 1923, with the great real estate boom under way, they went on to Miami, which Ellis described as "the gayest place I ever was in. It is beautiful—that is Miami Beach, where the Flamingo Hotel is, is beautiful, the town of Miami is like a circus. . . . There were at least two parties every day. We went on picnics in speed boats (with Gar Wood among others)—watched polo games—went sailing—surf swimming etc. It was too gay for me. I like Belleair better."

One of the attractions that had drawn them east was the theater, and, with Manhattan half an hour away, they went often, usually to opening nights. Ring was especially interested in musicals and he would carry away the main tunes of a Kern or a Romberg or a Gershwin score in his head and play them for us on the piano next day.

He was engaged by Ziegfeld to write some sketches for the *Follies of 1922,* two of which were used and favorably received by the critics, including Robert Benchley and Heywood Broun. The one they particularly hailed was "The Bull Pen" featuring Will Rogers as a veteran pitcher and Andrew Tombes as a rookie. It was the only time, I think, until his movie career began in the thirties, that Rogers used another writer's material, and the relationship between him and Ring was, and continued to be, an uneasy one. Even when Rogers visited him in the hospital ten years later and wrote about it in his syndicated column, Ring reacted adversely to the line "There's a man that's forgotten more humor than the rest of us ever knew." It wasn't the ambiguity itself that bothered him so much as the fact that Rogers, pouncing on the first cliché that came along, was probably unaware there was any ambiguity.

The other sketch was not so widely admired, but the reviews treated it as amusing and none of them took exception to its content. It was called "Rip Van Winkle" and its hero awoke after twenty years to find everything taken over by Jews, including the Presidency and Vice-Presidency. The big laugh line, which Ring said was rewritten by Al Shean, a Jewish comedian, was in answer to Rip's query as to whether the incumbents were Democrats or Republicans: "Neither. They are Jewish. Everything is Jewish; even the Knights of Columbus."

We boys started going to the theater at an early age; the first show I can remember was *Rose Marie* when I was nine. We saw the original productions of *Show Boat, Good News, No, No, Nanette, The Grab Bag, Manhattan Mary* and *Simple Simon* (the last three starring Ring's friend Ed Wynn). I recall the Wynn shows particularly because the comedian, forewarned of our presence, would work in some ad lib about "Bill Lardner's birthday" or whatever the occasion might be. And a comedy-mystery called *The Spider*, that wasn't too memorable otherwise, stays with me because the production was halted for the announcement from the stage that Lindbergh had landed in Paris.

Ring did continue to go to certain sports events occasionally, both for material for his weekly column and because he was still a fan, especially of football and boxing and of tennis at nearby Forest Hills in the years dominated by Bill Tilden. He covered the Dempsey fights with Willard, Carpentier and Firpo, and the first one with Tunney, and the World Series his first three years in the East. Then after a gap of three years he went to the Series again in 1925, explaining in a letter to the Fitzgeralds in France:

I had forgotten what terrible things world's series were so I consented to cover this year's. I got drunk three days before it started

145

in the hope and belief that I would be remorseful and sober by the time I had to go to it. But when I got to Pittsburgh, it seemed that I was the only newspaper man in America who had reserved a room; all the others moved in with me and there wasn't a chance to eat, sleep, work, or do anything but drink. The result was two fairly good stories and seven terrible ones out of a possible nine, including rainy days.

His disenchantment with baseball had clearly begun with the "Black Sox" Series of 1919, but I feel the extent of it has been exaggerated, along with the idea that he came to hate the whole human race.

The great scandal, involving the corruption of eight players on the club with which he had been most closely associated, was not exposed publicly until eleven months later, but Ring was so disturbed by the timing of the Chicago pitcher, Eddie Cicotte, on what could have been a double play in the first game that he invited Cicotte, whom he had described in 1915 as the best all-round ball player among Major League pitchers, to his Cincinnati hotel room afterward for a drink, and asked him point-blank if the defeat had been deliberate, which Cicotte naturally denied. By the end of the second game, when many Chicago fans were laying down fresh money on a White Sox comeback, Ring knew the fix was in.

That evening, either in a saloon across the border in Kentucky or right in front of the offending team in their Pullman car on the way back to Chicago, or both (each version has been reliably reported), he sang a lyric of his own devising to the hit tune "I'm Forever Blowing Bubbles":

> I'm forever throwing ball games,
> Pretty ball games in the air,
> I come from Chi,
> I hardly try,
> Just go to bat and fade and die.
> Fortune's coming my way,
> That's why I don't care.
> I'm forever throwing ball games,
> And the gamblers treat us fair.

I was only four at the time and can't testify directly to my father's reaction, but I don't think a deeply disillusioned man could dash off that lyric, and the way he spoke about the event later gave me the feeling he was at least as concerned about losing a substantial bet (three months after his and Willard's defeat at Toledo) as he was about the moral turpitude of the players. Ring took his gambling seriously and did not, as Maxwell Geismar writes in *Ring Lardner and the Portrait of Folly,* always lose money on his bets; in 1927, for instance, he won thirty-two hundred dollars against odds by his selection of the Pittsburgh Pirates to win the National League pennant.

There was something else that had happened that changed his attitude toward baseball, and that was the introduction of the "crazy" or livelier ball, which made it a hitter's instead of a pitcher's game and which he maintained had been done deliberately to make Ruth's home runs possible. But he still took us to ball games as long as his health allowed it, making sure we understood the fine points of the action, and he followed the pennant races every year, usually placing at least one bet with Jack Doyle, the bookmaker. And in the last decade of his life he wrote about the game again in two short stories, a play and a magazine series that became a book.

On July 2, 1921, two next-door neighbors on East Shore Road traveled to Jersey City to watch the first "million-dollar gate" fight between Jack Dempsey and Georges Carpentier, and both wrote about it under the title "The Battle of the Century." For Herbert Swope the evening proved that "Carpentier is in all probability the most formidable boxer in the world except Dempsey," and he noted that "There will always be speculation as to what would have happened had Carpentier not broken his hand in the second round." To Ring Lardner there was never any ground for speculation about the outcome from the moment the hopeless mismatch was announced. Skirting libel laws in thinly disguised fiction, he accused the promoters of selling tickets (fifty dollars for "ringside") with a phony build-up of "a pale, frail boy that if he'd went to college the football coaches would have rushed him for cheer leader."

These contrasting reactions to the same spectacle are indicative of a basic difference between the two men that explains why they never became really close in those eight years of proximity. Swope was a classic extrovert, gregarious in the extreme, with enthusiasms that sometimes approached manic intensity, a booster of the status quo who glorified American institutions all his life with a staggering array of facts to back his arguments. Ring was reserved, laconic, uneasy in crowds, with a mask over his emotions and a deep-seated mistrust of face values, a cynic who felt that if something could be faked it probably was.

Five years later, when Dempsey lost his title to Gene Tunney in a ten-round decision in Philadelphia, Ring was in a minority, along with Benny Leonard, the great ex-lightweight champion, that felt that fight was a frame-up. To the Fitzgeralds he wrote:

> Heywood Broun refused, at the last minute, to cover it and as a favor to Herbert [Swope], and to my syndicate, I said I would do it. . . . I bet $500 on Dempsey, giving 2 to 1. The odds ought to have been 7 to 1. Tunney couldn't lick David [Lardner] if David was trying. The thing was a very well done fake, which lots of us would like to say in print, but you know what newspapers are where possible libel suits are concerned. As usual, I did my heavy thinking too late; otherwise I would have bet the other way. The championship wasn't worth a dime to Jack; there was nobody else for him to fight and he had made all there was to be made (by him) out of vaudeville and pictures.

Ring had visited Tunney's training camp with Ellis and the Rices for lunch a few weeks previously and had been unfavorably impressed. The fighter expressed the hope that Dempsey wouldn't think his (Tunney's) motion picture experience had "cosmeticized" him, and he kept a small leather-bound book at his side at all times, even taking it to the table with him when the meal was served. Telling us about it later, Ring said he was praying that no one would ask Tunney what it was, but the Rices' nineteen-year-old daughter, Florence (Floncy), disappointed him by putting the question. "Oh, just a copy of the *Rubaiyat* that

I'm never without," said the heavyweight contender.

Most experts disagreed with Ring's verdict that night in Philadelphia, and the doubts of others were effectively dispelled by Tunney's second ("long-count") victory a year later in Chicago. The way Granny Rice saw that first fight:

> . . . Gene Tunney, a superbly cool and efficient boxer, marched out of his corner at the opening bell and hit Dempsey, the fighter, with a high, hard right hand. That blow sealed Dempsey's doom. . . . Had the fight gone 15 rounds, the referee would have had to stop it. . . . I intended to give Tunney a fitting tribute in my overnight story that historical night. And I intended to go as easy on Dempsey as I could. I did neither.

The reason he did neither was that after filing his factual description from ringside, he was stricken at the hotel by a virus or Prohibition liquor or both. Ring volunteered, under at least one of these influences himself, to write the overnight story for his friend, and sent out a piece under Granny's by-line blasting the two fighters for a staged performance. It was some time before Granny could resume his previously friendly relations with both Dempsey and Tunney.

Ring never thought of himself as a writer of books, but he had eight of them published in the four years ending in 1921. They were all collections of material that had appeared in magazines and he did almost no editing of them, so it was natural for him to think of them as by-products providing some much-needed supplementary income. Only two of them, *The Young Immigrunts* and *The Big Town,* were at the top of his form, and none of them drew much attention either from the critics or the book-buying public. Most of Ring's letters to Bobbs-Merrill of Indianapolis, his publisher in those years, contain requests to "nudge" or "remind" the bookkeeping department to send along his royalty checks and the largest sum mentioned is five hundred and seventy-four dollars. The records I have are incomplete, but they indicate that his income from books came to about two thousand a year at that time, which I estimate to be a bit over 10 percent of his total. Clearly he was pressing to have his checks sent because he was living right up to his income and perhaps beyond.

That was always the pattern. Ring and Ellis never had any substantial savings account nor did they follow the prevailing practice among their friends of putting a portion of each year's income into the rising stock market. Only once, in 1925, did they accumulate enough surplus to consider an investment, and they chose to make a down payment on a forty-four-acre farm a few miles away. Fortunately for them, they needed the money back before the 1929 crash and came out with a pleasing profit.

What Ring did do, as long as his health enabled him to pass the examinations, was to keep increasing his life insurance and give top priority to maintaining his premium payments.

One way to make some extra money was to write for the movies, and as early as 1916 Ring contracted to write twelve baseball shorts for two hundred and fifty dollars each. In 1925 he undertook to write a scenario for Thomas Meighan, who was not only a Great Neck neighbor and major movie star but one of the few drinkers whom Ring classified with himself as a genuine "two-bottle man." The picture, directed by Lewis Milestone before he became famous with *All Quiet on the Western Front,* was a comedy called *The New Klondike* about a baseball player involved in the Florida real estate boom. It was well received except by Ring, who wrote in his weekly column: ". . . they was a couple of baseball incidence in it that would make a ball player wonder if the author had fell out of a toy balloon in his infancy." The choice of a gifted European director may have had some bearing both on the positive values of the picture and the technical defects Ring saw in it.

The price Ring set on his services was generally in inverse proportion to his esteem for the medium. James Thurber wrote in *The Years with Ross* that when his daughter was born at Doctors Hospital in New York in 1931, a young intern said to him: "There's a patient here who is a writer and he says he would rather write for *The New Yorker* for five cents a word than for

Cosmopolitan for a dollar." Thurber asked if his name was Ring Lardner "and the man was astonished at my perception or magic or whatever." Asked what he wanted for *The New Klondike* job, Ring figured out he could do it in a week, ascertained that Meighan's pay for a week's work was seventy-five hundred dollars, then demanded and got the same.

The following year an MGM executive asked him to do a baseball picture for the comedy star Karl Dane. "I told him I didn't know what authors were getting," he wrote the Fitzgeralds. "He said, 'Well, we are giving Johnny Weaver $7,500 and Marc Connelly the same,' so he asked me again what I wanted and I said $40,000 and he threw up his hands and exclaimed, 'Excuse me, Mr. Lardner, for wasting your valuable time!' " Six months before Ring died, Harold Lloyd came with an entourage to visit him at La Quinta on the California desert, but negotiations broke down when it turned out all Lloyd wanted was the bare idea told in two paragraphs from which his scenarists and gag men would take over. Ring wrote about it in a joint letter to the four of us and our cousin Dick Tobin, who was then living with John in New York: "Well, to be modest, this was like sending Babe Ruth to bat and letting him stand there till the umpire had called one ball, then taking him out and substituting a good hitter."

Ring was not a close observer of the Hollywood product. After seeing a handful of talking pictures, he made a firm prediction that films would return to their natural state of silence once the novelty had worn off. The movie version of *June Moon* in 1931 did nothing to shake this belief. He didn't actually see it himself, but his collaborator, George Kaufman, did and wired him about it, recalling that they had deliberately used a cliché plot as a framework for comedy scenes that worked. The movie, Kaufman said, kept the plot intact and threw out all the comedy.

That was Kaufman's opinion. But his was necessarily a subjective reaction and he had an abiding contempt for the medium. A fairer presentation of the actual merits of the movie might be found in a couple of reviews from popular magazines of the day. The two I have chosen, *Judge* and *Life,* were both primarily humor magazines, but their critical departments were quite serious. (*Life* had no connection other than the name with the later picture news magazine.)

From *Judge:*	From *Life:*
A play by two of the wittiest men . . . was tossed into a conference room, and when the supervisors, re-write men, censors, sales managers and directors finished with it, *June Moon* no more resembled the Kaufman-Lardner play than Franklin Roosevelt looks like the future president. . . . I cannot tell you of one thing the director could have done to *June Moon* to make it any worse than it is.	By the simple means of sticking closely to the stage version, and selecting a cast with reasonable intelligence, Paramount brings *June Moon* to the screen with all of its entertainment qualities intact. The lines and situations created by Ring Lardner and George Kaufman are very nearly foolproof. . . . You will enjoy this picture.

The incidental political analysis in the *Judge* review was written eighteen months before Roosevelt's election.

Ring also had dealings with film companies involving the rights to the play *Elmer the Great,* which became a movie twice, as *Fast Company* in 1929 and under the play title in 1933, and to *You Know Me Al* and the short story "I Can't Breathe," neither of which was ever filmed. One of his objections to picture executives and other self-important people was that they violated his standards of telephone etiquette. Ring never had anyone else make a phone call for him and he expected the same courtesy in return. If he picked up the phone and a secretary announced that Mr. So-and-so was calling, he hung up. The caller usually got the point.

June Moon was readapted under the title *Blonde Trouble* in 1937 and emerged no better than the first time (as viewed by Kaufman and *Judge*). *Fast Company* was also the basis of a 1939 movie called *The Cowboy Quarterback,* which sounds peculiar if you know it was a baseball play and don't know how the B-picture department at Warner Brothers operated in those days. But I do know because I was there up to within a few months of that remake, and more than once I was summoned to receive a writing assignment from the remarkable head of that department, Bryan Foy of the famous theatrical family. "Brynie" turned out a completed feature film every two weeks, and when it was in the can he would place a copy of the screenplay at the bottom of a stack (the most distant of several) on his office floor. When he called in a writer, he didn't know what the assignment was going to be until you sat down opposite him and he reached over for the top script on the nearest stack, which had traveled many years across the floor.

"Let's see," he would say before he handed you the script to go to work on, "this one was about speedboat racing. Why don't we do it about motorcycles this time?"

After Ring died Ellis made several deals with movie companies. "The Golden Honeymoon" and "Haircut" were bought but never made. *Alibi Ike* became a vehicle for Joe E. Brown in 1935. After the war a new company founded by Stanley Kramer and Carl Foreman produced creditable adaptations of two Lardner works. The first, *So This Is New York*, based on *The Big Town* and starring Henry Morgan, was their initial production and failed so miserably at the box office it nearly sank the company before it was fully launched. The second, *Champion*, put the company across and made a star of Kirk Douglas.

Scott Fitzgerald was the catalytic agent in the transformation of Ring Lardner from a journalistic funnyman to a literary figure. Just as he was to do with his next year's "find," Ernest Hemingway, Scott persuaded Ring and Max Perkins of Scribner's that both parties would benefit from an affiliation. The specific idea, which had apparently never occurred to Ring, was to make a book of a selection of his short stories, and the sample Scott presented to Perkins was the one the *Saturday Evening Post* turned down, "The Golden Honeymoon," which Ring had written on a train trip from Florida to New York. Ray Long, editor of *Cosmopolitan*, had bought it for fifteen hundred dollars and published it in his July, 1922, issue.

After reading it Perkins wrote Ring for copies of other stories, creating an impasse. Money was just one of the paper goods Ring never bothered to save. He casually threw away almost all the letters addressed to him, including a great many from people already famous or soon to be. He never made a copy of his own letters, or of his stories, sending the originals to magazines and never keeping the magazines after they were published.

Ring, Scott and Perkins met for dinner at René Durand's restaurant and speakeasy, across the tip of the bay from East Shore Road, to address themselves to this problem. After a long and liquid session, Ring got into his car and drove home. The other two men got into Scott's car and Scott drove them into Durand's lily pond.

Of the three Ring seemed the least interested in locating copies of the stories. He would say that "The Facts," for instance, had appeared in either *McClure's* or *Metropolitan* during 1916 or possibly 1917, and Perkins would send an assistant to the library to check it out. Seven months later he was still writing Ring about such matters as that *McClure's* had no copy of their August, 1915, issue (containing the story "Harmony") and that the *Saturday Evening Post* was indexed only from 1920 on, which meant he would have to have it "looked through in the library between 1914 and 1919 . . . and I think we can arrange to have the stories copied out."

Ring's only contributions to the correspondence in all that time were, in their entirety:

Great Neck, New York
December Fifth

DEAR MR. PERKINS:—

I enclose a (and, I guess, the only) copy of "Champion", which Scott tells me you have been looking for. I'm sorry to have kept you waiting.

And:

DEAR MR. PERKINS:—

The arrangement and terms are satisfactory to me. I'm sorry you have had so much trouble gathering the stuff. Why not visit Great Neck again? It's safer now as Durand's pond is frozen over.

There was a lot of talk about a title before they decided on *How to Write Short Stories (With Samples),* which was Scott's idea, but all three men should be faulted for not anticipating that it would be classified in library catalogues with textbooks on writing. I think Ring accepted it because it gave him an idea for a preface. He regarded all prefaces (and most literary criticism) as nonsense, but they were practically obligatory in those days for such collections, so his solution was to write nonsense prefaces. This first one said in part:

. . . But a little group of our deeper drinkers has suggested that maybe boys and gals who wants to take up writing as their lifework would be benefited if some person like I was to give them a few hints in regards to the technic of the short story, how to go about planning it and writing it, when and where to plant the love interest and climax, and finally how to market the finished product without leaving no bad taste in the mouth. . . .

A good many young writers make the mistake of enclosing a stamped, self-addressed envelope, big enough for the manuscript to come back in. This is too much of a temptation to the editor. Personally I have found it a good scheme to not even sign my name to the story, and when I have got it sealed up in its envelope and stamped and addressed, I take it to some town where I don't live and mail it from there. The editor has no idea who wrote the story, so how can he send it back? He is in a quandary.

And then, typically, he turned his sights on his very sponsors. Perkins had published a Fitzgerald collection called *Tales of the Jazz Age,* in which each story title was followed by a couple of explanatory (and clearly superfluous) paragraphs about its contents and the circumstances in which it was written. Ring parodied this device, too. His foreword to "A Frame-up," for instance, which deals with a prizefighter from rural Michigan, read:

A stirring romance of the Hundred Years' War, detailing the adventures in France and Castile of a pair of well-bred weasels. The story is an example of what can be done with a stub pen.

His second collection had the preface by Sarah E. Spooldripper I quoted at the beginning. Referring to Ring as "the Master" and Ellis as "Junior," it described the former's death from a

fatal attack of conchoid, a disease which is superinduced by a rush of seashells to the auricle or outer ear. Present during the last hours were only myself and the wolf, Junior having chosen this time to get a shampoo and wave in preparation for the series of dinner dances that were bound to follow.

The reviewer in the *New York Times* Sunday book section chose as a stylistic device to take this obituary seriously and a subhead read: "A Victim of 'Conchoid,' or Rush of Sea Shells to the Outer Ear, He Leaves a Characteristic Collection of Stories." The result, Ring reported in a letter to "Dear Scott and Darling Zelda" in France:

was that Ellis was kept busy on the telephone all that Sunday evening assuring friends and reporters that I was alive and well. It just happened that I was at home and cold sober; if I'd been out, she might have worried a little. Or maybe not.

One has to assume that these callers were people who didn't even bother to finish the review. Certainly the preface itself was too broad a burlesque for any reader without at least a master's degree to plumb for deeper significance. *The Story of a Wonder Man,* a mock autobiography in 1927, was also introduced in the same style by Miss Spooldripper, with her occupation slightly changed:

The publication of this autobiography is entirely without the late Master's sanction. He wrote it as a pastime and burnt up each chapter as soon as it was written; the salvaging was accomplished by ghouls who haunted the Lardners' ash bbl. during my whole tenure of office as night nurse to their dromedary.

Some of the copy was so badly charred as to be illegible. The ghouls took the liberty of filling in these hiatuses with "stuff" of their own, which can readily be distinguished from the Master's as it is not nearly so good. Readers and critics are therefore asked to bear in mind that those portions of the book which they find entertaining are the work of the Master himself; those which bore them or sound forced are interpolations. . . .

Perhaps the severest strain on the critical mind is to accept a writer who appears not to take his work seriously, and accordingly it fantasizes that his levity masks a hatred of the world and himself. To the reviewer of *How to Write Short Stories* in the New York *Tribune:*

> There are times when it seems to us a little indecent for a man to make fun of himself. . . . If reverence has a place in this world it should be found in a human's attitude toward the best work he can do. In Mr. Lardner's case his best is better than almost anyone's.

Edmund Wilson, on his way to becoming the pre-eminent critic of his time, complained of Ring's lack of

> artistic seriousness . . . he compiles a book of the best things he has written and then, with his title and his comic preface, tries to pretend that he has never attempted to write anything good at all. Yet he has qualities which should make it more nearly possible for him than for perhaps any other living American to produce another *Huckleberry Finn.*

In 1933, six months before Ring's actual death, Clifton Fadiman came up with the revelation that Miss Spooldripper represented the compulsive need for "ironical self-castigation" of a writer who had "gone farther on hatred alone" than anyone since Swift. . . . I believe he hates himself; more certainly he hates his characters; and most clearly of all his characters hate each other."

Ring read Fadiman's piece, made no public answer to it and sent a newspaper résumé of it to a friend with no comment except his signature to the accompanying letter: "A Born Hater."

Thirty years later in his introduction to *The Ring Lardner Reader,* Maxwell Geismar wondered why Ring "insisted on describing his own best work in curious terms of disparagement" and found that "the self-depreciating strain in Lardner's work from the beginning . . . had become a kind of self-loathing." In *Ring Lardner and the Portrait of Folly,* published in 1972, Geismar's reading between the lines had grown more assured:

> These curious prefaces to the stories are an ironical and farcical statement of Lardner's true feelings about himself, his career, his work. He wasn't just kidding; rather their morbid humor allowed him to confess his true state of mind. That "wolf at the door," which represented Lardner's constant fear of not being able to make enough money to maintain his family's standard of living—a standard he himself insisted on for his wife and children—led him to some dark reflections on his own writing career, to wish he had never been born.

The ordinary reader, of course, read the same prefaces and found no such hidden significance. He just thought they were funny, or perhaps not so funny, depending on his taste. But he had no doubt about the intention behind them. Which brings us pretty close to the difference between a reader and a critic. The former may have invoked his unalienable right not to read scholarly introductions, but he had skimmed enough of them to know whom Ring was kidding. The parodies were directed not inward at the author himself but at the heavy-handed academic types, the literary essayists and authors of prefaces. They were thus an integral part of Ring's work as a whole, in which the main target was always pretense and pomposity.

Literary critics and historians, whose lethal occupation is the dissection of living prose, had trouble with Ring from the start. For one thing, their preferred pattern for an artist of any stature is that his talent be recognized initially by a few critical pioneers, who then proceed to their secondary function of elevating the general public to an appreciation of his merits. Sometimes, however, popular acclaim comes first, and the critics, gradually, reluctantly, have to accept the prior judgment of the common people. So it was with Dickens and Twain, with Chaplin and Gershwin, and so it was with Ring, in whose case the reluctance lasted more than a decade.

He was not an easy man for the arbiters of American literature to take to their bosoms. He wrote for, and managed to please, the conspicuously nonintellectual readers of the popular magazines. His stories dealt with ballplayers and other denizens of the lower depths of American culture. They made people laugh rather than think and they were written in a version of English without literary precedent.

Even after the decision was finally official, even now when the lines of his influence have been traced from Hemingway and Farrell and Anderson through Wolfe, Thurber, Hammett, O'Hara, Salinger and a continuing succession of American writers, his greatest admirers in higher critical circles are still uncomfortable with him. They strive, out of their own need to justify their function, to discover a deeper purpose beneath his most casual efforts and especially a tragic symbolism behind his freest flights of nonsense.

Of course some of his stories expose their principal characters so devastatingly the reader who went no further might suspect the author of misanthropy. But his tolerance and even affection for other characters he invented are equally obvious. As often happened, Dorothy Parker said it better in a few words than her fellow critics did in paragraphs when she wrote of "his strange, bitter pity."

It is also true there was a mordant side to his nature that developed with physical illness into periods of melancholy. The fact that he sought and failed to find release in alcohol has led to speculation about the roots of the despair that presumably provoked the addiction. But my empirical research into this particular disease leads me to believe that it is more likely to be the cause of depression than the result of it. The alcoholic is dismayed by his failure to conquer the addiction and he takes to drink to relieve his dismay, but the end result is that he increases it instead. In Ring's case the vicious circle was aggravated by his staunchly Protestant conscience.

Although he never kept copies of his stories, he did get reviews of his books, and later of his plays, from a clipping service. I never actually caught him at it, but I'm quite sure he read them in the privacy of his workroom. And he gradually came to realize he had made a name for himself in American literature. As an increasing body of critics followed the lead of F.P.A., H. L. Mencken, Burton Rascoe and Gilbert Seldes in recognizing his special quality, he responded by writing parodies of literary criticism. But that was just a defensive reaction, a necessary façade for a man whose work was a continuous indictment of people who took themselves too seriously. He knew perfectly well how good he was and better than anyone what an effort it was, especially in the later years, to live up to it.

Two other Fitzgerald proposals were undertaken by Scribner's that same spring *How to Write Short Stories* came out. One was the reissue, with the prestige of the Scribner aegis, of *You Know Me Al, Gullible's Travels* and *The Big Town.* The other was a collection of nonfiction syndicate pieces under the title (suggested by Grantland Rice) *What of It?* A year after the first publication of *How to Write Short Stories,* a critical and commercial success that surprised and pleased Ring, it reappeared as part of a uniform edition with the other four titles. Thus in the year 1925 critics, scholars and the reading public were confronted with an impressive set of five volumes from a name that was already extremely well known but almost wholly in association with newspapers and magazines.

8

Scott and Zelda made a strong impression on me in those days, even though I wasn't nine yet when they left Great Neck for the South of France. I never did see her again and my next encounter with him was at an exhibition of her paintings Ellis and I went to in 1934. I was a sophomore at Princeton, where I had gone because he had told me I should all those years before, and we talked about that as well as my father's recent death. Then I knew him again in Hollywood the last three years of his life, when his personality, at least with nonintimates, was all but extinguished.

We all liked him in that Great Neck period, mostly, I suppose, because he seemed to like and be interested in us. He told us stories and did card tricks for us and we felt he genuinely cared, as opposed to Sinclair Lewis, for instance, whom we didn't like because he communicated with us only to demonstrate to the other adults some theory of his about children's responses.

But on me at least it was Zelda, whom I didn't see as often, who left the deepest imprint. There were grown women I thought of as beautiful, including my mother, but Zelda was twenty-two years old when we first knew her and Ellis already thirty-five. I have never seen a photograph of her that conveyed any real sense of what she looked like, or at least the way she looked to me. A camera recorded the imperfections of her face, missing the coloring and the vitality that transcended them so absolutely. She didn't pay as much attention to us as Scott did, but we were used to that from visiting children, and that was how we thought of her, as another child, free and impulsive in saying or doing whatever she felt like. I have never known another adult, except my Aunt Anne, who seemed to say exactly what came into her head as it came, without any apparent exercise of judgment. I watched and listened to her in total fascination until the time came when grownups and children went their separate ways and she was unfairly borne off with the former.

Ellis liked her and found her stimulating, but she withheld complete approval from either Fitzgerald because of a self-indulgence and exhibitionism her standards simply could not embrace. And her reservations were enhanced by the fact that they were still young enough to drink a lot without the immediately serious consequences Ring was beginning to experience. Ring, however, in many respects the less tolerant of the two, found so much he liked in Scott and Zelda that he waived all his normal criteria and displayed more affection for them than for anyone else outside his family. The long letters he wrote (one, he noted, ran "about 2,500 words and I'm not getting a nickel for it") were mostly addressed to both of them, and there is other evidence that Zelda ranked, among his women friends, second only to Kate Rice, who was also from the Deep South. A verse "not to be opened till Christmas and then only for a little while" began:

> Of all the girls for whom I care
> And there are quite a number,
> None can compare with Zelda Sayre,
> Now wedded to a plumber.

And when they sailed to make a new home near Hyères on the French Riviera, Ring wrote her another that worked up after five stanzas to a specific proposition:

> So, dearie, when your tender heart
> Of all his coarseness tires,
> Just cable me and I will start
> Immediately for Hyeres.

To hell with Scott Fitzgerald then!
To hell with Scott, his daughter!
It's you and I back home again,
To Great Neck where the men are men
And booze is 3/4 water.

There was a porch on the side of our house facing the Swopes',
and Ring and Scott sat there many a weekend afternoon, drinking ale or whiskey and watching what Ring described as "an
almost continuous house-party" next door. Though their entertaining fell a whit short of Gatsby's, the location of the Swopes'
house was just right for the view of Daisy's pier across the bay.
And while there is no other significant similarity between Herbert Swope and Jay Gatsby, Swope's friend Arnold Rothstein
was reputed, like Gatsby's friend Meyer Wolfsheim, to have
fixed the 1919 World Series. Beyond those facts there is only the
knowledge that this was the period of gestation for *The Great
Gatsby.*

Sometimes Ring and Scott talked and drank right through the
night, either alone together or with their wives and perhaps a few
friends, usually at the Fitzgeralds', where Scottie, only two and
a half when they left Great Neck, was too young to notice such
irregularities. As for us, Ring would wait to come home on a
weekday morning till after we had left for school.

It was a remarkable friendship in view of the disparities in
temperament and age. (Ring was thirty-seven, Scott twenty-six
when they met.) Their joint dependence on alcohol was certainly
a factor. A decade later, when Scott was approaching thirty-
seven, he wrote Perkins:

> I was in New York for three days last week on a terrible bat. I was
> about to call you up when I completely collapsed and laid in bed for
> twenty-four hours groaning. Without a doubt the boy is getting too
> old for such tricks. Ernest [Hemingway] told me he concealed from
> you the fact that I was in such rotten shape. . . . Am going on the
> water-wagon from the first of February to the first of April but don't
> tell Ernest because he has long convinced himself that I am an

incurable alcoholic due to the fact that we almost always meet on parties. I am *his* alcoholic just like Ring is mine and do not want to disillusion him, tho even *Post* stories must be done in a state of sobriety.

The self-understanding in these words is outweighed by the self-delusion. By the time they were written the disease had developed in him to about Ring's stage at the time of their companionship. (Actually, for all the similarities, each case of alcoholism is unique. Ring, for instance, maintained his capacity for drink and his physical coordination when drunk for many more years than Scott did.) I think one of the things about Ring that fascinated Scott in the Great Neck days was the image he saw of his own future. He probably felt satisfaction that he could sleep off a drunk and get back to work with much more ease than his older friend, but he must have known he was heading in the same direction. Even the pattern he came to of setting a specific beginning and ending date for going on the wagon was Ring's. In his bachelor days and right up to his seeing in Prohibition a possible enforced solution of his problem, Ring thought in terms of giving up alcohol for life, but during the 1920s he regarded that as an unattainable goal and would set himself a fixed period of abstinence and a fixed quota of work to accomplish in it. When he did finally stop drinking for good in the last few years of his life, the state of his health made it an almost involuntary decision.

Groucho Marx said on the Dick Cavett show a few years ago that Ring Lardner used to take a New York hotel room, fortify himself with a quart or two of whiskey and then knock out a short story. That is nonsense, but it can be said in Groucho's defense that he might have heard it from Ring himself. James Thurber reported that Harold Ross, editor of *The New Yorker,* told him: "I asked Lardner the other day how he writes his short stories, and he said he wrote a few widely separated words or phrases on a piece of paper and then went back and filled in the spaces." Ross believed this; as a writer Thurber knew it was a joke.

Once, getting into a taxi with a friend, Ring dropped a manuscript and the pages scattered in the street. The friend gathered what he could, but there were two pages missing. "Makes no difference, it's for *Cosmopolitan,*" Ring said. That was his public attitude toward his work, not to be confused with reality. He learned about mixing drinking with writing the same way Scott did, and he once said to me, probably with educational intent: "No one, ever, wrote anything as well after even one drink as he would have done without it."

Scott's line about Hemingway considering him an incurable alcoholic contains the implication at least that he, Scott, did not yet regard himself as an alcoholic, and the obvious conviction that there is such a thing as a curable alcoholic. I think he was deluded on both points. Anyone who goes on a three-day bat with a twenty-four-hour recovery period is seriously addicted to alcohol. And one incontrovertible fact established by modern research on alcoholism is that it is a progressive disease and so far from curable that a person who has it can go twenty years without drinking and return, if and when he resumes, to the same symptomatic level he was at when he stopped, or, because his organs have aged meanwhile, a worse one. Knowing this, speakers at meetings of Alcoholics Anonymous always introduce themselves with the words "I am [never "I was . . ."] an alcoholic." Sometimes there is a qualifying adjective: a "sober" or a "recovering" alcoholic, but the present tense is inviolate.

To think you are not an alcoholic, or at least not an "incurable" one, because you can sober up to write a magazine story is simply not facing the truth of your dependence on the most ravaging drug known to man. Addicts have arrived at permanent sobriety by a number of methods, which range in success ratio from sheer unaided will power up to the collective effort and group therapy of A.A., but the rarest phenomemon of all is to reverse the path from moderate to heavy drinking.

Ring and Scott also had in common a respect for each other's work, tinged in both cases by secret reservations about the scope of the other man's talent. Ring never told Scott where he thought he fell short and certainly never expressed himself in public on the subject, but he did write Mencken that his appraisal of *Gatsby* was "close to perfection in criticism," after Mencken, while praising the style and social commentary of the book, had found the plot improbable and the characters, other than Gatsby himself, false.

Scott was the most valuable booster Ring ever had, and he continued to be interested in the sales and critical estimates of the books he had done so much to get published. He thought Ring should write a novel, though he was willing to settle for a novella, and he felt it should be about Great Neck. I don't know exactly what Ring said to him, but when I asked my father if he would ever write a novel, he said that after one chapter he would be even more bored than the reader.

In any case Scott was disappointed that his suggestion was not accepted, and in his affectionate obituary piece about Ring for *The New Republic,* he dealt with what he considered his friend's limitations as a writer. Ring's accomplishment, he wrote, "fell short of the achievement he was capable of. . . . However deeply Ring might cut into it, his cake had the diameter of Frank Chance's diamond. . . . So one is haunted not only by a sense of personal loss but by a conviction that Ring got less percentage of himself on paper than any other American author of the first flight."

Christmas was a major event in our family, especially for Ellis, who provided presents not only for her own household, including a new musical instrument for Ring each year, but for more than twenty nieces and nephews. Ring's annual contribution was a new Christmas card that went out to a long list of people. One year his message read:

> We combed Fifth Avenue this last month
> A hundred times if we combed it onth,
> In search of something we thought would do
> To give to a person as nice as you.

We had no trouble selecting gifts
For the Ogden Armours and Louie Swifts,
The Otto Kahns and the George E. Bakers,
The Munns and the Rodman Wanamakers.

It's a simple matter to pick things out
For people one isn't so wild about,
But you, you wonderful pal and friend, you!
We couldn't find anything fit to send you.
                              THE RING LARDNERS

The following Christmas they got this from the Fitzgeralds:

To the Ring Lardners

You combed Third Avenue last year
For some small gift that was not too dear
—Like a candy cane or a worn out truss—
To give to a loving friend like us.
You'd found gold eggs for such wealthy hicks
As the Edsell [*sic*] Fords and the Pittsburgh Fricks,
The Andy Mellons, the Teddy Shonts,
The Coleman T. and Pierre duPonts,
But not one gift to brighten our hoem
—So I'm sending you back your God damn poem.

After the Fitzgeralds left for France in the spring of 1924, Ring took over some unfinished business concerning the transfer of their lease to new tenants, various local bills they had left behind, and the bank account they continued to maintain in Great Neck. That fall Ellis and Ring went to Europe for two months, during which they visited Zelda and Scott in their new home. The following March Ring read the galleys of *The Great Gatsby* and corrected a few errors of fact regarding various locales used in it. Scott's next book, *All the Sad Young Men,* was dedicated "To Ring and Ellis Lardner."

The correspondence continued for another five years, but there were only a couple more encounters between the men, the last in 1931 when Scott visited Ring in the hospital and found him, according to the obituary piece, looking "already like a man on his deathbed—it was terribly sad to see that six feet three inches of kindness stretched out ineffectual in the hospital room; his fingers trembled with a match, the tight skin on his handsome skull was marked as a mask of misery and nervous pain."

The Lardners' closest friends over a long period of years were Kate and Grantland Rice, whom most people called "Granny" and Ring called "Grant." The two men had a common interest in sports, they liked to play bridge, poker and golf, and they were both gambling men. Otherwise the contrast between them was even more extreme than between Ring and Scott. Ring was a debunker of sports heroes, Granny a glorifier of them. Ring was reserved and taciturn, Granny outgoing and loquacious. Ring's views tended to be pessimistic with a sardonic flavor, Granny's optimistic and tinged with sentiment. There was a whole side of Ring most people never saw because he couldn't be relaxed except with his family and a few close friends. Granny was at his ease everywhere and with everybody; he knew an astonishing number of people by name, but that was only a fraction of the number that knew and greeted him.

Despite their differences each man had deep affection and respect for the other, but it was Kate and Ellis who really forged the bond between the two couples. In her own way Kate was as original a Southern belle as Zelda or Tallulah Bankhead, but notably easier to get along with. Her wit produced as much laughter as that of any nonprofessional on the New York scene, but she was practically unique among comics in her ability to transform herself into the most sympathetic of listeners. Like Granny she had the knack of getting along with all kinds of people, but she had a special regard for Ellis's integrity and judgment, looking up to her as, relatively speaking, an intellectual.

The winter trips the Lardners and Rices took together almost every year during the 1920s were meant to be vacations, but Granny would set aside an hour or two most days to turn out his

Ring, Floncy Rice, Ellis, Kate Rice and Grantland Rice—on one of their briefer excursions

syndicated column, and once Ring stayed in his hotel room for three days and produced two short stories for *Cosmopolitan.* In the winter of 1926, accompanied by Floncy Rice, they lived together on trains and in hotels for three months, traveling from New York to Belleair, to New Orleans for the Mardi Gras, to Coronado Beach, California, to Los Angeles, Monterey and San Francisco. Midway in the trip Ring wrote Scott and Zelda, "The Rices have been with us right along and we are still all speaking."

He also reported that "We had two long and entertaining sessions with Sherwood Anderson and wife in New Orleans." Anderson wrote in his account of one of these occasions:

> There was something loose and free in the little room. How shall I describe it? It was Ring. What we all felt for him was warm affection. . . . We poured it over him as we poured the wine down our throats. We loved him. I cannot help thinking it was a rich and rare evening in his life. He laughed. He talked. He drank the wine. He told stories. It was a good evening for him. It was something more than that for the rest of us. Two years later, I was in the same little restaurant, and the chef, that fat Frenchman, came to my table. I was alone and he brought a bottle of wine. He had come in from the kitchen and had on his white apron. He stood beside my table and poured wine for us both. "To that man you brought here that time . . . to Ring Lardner," he said, lifting his glass.

Anderson also reported the other occasion in a different context. Writing of the difficult situations that arise when people are introduced to authors whose books they haven't read, he described how that happened to a woman at a large party in New Orleans where Ring and he were the celebrities. She gushed to Anderson that she had been longing to meet him and that that last book of his had been so very, very beautiful. Then she was stuck for anything more specific to say and

> There was this terrible waiting time and then Ring, out of the kindness of his heart, helped her out.
> "You mean of course *The Great Gatsby,*" he said, and there was a look of joy and gratitude on that woman's face that I'll never

forget. It was the kind of good deed on Ring's part that inspired other good deeds. It inspired me and I told the woman that Ring was the author of *Sister Carrie* and of course she ran about and told all the others. It made everything all right. It made an evening that had started to be a complete flop a great success.

Two years after that trip the Lardners and Rices were not only still speaking but so compatible they jointly bought land on the ocean at East Hampton and built houses separated by an unbroken stretch of lawn with no indication of a property line.

The move was overdue for Ring and Ellis. Commenting on the Fitzgeralds' departure four years earlier, Ring said it was necessary because their New York friends thought they were running a roadhouse. Our Great Neck house, chosen partly for its relative isolation, lost that status abruptly when the Swopes moved next door the year after we came. A large percentage of their guests either knew Ring or had some connection they could invoke. According to his Sunday feature, "They wander in at all hours, demanding refreshment and entertainment at the place that happens to be nearest at the moment."

The acre or so of lawn in front of the Swopes' was transformed into a large-scale croquet court, and on weekend afternoons we could watch such devotees as Harpo Marx and Alexander Woollcott play the game with an earnestness that reflected the large wagers at stake. One evening Ring and Ellis were sitting on their porch with Dorothy Parker and Marc Connelly when they saw the cars across the way begin to move around as if the guests were leaving. This was remarkable because it was not yet ten o'clock and, though dinner was over long since at the Lardners', that was about the time the meal was apt to be served at the Swopes'. Soon they observed that the cars were being arranged so all the headlights converged on the croquet court, and full realization dawned when they heard the familiar daytime sound of mallet striking ball. "Jesus Christ," Dottie exclaimed, "the heirs of the ages!"

Ring was both repelled and attracted by the incessant social activity a hundred yards away, and the latter force could become the stronger, especially when he was drinking. Sometimes he would go over and perform at the piano, playing and singing compositions of his own like one called "Gretchen, I'm retchin' for you." Sometimes he would sit in a corner watching the goings-on. Once when he was there with his brother Rex, a newly imported Swedish actress and her fiancé were among the guests. The young woman drew attention by moving from one male lap to another, causing Rex to observe, "She's not a Swede, she's a Laplander," and Ring to add, "And she manages to keep one lap ahead of her fiancé."

Reporting a surprise visit from Michael Arlen in his column, Ring explained that it was a surprise not only to the hosts but to the visitor, who thought he was ringing the Swopes' doorbell. "That is how we get most of our celebrities," Ring wrote, adding that "Mike stayed long enough to take off his coat and reveal that his pants depended for sustenance on neither belt or galluses but just naturally constricted themselves at the waist like the top of a tobacco pouch."

The phenomenon of Arlen's abrupt leap to fame with the publication of *The Green Hat* intrigued Ring and he wrote about it several times in print and in letters to Fitzgerald, who referred to Arlen as "my successor" because of the similarity to his own sudden celebrity five years previously.

Arlen, Ring wrote Scott,

said he thought *How to Write Short Stories* was a great title for my book and when I told him it was your title, he said he had heard about you and was sorry to miss you. He also said he had heard that Mrs. Fitzgerald was very attractive, but I told him he must be thinking of somebody else. Mike is being entertained high and low.

And again a few months later:

New York is all agog over Michael Arlen and Noel Coward. Heywood, George Nathan and one or two others have taken some awful socks at Mike, but the large majority are mushy over him.

And:

> Some of the Algonquin bunch was sort of riding Michael Arlen, I
> don't know why. Anyway, when Edna Ferber was introduced to him,
> she said: "Why, Mr. Arlen, you look almost like a woman!" "So do
> you, Miss Ferber," was Michael's reply.

Ring and Ellis envied the Fitzgeralds their mobility, but
uprooting a family is a major operation when there are three
children in school and a fourth just starting; moving, like Scott
and Zelda, to a whole new country was virtually unthinkable.
But for Ring especially, and Ellis to a lesser degree, the very
closeness to New York that had attracted them to Great Neck
in the first place was becoming a liability. There seemed to be
no practical way to avoid the intensive social life that prevailed
in the community, especially when their attitudes toward it were
ambivalent.

The truth is that while Ring and Ellis may have been her-
mits by Swope standards, they actually went out and entertained a great deal, as all prosperous people did in those days
in an environment where three were a modest domestic staff.
Most of their guests were celebrities of one sort or another,
with the emphasis on the fields of theater and popular music.
Dinner guests were often taken on a tour of the house, which
included an inspection of the boys, generally at some stage of
preparation for bed. Several people told me decades later,
Beatrice Lillie and Dorothy Parker among them, that their
first glimpse of me had been in a bathtub along with my
three brothers. In actual fact, there were never more than
three of us in the tub at once.

When the guests included people who could be expected to
perform, two or three of us were generally at the top of the front
stairs in our pajamas. I don't think we ever had express permission to be there, but neither was it a punishable offense. That was
how we heard "Under the Bamboo Tree" sung by its composer,
J. Rosamond Johnson, and "On the Road to Mandalay" sung by
Reinald Werrenrath, the concert baritone, whose favorite en-

core it was. Jerome Kern and Vincent Youmans played their latest songs, and on two different occasions George Gershwin came and played what must have been just about everything he had written to date.

Having become a fiction writer through external pressures and then having discovered there was an ever-growing market for his comic commentary, Ring might never have written another short story after "The Golden Honeymoon" in 1922 if it hadn't been for Scott Fitzgerald and Max Perkins. Even with their prodding, he devoted himself for nearly three years after that to the weekly syndicated column, nonfiction magazine pieces, a couple of abortive theater projects, and the comic strip.

It took the unexpected success of *How to Write Short Stories,* the extent to which reviewers hailed him as a master of the form, and unremitting pressure from Perkins to bring him back to the work on which his reputation was ultimately to rest. At the end of 1924 he wrote Perkins:

> I think I am going to be able to sever connections with the daily cartoon early next month. This ought to leave me with plenty of time and it is my intention to write at least ten short stories a year. Whether I can do it or not, I don't know. I started one the other day and got through with about 700 words, which were so bad that I gave up. I seem to be out of the habit and it may take time to get back.

Within three months he had published "Haircut" and if he didn't quite make his quota, he did turn out more than fifty stories in eight years of declining health, along with a considerable body of nonfiction, two produced plays and three unproduced musicals.

The overwhelming bulk of his work up to that point had been written in the first person, either in the words of a fictional character, usually uneducated, or in the colloquial style of his syndicated pieces. There were two third-person stories in *How to Write Short Stories,* but they had been written eight years before and the month before that book came out he told Edmund Wilson he couldn't write straight English. "I can't write a sentence like 'We were sitting in the Fitzgeralds' house and the fire was burning brightly.' " Nevertheless, when he started writing stories again the following year, he began to experiment more and more with third-person narration, and that is how five of the nine stories in his next collection are written. Nine months before he died he told an interviewer he thought all stories should be written in the third person, going as far as to add: "Hemingway had the right idea in 'Fifty Grand' but in my opinion he should have done it in the third person."

The latter judgment is debatable, and the dogmatic generality is clearly refuted by Ring's own work. Can anyone conceive of "Haircut," "The Golden Honeymoon" or "Some Like Them Cold" being improved by recasting them in conventional narrative mold?

He rarely had anything serious to say about his own work. When he was in Boston in 1930 with a Ziegfeld musical, a reporter asked him how he came to write lyrics and Ring said, "Someone gave me a rhyming dictionary for Christmas once and I couldn't exchange it for a tie." When a feature writer he had known on the Chicago *Tribune* did a symposium on "What book would you rather have written than any other?" his reply was "The Newfoundland-Punjab volume of the New International Encyclopedia." But he was part-way serious when he said he would rather do almost anything than write short stories but had no choice "because I have four children and a wife who has extravagant ideas about a garden." And he meant it when he complained: "Where do they get that stuff about me being a satirist? I just listen." Most revealing of all was his response, with only family present, to a nephew's contention that Dickens was sentimental and sloppy. "How can you write if you can't cry?" he said.

In that last interview he gave the year he died, he asserted that he didn't worry much about plots:

I just start writing about somebody I think I know something about. I try to get him down cold. The other characters seem to walk into the story naturally enough. . . . I keep pretty close to the deadline, and sometimes I have to write a story when it's the last thing on earth I feel like doing. Once when a story was due, I had to go to the funeral of a friend in Indiana. I had to write it, so I took a drawing room on the train and brought my portable typewriter. The train left at five-thirty and I started to work. As usual, I had no definite idea at first what it was going to be about. The train went by a golf course and several big estates. An idea came to me about a very wealthy man who had a big country estate. He was crazy about golf, but played a poor game, and was sensitive about his scores. He had a private course on his estate, and got so he would play only there, with his chauffeur for caddy. . . . I had the story finished when we came into Buffalo. I called it *Mr. Frisbie.*

That was it. If he had remembered to bring along stamps and an envelope, he probably gave it to the Pullman porter to mail in Buffalo. One of the major sound effects I retain from my childhood is silence, prolonged to the point of acute tension, followed by a sustained burst of rapid two-finger typing. He would think out a page or two of a story in meticulous detail and then set it down at high speed, rarely returning to it except for a copyreading when he was all through. The only real revision he ever did was for the theater, where he generally worked in collaboration and where rewriting is a way of life.

In the case of the play *Elmer the Great,* most of the revising was done by George M. Cohan; then Ring would try without much success to restore a few of his jokes. It is difficult to convey to present-day readers what a phenomenon Cohan was. The James Cagney impersonation in *Yankee Doodle Dandy* thirty years ago did show the variety of his talents and the magnetism of his personality, onstage and off, but it didn't begin to suggest the appalling taste and utter mindlessness of some of his patriotic creations. There is a special irony in Ring's collaborating with the author of "Over There" because Ring had collected, as a connoisseur of bad taste, the sheet music of the most outrageous recruiting songs of World War I: "That's a Mother's Liberty Loan," "America, Here's My Boy," "The Bravest Heart of All," "Send Me Away with a Smile," "Set Aside Your Tears Till the Boys Come Marching Home."

In so doing he was pursuing an interest he had shared as a child with Rex, Anne and their mother in unconscious humor and the abuse of the English language by the semiliterate. They delighted in passages of prose or verse that were intended quite seriously by their authors, and some of the funniest lines in Ring's work, especially in the earlier stories and the plays, are ones the narrator or speaker doesn't realize are funny ("I treat every woman like they was my sister, till I find out different"). One of the great moments in Anne Tobin's life was her discovery of *Musings of a Coroner,* a book of privately printed verse containing a line that became a family favorite: "If by perchance the inevitable should come."

The richest source of such humor lay in songs tailored for patriotic and other special occasions, a field in which Cohan was a major offender. One that particularly appealed to Anne and Ring, perhaps because of the total absence of rhyme, a rare occurrence in song lyrics, was discovered by Ring in a music store on the boardwalk at Atlantic City, New Jersey:

> Oh, you Atlantic City Guards,
> You are the idols of my dreams.
> From early morn till late at night
> Guarding the gay bathers with your life.
> If bathers venture out too far,
> Risking your lives you bring them back to shore.
> Heroes seven times a day,
> Oh, you Atlantic City Guards.

The interest in special-occasion songwriting continued into our generation and my brother Jim made a comprehensive study of the subject for a magazine presentation in 1936. Some of the choicer items he found were inspired by the deaths of public figures (Enrico Caruso, Rudolph Valentino, Huey Long, Will Rogers) or the abrupt fame of hitherto obscure ones (Charles Lindbergh, Bruno Richard Hauptmann, Gertrude Ederle, John Dillinger). In the first category Jim had a particular affection for "They Needed a Songbird in Heaven (So God Took Caruso Away)" and "There's a New Star in Heaven Tonight," which found solace for the passing of Valentino in a new thespo-astronomical concept:

> Stars may come and stars may go
> Up there in that starry space.
> But when one falls, God always calls
> A star to take its place.

Jim found three Cohan lyrics worth quoting for their sheer exuberance, but one of them stood out because it contained the only known instance of the use of a song to plug another song by the same author. It was written in anticipation of Lindbergh's return after his landing in Paris:

> The cannon's roar you'll hear in the air,
> A thousand bands will play *Over There.*
> Oh! say what a day for poet and poem
> When Lindbergh comes back from across the foam
> To his Home Sweet Home.

Jim didn't live to see this whole school of songwriting die out after reaching its possible high and low points in the frenetic months following Pearl Harbor. The high, introducing the first unmistakable talent of the whole genre, was Frank Loesser's "Praise the Lord and Pass the Ammunition." The low, and the only one of a host of songs inspired by the Japanese attack that had to be suppressed as a matter of national policy, was "The Japs Ain't Got a Chinaman's Chance." As far as I know the destruction of Hiroshima was not marked by any lyrical effusion, and it may have been their failure to rise to that challenge that made the special-occasion songwriters realize they were practicing a dying art.

Ring wrote the Fitzgeralds on September 25, 1927: "If you care to know anything about my affairs, I had quite a wet summer, but have now been on the wagon since the 22nd. of August. During the dry intermissions, I wrote a baseball play which George Cohan accepted. He says he is going to put it on this fall. . . ." That was Ring's understanding of what had happened, but a week later Cohan sent him a contract which provided that Cohan would rewrite the play and become entitled to half the royalties; also that Ring would become a nonvoting partner by putting up 25 percent of all production costs. Since these included the advance of one thousand dollars to the authors, Ring contributed a quarter of that sum and received half of it, for a net advance of two hundred and fifty.

Cohan retained control "to the same full extent as if I were the sole owner," and he exercised it by removing all the special Lardner quality from the play. After tryouts in Boston and Chicago it opened in New York a full year, less one day, from the letter to Scott and Zelda. The reviews weren't bad, with most of the praise going to Walter Huston in the title role, but it closed after forty performances. During their association Huston introduced Ring to his young son John, who had written a short story Ring liked. Ring called it to Mencken's attention and it was published in the *American Mercury*.

"The look of eagles"

9

It was only a month or two after *Elmer the Great* closed that George S. Kaufman called Ring and said he thought there was a good comedy play in the story "Some Like Them Cold." How about a collaboration? But the wounds were still fresh from the struggle with Cohan, and Ring said no. After a lifetime of being stagestruck, he was so recovered from that condition that he had resolved never to work in the theater again or permit a story of his to be adapted. It was such a definitive response that George made no further attempt to persuade him.

Early in 1929, however, Ring called George and asked if he still felt the same way. If so, Ring said, he was willing to try, adding, almost as if it were his only reason for reconsidering, the condition that they write in a part for Floncy Rice. A surpassingly beautiful girl whose overlapping romantic involvements had been the basis of Ring's story "I Can't Breathe," Floncy had decided on an acting career, and Ring resolved to launch it with a Broadway part specially designed for her . . . showy, with some good lines, but not too demanding in view of her inexperience.

An only child and five years older than the oldest Lardner boy, Floncy had been part of her parents' social life for several years, making winter trips with them and the Lardners, and she was the only young female with whom Ring and Ellis had any sustained contact. They both regretted not having a daughter and Floncy got some of the affection they would have lavished on one, as did their nieces Anne and Blanche Tobin when they came visiting from Niles.

The basic method of the collaboration was for Ring to write the first draft, George the second and Ring the third. By summertime their play, *June Moon,* had been written, cast, rehearsed, tried out in Atlantic City and judged by its authors to collapse completely after a promising first act. On the boardwalk Ring met an old friend who hadn't heard of his new venture and asked what he was doing in such an improbable place. "I'm down here with an act," Ring said.

They spent the whole summer rewriting and the new version was first performed in Washington in September with a gratifying response. Sam Harris, the producer, who had left Ring and George alone up to this point, now told them his opinion that they had a hit which could become a smash with the addition of one missing element. What was lacking, he said, was sympathy or rooting interest for just one of the characters. The logical person to be given that sympathy was the girl, Edna, and it could be supplied by a tender love scene between her and Fred, the male lead. He implored them to this one last effort that would make all their fortunes.

Unhappily for Harris's purpose, he had the wrong writers. Nothing resembling a love scene can be found in the complete works of Ring Lardner, and George Kaufman had a standard speech to his collaborators: "Count me out. I'll walk around the block while you do the love scene." But with the double incentive of pleasing their producer and enriching themselves, they strove mightily to create what he wanted. I don't know how close they came because no preliminary draft remains. But when they had completed the standard Kaufman process of honing the scene down to its essentials, what survived was:

FRED: We used to have a lot of fun together. Remember that day in Van Cortlandt Park when I lost my watch and that little boy found it.

EDNA: You gave him a nickel.

182

FRED:	It was a dime. And he said, "Keep it and buy your wife a raddio set." He thought we was married.
EDNA:	I remember.
FRED:	You was embarrassed, all right. You got red.
EDNA	Any girl would.
FRED:	And then coming back we forgot to change at Seventy-second Street. That is, you forgot. I didn't know any better.
EDNA:	I just wasn't thinking.
FRED:	We had to go all the way down to Times Square. That's when we saw the flea circus.
EDNA:	You said one of the fleas reminded you of a man in Schenectady.
FRED:	Yeah. Perry Robinson. He always walked like he'd just picked up a nail.

With that measure of heart-warming sentiment added, the play opened in New York on October 9, 1929, less than three weeks before the debacle on Wall Street. It was a distinct and satisfying hit that ran through the theatrical season and then went on the road with considerable success over the next two years. Despite his initial uncertainty Ring enjoyed the whole process, even to dropping in backstage during the run or just standing outside the Broadhurst Theatre watching the crowd.

Once he actually sat through a performance and experienced the occupational trauma of the novice playwright who doesn't realize that unsupervised actors will work at improving, not their mastery of their parts, but the parts themselves. He called George in haste and a special rehearsal was convened to restore the play to its original form.

John had started Harvard that fall; Jim and I were rooming together at Andover; and the major event of Christmas vacation for us, and I think for Ring, too, was the night he took us to see the play. I can't remember whether David, ten years old at the time and going to day school in New York, went with us or not; the chances are he had already seen it.

The play, which presented an hilariously unfavorable view of the American popular-song business, contained several numbers that were, according to the credits, "eavesdropped by Ring Lardner and George S. Kaufman." Actually, Ring wrote the words and music, which were intended to parody prevailing trends on Tin Pan Alley. Two of the songs had quite pretty though familiar melodies; of one of them a character in the play said, "It's a tune that's easy to remember, but if you should forget it, it wouldn't make any difference." There were a couple of "novelty numbers," which were close relatives of the special-occasion songs. One of them was about a man who falls in love with the picture of a Japanese girl on a magazine cover and calls her over the newly installed Pacific telephone cable:

> Hello, hello, Tokio!
> Girlie, you'll excuse it, please,
> If I no spik Japanese.
> This little call will leave me broke-e-o,
> But I simply had to say, "I love you so."
> Believe me, dearie, it's no joke-e-o;
> I'd gladly fly through fire and smoke-e-o
> To share with you the marriage yoke-e-o,
> Fairest flower of Toki-oki-oki-o!

The other was the occasion for a variety of snide remarks from our schoolmates after *Time*'s review of the play was illustrated by a picture of my father with the couplet in quotes beneath his name:

> Should a father's carnal sins
> Blight the life of babykins?

Another added contribution of Ring's was to write the "Who's Who in the Cast" for the program. Some samples:

NORMAN FOSTER, who portrays the role of Fred Stevens, is well qualified to act the part of a song-writer as he is the stepfather of Stephen Foster, who turned out such smash hits as "Swanee River," "Celeste Aida" and "Old Black Jolson." Norman (as you begin to call him after a while) is married to Claudette ("Peaches") Colbert, who cannot be with us tonight, but sends regards.

LINDA WATKINS won instant recognition from the critics by her portrayal of Ibsen in the play of that name, but first sprang into prominence as a stowaway when Gertrude Ederle swam the Nile.

JEAN DIXON is a great favorite with the producers and authors because she won't accept a salary. "It's just fun," is the way she puts it. She makes a good living betting on the whippet races at Grant's Tomb.

FLORENCE D. RICE is the daughter of Grantland Rice, the taxidermist. Miss Rice's parents have no idea she is on the stage and every time she leaves the house to go to the theatre, she tells them she has to run down to the draper's to buy a stamp. On matinee days she writes two letters (that's what they think). . . .

FLOBELLE FAIRBANKS . . . is the paternal grandmother of Douglas Fairbanks, the Hollywood mummer, and has doubled for her distinguished grandson in most of his screen triumphs. . . . Once, when maneuvering her plane in a particularly dangerous stunt, she fell several thousand feet and was instantly killed. Miss Fairbanks resents applause, and will leave the theatre in a sulk at the slightest indication of a curtain call.

As a result of *June Moon* Ring formed friendships with two remarkable women with whom he remained in touch for the remaining four years of his life. One was Claudette Colbert, who had met Foster two years previously, when they were in a play together. That play won her a leading role in a silent movie, *For the Love of Mike,* which was such a failure its director, Frank Capra, returned to his job as a gag man for Mack Sennett, and Claudette herself swore she would never face a camera again.

By 1931, when she came to visit Ring in Doctors Hospital in New York, she had broken her vow to such conspicuous effect that she was one of the emerging stars of the talking screen. According to Ring's account in *The New Yorker,* fifteen interns who had previously "treated my room as vacant" suddenly appeared to take his temperature.

The other good friend was Jean Dixon, for whom *June Moon* was a turning point. Before it she had played a variety of roles, each one a struggle to land. After it she had offers to choose from and they were all the same part. She stopped the show opening night with the weary, incredulous, scathing look she gave her composer husband as he auditioned his latest number. When the New York run was over, she went directly into a leading role in *Once in a Lifetime,* and on to Hollywood and a succession of wisecracking, best-friend-of-the-female-star roles.

It was Ring's first sustained experience with what a gifted performer with the mystical talent called timing could do to a speech or a piece of action that seemed only moderately amusing on paper. For George the phenomenon, while hardly novel, was always stimulating, and the two of them spent many hours devising new lines and bits of business for her, or working out refinements in existing ones to produce more laughter. Jean contributed to the process as in the following exchange:

LUCILLE: Has he ever said anything half-way definite? About marrying, I mean?

EILEEN: Not in words, exactly.

LUCILLE: What did he say it in?

A layman might expect that the two men who had conceived that last line would know how it should be said, especially when one of them was the foremost comedy director of his time. But figuring out what will make an audience laugh is no more an exact science than prophecy generally. In this case the line might be read with the accent on any one of four of its six words . . . any but "he" and "it." They had tried other variations unsuccessfully and George was ready to throw out the line when Jean asked if she could try "What did he say it *in?*" From no laugh at all it became a big one. None of them could explain why.

For her part Jean was well aware what an opportunity it was

to have those two men striving to create funny lines for her. But early in the association she thought she had blown it. The night after the play opened in Washington to excellent reviews, the publisher of one of the papers, whom Ring knew, came up to him in the theater and congratulated him. Ring responded that he couldn't congratulate him on his critic since, in an otherwise laudatory notice, the man had failed to mention Jean Dixon. As a result of this encounter a reporter for that paper sought Jean out for an interview, which surprised her because Foster and Linda Watkins had the leading parts. In the interview she was quoted as saying:

With all Mr. Lardner's brilliance, he is very like a child and loves whatever praise he receives. It's like an *Alice in Wonderland* thing, this whole production, and during every show Mr. Kaufman and Mr. Lardner sit in the back row and with great black pencils write ridiculous words on the back of a torn envelope. After the performance we have to rehearse the new lines born that night.

On the call-board shortly thereafter a telegram was posted signed Ring Lardner which said that "a certain actress" in the play would no longer have to worry about having any more jokes written for her. Jean, who scarcely knew Ring at this point, was devastated. Miss Watkins announced to George from the stage that she refused to rehearse that day because of Ring's rudeness to Jean.

Appalled that his joke had misfired, Ring came onstage from the back of the theater to apologize and tell Jean for the first time what an ardent fan he had become. And from that time on there was no uncertainty in their relationship. No matter what his telegrams said, and there were many (it had become his favorite means of communication) and they were sometimes insulting, she was confident of the affection behind them.

While they were still on the road, Jean, who had just acquired an apartment of her own in New York for the first time, asked Ring if he would drop in on a particular night about three weeks after the New York opening. She promised she would also invite

Claudette and Norman, and no one else. Ring agreed to come.

Before New York the play went to Newark and after the last performance there Sam Harris invited the company to his Manhattan office to drink to its success from a keg of beer he had secured for the occasion. Jean asked Ring if he would go along and he said no. When she pressed him, he said, "You've never seen me drunk, have you?" She said she'd never seen him even take a drink. He told her she wouldn't like him if she saw him drunk and that the reason he wouldn't go was that if he smelled the beer he would drink it and if he drank it he would go on to something else.

Avoiding liquor that particular night was apparently a matter of timing, whether consciously or not, for, as Ring wrote Scott at the end of February, 1930, "When the New York opening was over, I went on a bat that lasted nearly three months and haven't been able to work since, so it's a good thing the play paid dividends."

When the night came that Jean had invited him for, nobody connected with the play had seen him since the opening and it was common knowledge that he had gone off the wagon, so she didn't expect him to show. But Claudette and Norman came anyway, and after they had been there an hour or so, Ring arrived looking even more solemn and dignified than usual, which was characteristic of his drinking periods, and it turned out to be quite a satisfactory occasion. The next time Jean heard from him he had committed himself to a hospital to recuperate, and asked her to come to see him there. It was the first of a number of times she visited him in a hospital.

During the period in which he met the Misses Colbert and Dixon, he also established warm relationships with two of Kate Rice's sisters, Mildred Luthy and Lizabeth Vereen, who lived in their native Georgia but occasionally ventured to New York or East Hampton to visit the Rices. He did not make any new masculine friends in those years; I think he found it easier to speak or write to women on a personal level.

If there was a sexual element in his feeling for any of his

women friends, a son of his would have been in the least likely position to be aware of it, so I speak with impeachable authority when I say he never wavered in his devotion and fidelity to Ellis. I feel this could be true, especially of a drinking man, despite an occasional sexual episode, but my father's standards were something else, and it would have been uncharacteristic not to apply them as rigidly to himself as he did to others. For this reason I question, though I certainly can't disprove, the only assertion I'm aware of that he had an extramarital involvement.

I happen to have a lot of affection and respect for the asserter, who is Lillian Hellman in her memoir *An Unfinished Woman.* Speaking of Dorothy Parker she wrote, "She had had an affair with Ring Lardner. . . ." Before publishing that Lillian verified with my son Jim, then a student of hers at Harvard, that Ellis was dead, and asked him to ask me if there was anyone else who might be hurt by the statement. I replied that the only possible casualty was the truth. At the time and in a subsequent discussion while writing this book, I reminded her that Dottie had not been a paragon of veracity, especially on the subject of her love life. Lillian's response was that to her Dottie didn't lie.

I know Ring liked Dottie and was amused by her, and the way she spoke of him when I knew her in Hollywood and New York the last thirty years of her life was close to reverential. Once I took my mother to a party at her house in Beverly Hills and they greeted each other warmly, but Ellis told me she could never quite forgive Dottie for one incident. Dottie had complained to Ring at a party in the Great Neck days that she couldn't get the solitude she needed for work, and he invited her to come and stay in one of our guest rooms and enjoy absolute privacy. When she came, they left her entirely alone as she presumably wanted, and she couldn't stand it after a week and left. A short time later it was reported back to Ellis that Dottie, asked how things had gone at the Lardners', had said she had to escape because Ring was after her all hours of the day and night.

Ring's version, I learned later when I read a letter he wrote Scott at the time, was somewhat different:

She had been having an unfortunate affair and for some reason or other, I thought a visit to us would cheer her up. I got into this sympathetic mood on the seventh of May and it lasted till the tenth of July; during the two months I was constantly cock-eyed, drinking all night and sleeping all day and never working. Fortunately I was eight weeks ahead in syndicates before the spree started.

In a *New Yorker* article about some events during his post–*June Moon* lapse from sobriety, Ring wrote: "So the next night at eight I ran into Dorothy ('Spark Plug') Parker and we went places until I got tired of her and I landed at the stagedoor of the Broadhurst. . . ."

Dottie's kindness to me in later years could be taken as an indication of her feeling for Ring. When I was twenty-one, Budd Schulberg and I did a few added scenes for *A Star Is Born*, including the ending, which involved Janet Gaynor saying "This is Mrs. Norman Maine . . ." into a microphone outside Grauman's Chinese Theatre, and Dottie, whose screenplay it was in collaboration with her husband, Alan Campbell, proposed that we should be given some sort of screen credit for our contributions. It was a generous offer, which we would have rejected as unjustified if David Selznick hadn't already done so in our behalf.

The year before she died I spent a number of hours with Dottie in a hospital to which she was confined after an alcoholic accident. She was wavering quite unpredictably from perfectly good sense, with flashes of the old wit, to a state of disorientation in which she lost her grasp of where she was and with whom. In some of these moments she confused me with my father, then dead for more than thirty years, and referred to incidents they had been through together. But nothing of what was once known as a compromising nature.

I realize all of this doesn't make much of a case one way or the other. But I remain skeptical about the "affair," not only because he had such hyper-Puritan ideas about what was right and wrong, but also because his alcoholism never reached the stage of personality deterioration where there are complete reversals of behavior, as when a normally gentle man becomes aggressive and violent. All the testimony is that when drunk he remained as unsmiling and taciturn as ever, and just as intolerant of "funny stories," especially "dirty" ones.

He was the kind of drinker for whom the drug was a problem almost from the start. When he was first introduced to George M. Cohan, many years before their collaboration, Ring attracted Cohan's attention by saying: "Mr. Cohan, you've been in the theater for twenty years. You write songs and sing them. You dance. You write plays and produce them. You know everything there is to know about the theater. You're the one man who can tell me what I want to know. Mr. Cohan, how the hell does a guy get on the water wagon?"

By the age of twenty-five, as the letters to Ellis reveal, he was already into the pattern of alternate periods of indulgence and total abstinence, and it seemed to him a matter of course that he would have to stop drinking entirely to turn himself into an acceptable husband. And she knew enough about his weakness to agree with him.

I don't know how long he actually abstained after their marriage or how long either of them maintained the illusion that eventually he was going to abstain for good. But at some point the alternating routine was resumed and he adopted the more realistic practice of setting a fixed period of weeks or months during which he would refrain from drinking. I feel safe in saying there was never a year during the rest of his life when the sum of the abstinent periods wasn't greater than the drinking ones. Otherwise, considering his kind of addiction, which led to sustained drinking bouts rather than nightly intoxication and daytime sobriety, he couldn't have turned out as much good work as he did in those first married years. And the later years I know about from my own observation.

Marital discord is a natural by-product of alcoholism, but my parents somehow succeeded in avoiding all but the most private manifestations of it. I remember a few occasions when Ring made a dry comment on something Ellis had said that she might have taken as a put-down, but I never once heard either of them use a raised voice or display any antagonism toward the other. My cousin Anne Tobin Willcox remembers being aware as a young girl, probably through her mother, that Ellis was "mad" at Ring because of his drinking, but even close friends of Ellis's outside the family have said they never heard her speak of it. It was the overriding problem, insidious and insuperable, of their lives and they both tried to pretend it didn't exist.

That effort probably caused as much psychic damage as the opposite kind of strain on a different sort of couple with the same problem who yell at each other in endless, futile argument. For Ellis there was the knowledge that he had intended to quit and failed to do so despite material success, growing fame and children in whom he clearly delighted. If instead of satisfaction he displayed increasing depression and the need of the drug to escape it, mightn't that be because she had fallen short of his expectations? And along with the self-doubt there was anger at the unfairness of it all, a great mass of stored anger whose existence she never even admitted to herself until she sought some psychiatric aid in the last years of her life. What she did instead of expressing how she felt was simply to remove herself, first into a bedroom of her own, and then into a separate existence whenever he was fully launched on a binge. More often than not, removing herself from him took the form of staying home instead of joining him on the town.

One reason we boys had only limited knowledge of his drinking was that he did much of it away from home, staying in New York for two or three days at a time and sleeping, if at all, in a hotel room. Since he was also in the habit of isolating himself in a New York hotel when he needed to catch up on work, we were led to believe in that explanation for all his absences.

Although he set an increasingly high value on solitude during sober times, when drinking he liked to be where the action was, even though he generally didn't take part in it. Sometimes he himself provided the entertainment he craved, wandering from one speakeasy or party to another with a piano player and magician he hired for the evening. He liked to play the piano and sing, especially as part of a quartet, but he also liked to listen to music and would always yield to a professional he respected.

Occasionally he joined the poker games of the Thanatopsis Literary and Inside Straight Society, whose members included Adams, Broun, Kaufman, Connelly and Woollcott. One of his favorite hangouts was the Lambs Club on West Forty-fourth Street, where the pleasures of running into his favorite composers outweighed the hazards of encounters with actors, of whom he tended to be intolerant. Once he was sitting alone in the bar when a member of that profession insisted on declaiming a long speech from his current engagement. When he was through, Ring invited the man to join him and repeat the recitation at closer range. The actor complied happily, whereupon Ring requested a third performance. Overjoyed, the actor asked, "Do you really like it that much?" "No," Ring told him, "but I was a bad boy last night and this is my penance."

In those days actors, especially Shakespearean actors, were distinguishable from ordinary citizens by the flamboyance of their clothing and coiffures. Ring accosted one such in the Lambs and asked, "How do you look when I'm sober?"

But the longest of what he called his "sitting-up exercises" took place at the Friars on East Fifty-fifth. He dropped into the club, of which he was not even a member, in evening clothes one night after an opening and remained until the end of the third day following. Writing about it in *The New Yorker* years later, he recalled that the urge to go home came only at high noon when "it would have been kind of embarrassing passing all those policemen in dinner clothes instead of the conventional pajamas." So he lingered. During the session "five of the best music-writers in New York played their latest stuff" and "I and whoever happened to be with me at the moment ordered five meals and rejected them as fast as they were brought in." At the end of the third day a man came up to him and said, "Have you heard the one about the . . . ?" Ring rose abruptly to his feet and quit the premises. A short time later a member looked in and said, "My God, the statue's gone!"

He didn't just vanish when he went into New York to drink. Ellis always knew where he was and how to get in touch with him if she needed to. He realized how much more she would worry otherwise and he spared her that because he was an extreme worrier himself, usually foreseeing the worst possible result from a given situation. That was why he persuaded Ellis to give up driving after her 1913 accident and why he fretted so whenever one of us didn't show up at the moment he had said he would, especially if he was out in a car. Once, a couple of hundred yards out in the ocean in front of our house in East Hampton, I decided to swim to the Maidstone Club a mile away. From his upstairs screened porch Ring saw me head gradually out of sight moving parallel to the shoreline. When I reached the club, I found I was the object of a Coast Guard search.

As the two diseases, tuberculosis and alcoholism, progressed, along with a few subsidiary ailments, a spell of drinking would leave him in such a weakened state that he was more apt to admit himself to a hospital at the end of it than to return home. But he would have first stopped drinking of his own accord; he didn't believe in the institutions that practiced the therapy of restraint. In October, 1927, Max Perkins wrote him that "Scott did not seem at all well, and I have had him on my mind ever since. I wish he would go to Muldoon or some such place for a month to straighten out his nerves." Ring replied: "I wouldn't recommend Muldoon's as a cure for nerves, especially Scott's kind of nerves. From what I have always heard, it is so strenuous that when a person is released, he is inclined to go on a bat to make up for it."

One of the main effects on the individual of addictive drinking such as Ring's is a loss of self-respect. The addict knows that he should stop, he feels shame and guilt over the fact that he is unable to, and remorse over what he is doing to other people and himself. These feelings lead to episodes of depression under both drinking and nondrinking conditions. His image of himself deteriorates, sometimes even provoking suicidal impulses. At all stages the process is a cumulative and self-sustaining one: the more intense the depression, the greater the craving to relieve it with alcohol; the stronger the self-destructive drive, the less inhibitory the subject's realization that he is indeed destroying himself.

That is the usual cycle. Imposed upon it in Ring's case were a strong religious background, personal moral standards that were always more rigid than those of his contemporaries, and a highly idealized concept of love and marital bliss. The guilt in him must have been oppressive in the extreme. In a time when alcoholism was regarded as a character weakness rather than a disease, when the conventional image of the alcoholic was the town drunk like Huck Finn's father or the Bowery bum, the effect on the addict's self-esteem was catastrophic. One of the clearest benefits Alcoholics Anonymous brings to the neophyte member is the discovery that so many of his peers have been hooked in the same way he has, unsuccessfully fought the same cravings and suffered the same grim effects. The solitary struggler like Ring doesn't have the example and comradeship of those who have won the battle.

In the pattern of the disease as accentuated by his individual reactions to it lies, I believe, the major explanation of the melancholy and pessimism of Ring's later years. In his case at least, instead of the standard psychiatric assumption that neurotic maladjustment drives a man to drink, it is far more likely that pernicious dependence on drink drove him to a state of neurotic depression.

Despite Clifton Fadiman's analysis Ring never became misanthropic, but he did come to castigate himself for his inability to stay on the wagon. So I am not disagreeing with Fadiman or other critics like Geismar who subscribe to his thesis in the contention that my father arrived at a poor opinion of himself. What I am questioning, besides the general overstatement about hatred, is the assertion that his nonsense prefaces were a direct expression of that self-denigrating side of him. One reason is that he began writing them before it had developed to any significant degree. The other is the implausibility of the argument that a man who writes facetiously about his own work and career must therefore undervalue them. On the same level of criticism I might say that the nonsense of Lewis Carroll and Edward Lear, two favorites of Ring's, expressed a morbid incapacity to take life seriously.

As Ring's health disintegrated and his will to live ebbed, Ellis grew stronger and surer of herself, and a more exemplary person altogether. Like many very pretty girls, and some not so pretty, she had spent a good part of her young adulthood getting her share of the fun out of life. In addition to her appearance she had a lilting voice and a laugh that people found extraordinarily appealing. Even after bearing three sons in the first four years of her marriage, and another four years after that, she didn't let herself be bound by the confines of housekeeping and child-rearing.

Always allowing for her concern about Ring's drinking and his symptoms of ill health, she continued to find a variety of pleasures for herself. She cared a great deal about her surroundings, and every house she lived in was known for its beauty and taste inside and out. She favored early American antiques but was willing to mix them with other periods, and she put in long hours on the finer points of gardening in order to maintain an ample supply of cut flowers throughout the growing season.

In the spring of 1927 she refurbished the house on East Shore Road with new wallpaper, paint and upholstery, and Sheraton mahogany dining room furniture, but Great Neck was already becoming too much a part of the metropolitan area for the Lardners. In June my parents rented Victor Herbert's house in Lake Placid and we all welcomed the change. Even I remember the summer there with pleasure despite coming so close to drowning one day that I had reached a euphoric state as I settled to the bottom of the lake. I abandoned resistance and was yielding to my fate with serenity when John, observing my absence, dove to

Ellis contemplates a "mass of masculinity": Jim, John, David and "Bill"

where I was and bore me back to the surface.

Sometime that same year Ring and Ellis made the decision that resulted in their buying the seaside property in East Hampton with the Rices, who were already renting there. The Percy Hammonds and the Irvin Cobbs had acquired places there previously, and the John Wheelers soon followed. The Lardners sold most of their furniture along with the Great Neck house, and Ellis had another big job equipping the new thirteen-room one plus a two-room apartment over the garage. We moved there in the late spring of 1928.

Since I joined John and Jim at Andover that fall, East Hampton was the only home we had from then on, except for David, who went to day school in New York and lived with our parents eight months a year in an apartment hotel at Eighty-sixth Street and Madison Avenue. When the three of us came to town at Christmas and Easter, they rented a second apartment for us. Because they liked to be free to travel during the winter, Miss Feldman lingered on for another two years.

We thoroughly enjoyed East Hampton. We had done ocean swimming at various beaches in the New York area but generally in the very best of weather. Now we learned the pleasures of rough-weather swimming, diving through the great, cresting breakers and riding in with them. By the time I was sixteen the days we preferred to go out into the waves were those when the Coast Guard hoisted a signal flag to warn against swimming at all.

For Ellis the predominantly good times extended into 1929 and 1930. The year of the great crash was also the year of *June Moon* and the publication of Ring's definitive story collection *Round Up,* which not only sold well but was selected by the Literary Guild and occasioned an outburst of critical appraisals of his place in American letters, almost all of them laudatory. In 1930, when the unemployed began to sell apples in the city streets and many of the Lardners' friends had been wiped out in the stock market, *June Moon* was doing well on the road, Ring and George Kaufman were talking about another play, and the magazines had only just begun to cut their prices for short stories. Spring vacation that year, Jim and I went with our parents to lunch at the Astor Hotel and a matinee of a joyous musical, *Strike Up the Band.*

That fall Miss Feldman finally left, David entered the seventh grade as a boarder at the Riverdale Country School in the upper reaches of New York City, and John sailed for Europe. He had wanted to go directly to Oxford from Andover and had actually been admitted to a college there, the only American secondary school student we ever heard of to achieve that distinction, but he was advised to wait a year and had gone to Harvard instead. At the end of his freshman year in that spring of 1930, he persuaded his parents to let him leave and go not to Oxford but to the Sorbonne because he felt knowing French would help in a newspaper career. In Paris he found a place to live at something called the "Fondation des États-Unis, Cité Universitaire."

In October Ellis wrote him from the Hotel Elysée on East Fifty-fourth Street, where she and Ring had taken an apartment:

> Dad has been in Boston for a week writing lyrics for *Smiles.* Ziegfeld called up from Boston and wanted him to start up there in five minutes. The book is ridiculous. . . . Dad is not strong but seems to have stood the trip reasonably well. . . .
>
> Dad saw Jim and Bill—went out to Andover. He says Bill has shot up ahead of Jimmy again. I wish for Jimmy's sake he would grow faster.
>
> I have been doing a lot of theatering lately but there is nothing really good to see. While Ring was in Boston I went to the opening of the new night club Pierrot at the Hotel Pierre, danced and stayed until three in the morning. You had better come home and sit on me.
>
> I think of you every minute and miss you most frightfully and still don't know why I let you go.

It may have been that winter that Ellis and her two closest friends, Kate Rice and Tee Wheeler, formed a club whose sole function was to go to a matinee every week. It lasted for many years, so pristine in its exclusivity that no applicant was ever accepted for membership. Everyone from their set who tried to join got the straight-faced response that she had been blackballed by an unspecified member of the trio.

Ring became involved with *Smiles,* despite his distaste for the book and previous unpleasant experiences with Ziegfeld, because two of his friends, Vincent Youmans and Paul Lannin, were composer and musical director respectively. He also demanded and received "an unheard of advance royalty." In Boston he wrote or rewrote eight lyrics for the stars, Marilyn Miller and Fred and Adele Astaire. After he returned to New York he did two more, with Youmans whistling the tunes for him over the phone from Boston, but only six of his numbers remained in the show after it was cut. An indication of the confusion going on as well as of the producer's famous telegraphic style may be gleaned from the following:

LANNIN SAYS YOU LEFT OUT THE ENTIRE LINE IN THE RALLY ROUND ME LYRIC MARILYN OBJECTS TO THE LINE ABOUT THE DEVIL AND LINE I USED TO SHIRK MY WORK ETC I KNOW IT IS HARD TO WRITE A LYRIC LONG DISTANCE AND IT IS HARD ON ME SO NEAR OPENING THIS IS A TOUGH BUNCH TO HANDLE WILL YOU PHONE YOUMANS TO GET THE MUSIC RIGHT I WAS FINALLY COMPELLED TO GET A COURT ORDER TO PREVENT YOUMANS RUNNING THE SHOW THE ONLY THING HE FORGOT TO GIVE ME A CHEQUE FOR 200,000 DOLLARS WE ARE GRADUALLY GETTING INTO SHAPE AND WAYBURN IS DOING GREAT WORK AND THE COURT ORDER KEEPS YOUMANS FROM INTERFERING THAT IS A VERY IMPORTANT LYRIC PLEASE TRY AGAIN I THINK YOU HAVE GOT TOO MANY RALLY ROUND ME IN IT REGARDS

ZIEGFELD

Two days after Christmas Ellis reported to John:

The reason for my not writing more and oftener is the confusion that reigns in this apartment when three young Lardners are home from school for their Christmas vacation.

Dad, as I wrote you, was not getting any better so he and the doctor decided the best place for him was the hospital where they could see that he ate three meals a day of the right food and they could try some experiments to get him over the insomnia, and build him up. He went to the Doctors Hospital the 18th of Dec. It is a grand hospital on East End Ave. between 87 & 88th St. . . . I know he could not have stood the confusion of so many people in this little apartment. He came home early Christmas morning and went back in the afternoon. We had our dinner up here and had quite a jolly successful time—though times being hard with us, as with every-body, we were not as extravagant with presents as usual. . . .

The boys have seen Edgar Wallace's *On the Spot* and Joe Cook in *Fine and Dandy* and are going to see *Once in a Lifetime* and *Girl Crazy;* also a hockey game. We eat our meals here and there, though I get breakfast every morning . . .

It was a memorable group of shows. *Girl Crazy* introduced two young women, Ethel Merman and Ginger Rogers, and at *Once in a Lifetime* we went backstage to see Jean Dixon and George Kaufman, who had solved a major casting problem by himself playing the part of the playwright, Lawrence Vail. But Ring must have emerged at least one more day while we were home because I remember going into the Ziegfeld Theatre with him during a performance and standing in back to watch part of *Smiles.* Ridiculous was a kind word for the book, but the show somehow tottered through sixty-three performances.

10

In the first months of 1931 Ellis's enjoyment of life began a decline that was never to be reversed for more than brief interludes. Ring got out of the hospital in January and they went with the Rices and Floncy to the Flamingo, their old hotel in Miami Beach, where, Ellis wrote John, it was cold and rainy and "None of us wanted to come here anyway but with a cottage and meals free for three weeks we couldn't afford to refuse." Apparently it was all free because they were celebrities and therefore drawing cards. "The hotels are all practically empty and all the hotel people are facing bankruptcy."

She also told him: "I think Dad is going to do the newspaper work I wrote you about in spite of my protests—but who ever did pay any attention to my protests?" The work was a daily column of a hundred words or less for a consortium of the Bell Syndicate, Chicago *Tribune* and New York *Daily News.* This form of brief column, also called a "daily wire," had been pioneered by Calvin Coolidge and Will Rogers. The strain Ellis feared was not, of course, the quantity of writing involved, but the process of getting a daily idea that justified being set in a box on the front or other prominent page. Ring was temperamentally incapable of adopting Coolidge's solution, which was to go ahead and write whether he had an idea or not.

He began writing the column from Florida on February 1. The following week they went back to New York and took a suite

East Hampton, where we moved in 1928

East Hampton, after the storm in 1932 (the Rices' house in the background)

at the Vanderbilt Hotel on East Thirty-fourth Street. The same bad weather that had plagued them in Florida had stirred up Atlantic storms that cut into the dune in front of the East Hampton house, and while they were worrying about that Ring was told he had to go to Arizona, to the Desert Sanitarium in Tucson.

Ellis moved to a one-room apartment with kitchenette at the Carlyle Hotel on East Seventy-sixth, "a spick and span new building with dizzy modern decorations in the lobby." A few days later a hurricane struck the Atlantic coast and nowhere with greater force than the section of East Hampton beach where the Rices', Lardners' and one other house stood on an already ravaged dune. Once there had been a hundred feet of beach and then a hundred feet of lawn between the ocean and the houses. Now half of each house was hanging over the water, most of its foundation swept out to sea. Pilings were placed under them to prevent them from toppling, but it remained an open question for days whether they would be washed away or saved by moving them inland. It was nearly two weeks before Ellis was able to write Jim and me at school: "I think the house is safe. They have it all up on blocks, off the foundation, ready to move it and are getting the Rices' house ready to move now." She asked us to be very careful with the money she was sending for us to come home on spring vacation because of the terrible expense.

Ring returned in mid-April determined to find a sanitarium closer to home, which he never did succeed in doing. But Ellis went scouting various places in Pennsylvania for him between her trips to East Hampton to try to speed work on the house. Also, as she wrote John:

Then I think I wrote about David's falling and hurting his leg. We thought it was just a bone bruise and torn ligaments but found later from x-rays that the bone was cracked and he is hobbling about on crutches with his leg in a cast, so I have been up to school a good deal of the time. Our last calamity, which was very nearly a fatal one, was that Bill fell from a third story window in Johnson Hall. He missed a cement block by inches and so received no fatal or internal injuries but he broke his right arm very badly and is in the Mass.

General Hospital in Boston. He has to be flat on his back for two or three weeks with his arm stretched out at right angles to his body and weights attached. I just got back from Boston last night after being there three days. Before I left I had to get Dad moved to the Doctors Hospital because I did not think he was well enough to leave alone.

Do you think anything nice will ever happen to the Lardners again? I know of one thing anyway—you will be coming home in less than two months. Try *not* to make your homecoming coincide with Jimmy's commencement which is around the 12th of June.

In a subsequent letter she revealed a few more details of my accident, describing my injuries as

a compound fracture of the upper arm and a fracture of the pelvic bone. He was in bed three days recovering from shock before they were able to set the bone. We took him to Boston in an ambulance for the operation. He was there two weeks but is now back in the Infirmary at Andover. There won't be any serious results except financially and to my nervous system. . . . [Dad] hasn't decided what he is going to do this summer yet but the doctor doesn't want him to be in East Hampton.

It was technically inaccurate but excusable under the circumstances to say I had fallen from a third-story window. It was the third story of the dormitory in front, but because of the way the ground sloped there was another half-story in back, where I fell, and I had fallen not from a window but while trying to get from one window to another along a narrow ledge on the face of the building. The boy in the next room had received a package of goodies from home and inhospitably locked his door on them. I saw the opportunity to fill a void in my stomach and create a baffling mystery at the same time. Unfortunately, I was at an even more awkward stage than usual, having grown about six inches in a year, and when one of the window blinds I was holding onto flew open, I lost my balance and entered a free fall.

As of this writing I have been the sole survivor of the family for sixteen years, but such an eventuality would have seemed most improbable at that moment. I had had a close call as an infant with one siege of pneumonia after another, I had narrowly escaped drowning at age twelve, and now here I was hurtling downward at an acceleration rate of thirty-two feet per second per second.

Trained acrobats and parachute jumpers may be able to exert some measure of control over their bodies in descent, but I had none. My mind was fully occupied, not with any rapid review of the course of my life to date, but with the immediate question of the odds for survival, which seemed to rest on where and how I was going to land. I was intimately acquainted with the terrain below, which had been part of the view from my windows for two years, and I knew I was heading for the general vicinity of a block of cement several feet square outside the basement doorway. It turned out, as I was often reminded in the coming months by the spectators who converged on the scene, that I missed it by less than a foot. My right shoulder hit the grass first, with shattering results, followed almost instantly by my right hip, with sufficient impact to crack the pelvic bone.

My father wrote me from his hospital in New York to mine in Boston:

Monday night, April 27 [1931]

Dear Bill:—

I don't intend to allow a son of mine to show me up. If you can live in a hospital, so can I. I would like to trade ailments with you, for I have no excuse not to write letters; you have, which means that I shall hear from you almost as often as before.

I am on the ninth floor of this structure so that if I ever take a notion to step out of the window and stroll along the walls, the X-rays are likely to show a couple of fractured fingernails as well as the conventional arm and leg breaks.

Out in Arizona, the gent in charge of me said I mustn't do any work for six months at least, and preferably for a year. I had hoped for an order like that, from a competent physician for a long, long while, but I didn't like it so well when it was actually issued. So I said I wouldn't do anything excepting for a daily syndicate "feature" of about one hundred words; it was no strain, paid very well and couldn't really be classed as work. He said anything I had to think of every day was sure to be a strain and a handicap. I said maybe that was true, but I intended to keep it up. Well, you can imagine my blushes when I got back to this city (New York) and discovered that the various newspapers throughout the country were in thorough agreement with my Arizona doctor; not only did they feel that I mustn't do any work, but they also doubted that I had been doing any. The only reason I can think of is that readers of the few papers to which my stuff had been sold were dying with laughter in such numbers that the editors were afraid the entire circulation would soon be in the col', col' ground. Anyway, massa is temporarily among the unemployed and awaiting offers from magazine editors. I presume I shall have to ask for a squad of mounted police to keep them in line at the door.

A very unfortunate thing just happened to you. Your mother called up and reported that she had received a letter from you, written on a one-armed typewriter. If you can write to one parent, etc. But don't do it if tires you.

Sr.

That series of crises coming so close together in a two-month period is just an intensified illustration of what Ellis faced those last three years in East Hampton and New York. She supervised the lives of all four of us, writing at least weekly to each of those away from home, maintaining our allowances, paying our bills and coping with the current emergency that generally faced at least one of us; the year after that strenuous spring it was Jim's turn to worry his parents with a sudden academic tumble that caused him to be put on probation at the end of his freshman year at Harvard.

Taking care of four minor males and a major one must have made her crave another female in the house, but when her sister Jeannette (Jane) Kitchell suffered the same fate of four sons in a row, Ellis wrote her gallantly, "Believe me, however disappointed you may be in not having a daughter, four sons is a perfect family. I speak as one who knows. My disappointment never lasted but a few days."

That fourth son of Jane's died in infancy, and five years later she bore her last child, again a boy. Probably not remembering her previous letter, Ellis again rose to the occasion: "I know you were disappointed at first about the baby but after all we both know that boys are much grander and it makes us unique. It really is better when you have found you do a thing well to stick to your line."

Besides ministering to us in our crises, Ellis also gave all the attention she could spare to consulting with us on the courses we selected in school and our developing ambitions about our future careers, while continuing to exert what influence she could over the reading that continued to be the most important part of our education. Because of Ring's illnesses and absences she performed what are often considered paternal functions as well as maternal ones. The only area she couldn't bring herself to take over was the sex education of male children.

Even if Ring's contacts with us had been closer and more constant, I doubt if he could have conquered his inhibition against talking to us on the subject. As it was he never even gave it a try. And since Ellis didn't either, only Miss Feldman was left to fill another of the vacuums she abhorred. I think it was the year Jim was twelve and I was eleven that she cornered us and asked if we had any questions about, you know, babies and where they came from.

It is remarkable to contemplate now how lacking we were, in a sisterless household in the uptight culture of fifty years ago, of any direct knowledge of the matter. Fleeting observations of visiting girl cousins had left us with a general concept of the anatomical differences but not of their biological purpose. Our heads were full, however, of pieces of information from books that didn't quite fit together into a coherent whole.

Miss Feldman started to say something to the effect that when a man and a woman fell in love and got married . . .

"They don't have to be married," I said.

"Or in love," added Jim.

"Why do you say that?" she probed, cautiously.

"The Duchess de Chevreuse gave birth to Raoul de Brage-lonne after sharing a bed with Athos in an inn when she was disguised as a man," I said.

"And he was disguised as a priest," Jim said. "And they didn't even know each other so they couldn't have been in love."

"No," I said, "she just wanted to damn an abbé."

"She wanted to *what?*" Miss Feldman was getting close to her full depth.

"Damn an abbé."

"What about all those bastards?" Jim said. "The Bastard of Orleans, Edmund in *King Lear*—"

"And all the illegitimate children Louis the Fourteenth had," I said, and then typically went on to a display of scarcely relevant information. "With Louise de La Vallière and Mademoiselle de Tonnay-Charante and Madame de Montespan. And Charles the Second and Nell Gwyn . . ."

Miss Feldman said to stop showing off and get to our questions. What were we curious about?

Jim couldn't think of anything and neither could I. It was hard to figure out exactly what sort of questions she had in mind, and anyway we sensed instinctively that she was not the ideal fount of enlightenment in this area. She was determined not to volunteer any information but simply to satisfy whatever specific curiosity we expressed, and we were equally firm in not wanting to play her game. The session ended in a stalemate.

If Miss Feldman reported to Ellis at all, it could only have been that we weren't ready for the facts yet, so I was a bit taken aback a few summers later when the Tobin girls arrived for a visit at East Hampton and I wanted them to go swimming immediately and they said in an evasive way that they couldn't and my mother took me aside and asked almost harshly if I didn't have the sense to know there were times when girls couldn't swim. Well, of course, by that time I did, having been away at school for a year or two, but how, I wondered, did Ellis suppose I had gained the knowledge?

Increasingly those last years, as Ring's health and his income declined, Ellis was preoccupied with caring for him and keeping the household going on a tighter budget. And once the broken bones of 1931 were healed, we were all making enough progress toward self-sufficiency to lighten her maternal burden somewhat. That summer John, now nineteen, went to work for the New York *Herald Tribune,* and shortly afterward sold a piece to *The New Yorker.* When Ring and Ellis took a furnished apartment on East End Avenue in the fall, he moved in with them.

I believe there are always ego scars on a woman whose life is as wholly subordinated to her husband's as Ellis's was by this time, but I don't think she was consciously aware she was sacrificing a part of herself to her devotion. What struck you instead was how genuinely Ring and she seemed to enjoy being with each other, especially the way he continued to make her laugh. As always only more so, he was finding it difficult to come up with ideas for stories, and they spent a lot of evenings discussing possibilities before he went off to the typewriter, often for an all-night session. "She was the perfect foil for his intelligence," said my uncle, Richard G. Tobin, a close and astute observer.

During the years 1926 through 1934, there was always a Lardner boy at Phillips Academy, generally known as Andover from the Massachusetts town, long the home of the Abbott family, in which it is located. It would have been another two years if David hadn't been forced to transfer halfway through to the Taft School.

It is a commonplace among Andover graduates that a great many of them consider the school to have been a bigger influence on their lives than the college that followed. That was truer in the cases of John, Jim and me than in most because our college careers, at Harvard, the Sorbonne and Princeton, ranged from two to two and a half years, and were cut short because, for pretty much the same reasons, we found them unfulfilling.

During the time we were there, Andover stood out among American preparatory schools to a greater degree than it does now. It was not only the oldest but the richest of them, owing to its good luck in having graduated, during the last decades of the nineteenth century, a couple of students who grew up to be partners in J. P. Morgan and Company. Their contributions, along with others', to the endowment fund paid for an unequaled physical plant, a superior faculty and a system of student aid that made it possible for a full one-third of the student body (numbering in the six hundreds at that time) to be boys who could not otherwise have afforded to go there.

Because of that last factor there was a moderate difference between Andover undergraduates and those of the more exclusive New England schools. We had a wider geographical diversity and we included among us more scions of distressed middle-class and even working-class families. But still notably short of a cross-section. No girls, of course, not for four more decades. And the darkest face we ever had to contemplate belonged to "Sarge" Kahanamoku from Honolulu, brother of the famous "Duke" of the same name. As for Jews, they were kept, with an effort, to just about their proportion in the national population. (Without a quota system the proportion of Jews at Harvard and Yale is now over 25 percent.)

John started there at the age of fourteen in the lower middle year, equivalent to sophomore in normal high school terminology. He spent his first year in Williams Hall, a dormitory set aside for the youngest boys in the school, who were almost all in the class below him, making it doubly hard to catch up to his own classmates socially. His considerable shyness added to his difficulty in getting to know and be known by them, and he never did become a prominent figure in school life. Fellow students noted that he never volunteered in classroom (or had much to say generally) but usually knew the answers when he was called on, especially in English.

He made the editorial board of the school newspaper, but it is worth remarking, in view of his later journalistic achievements, that he was not voted into one of the executive positions. He was elected to be one of the athletic team managers, which was sort of a popularity contest, but the sport he managed was golf, a minor one. He was editor of the literary magazine, which was in the process of failing, and at graduation he was chosen class historian. More indicative of how he was regarded by his two hundred classmates are the votes he received in the "Class of 1929 Statistics," where he came in second in two categories, "Brightest" and "Laziest," third in "Best Student" and in a triple tie for fourth place in "Wittiest." The only explanation for his low showing in the last category is that some of the funniest things John ever said came out in an almost inaudible mumble.

He grew to his full height of six feet two during his years there, was slightly on the thin side, and his ears stuck out in a way that ceased to be noteworthy when his face and form filled out to match his height. Though generally regarded as silent and reserved, he did make close friends with a number of boys who were also not among the leaders of the class. One of them became a Texas cattle baron and another, who edged John out in the vote for laziest, is now a top executive in the world of book publishing. John won two prizes for English literature and composition, and was the only member of his class to graduate with honors in English.

Jim started the year after John did, in the junior or lowest class. There was a great contrast in the way they looked, not only in size but because John was dark-haired and dark-skinned, with Ring's heavy eyebrows, while Jim had light brown hair and fair skin. He was small and deceptively delicate in appearance, with a quality of innocence about him that appealed to everyone older and seemingly stronger than he was. As a result of an incident in which he was considered responsible for a canoe overturning, he was given the nickname "Skipper," which stuck throughout his school years.

The adult counselor on the third floor of Williams Hall was John Homer Dye, private secretary to Andover's formidable headmaster, Dr. Stearns, and later assistant registrar. A slight, gentle, balding man who wrote poetry, collected antiques and hid his native Tennessee accent under an acquired British one, Dye had made a favorite of John, but for Jim he conceived such an affection that his appraisal of him at the age of thirteen cannot be regarded as entirely objective. Nonetheless, Dye had observed a great many young boys from different backgrounds over the years and the qualities he found in this one are significant.

When John underwent three weeks' quarantine for scarlet fever and Jim himself was subsequently confined to the infirmary, Dye kept Ellis informed, referring to Jim as "a wonder, the kindest, most generous and one of the finest youngsters it has ever been my pleasure to know." He told her that since John's illness Jim "has been to me five or six times a day to know what he can do next." He had also been to visit every boy who had been in the infirmary from Williams Hall since school began. "He just goes, no one suggests it, he is thoughtful and kind." Jim was also good, Dye went on, about doing things for his own protection, seeking counsel about what to wear or about the safety of the ice for skating, "and he has always done as I advised."

He predicted that Jim would make six friends to John's one. He was maturing rapidly, was already popular and his career at school was bound to be a successful one. As a patient "Jimmy has captivated the hearts of the whole force at the infirmary and they love him." Noting that he was "terribly shy and at times absolutely inarticulate," Dye said it was a wonder how so many people were drawn to him, found him bright and interesting, and wanted to enjoy his company. He seemed to have a great "drag" with everyone who has anything to do with him. "He has been shamelessly favored by every table proctor in Williams Hall." Nor did all this attention have any adverse effect on him. Jim just pursued the even tenor of his disposition, never running to excess in any form, remaining friendly to everyone and always happy, full of energy and bubbling over with fun. "To use the word the boys use, he is an absolute 'whizz' and I wish we had a hundred like him."

Jim's impression on his classmates, like John's and unlike mine, was a quiet one. He didn't appear at all in the "Class of 1931 Statistics," but he was involved in a number of extracurricular activities, including the debating society and the dramatic club, for which he played a leading female role in Kaufman and Connelly's *Dulcy*. But his major concentration was the school newspaper, the *Phillipian*, which appeared every Wednesday and Saturday and could be practically a full-time occupation for its managing editor, which Jim became in the spring of his upper middle year. He was also assistant manager of basketball and manager of lacrosse, the only relevance of which is that he had still not developed into an athlete. The next year at Harvard, grown to his full height of not quite five eight and weighing a hundred and forty-five pounds, his only extracurricular activities were the freshman wrestling, rugby and lacrosse teams.

My first hours at Andover remain in my memory because after John had introduced me to Mr. Dye and left me at Williams Hall, I felt very much alone and wandered through the open door of the adjoining room and started a conversation with the boy there. He stuck out his hand cordially and said, "My name's Ring. What's yours?" And it wasn't a put-up job. His name actually was Ringland F. Kilpatrick. That was almost fifty years ago and I haven't met another Ring since.

In later years I have been described as laconic, reserved and less than articulate (some Hollywood friends called me "the Indian"), but by Lardner standards when I arrived at Andover in 1928, I was considered gregarious if not flamboyant. Like most fat kids I was ashamed of the way I looked, and I think I deliberately tried to call attention to myself in other ways to compensate. Embarrassed too by my intermittent stutter, I made a point of speaking in public, both as a member of the school debating team and in a number of prize contests that consisted of declaiming original compositions. I was also editor-in-chief of the newly revived literary magazine.

But the main way in which my Andover career differed from

John's and Jim's involved activities so distinctly extracurricular as to be quite outside the rules and regulations of the academy. I went on furtive night excursions, in the full and joyous knowledge that discovery meant probation or expulsion, to the amusements of Revere Beach, a half-hour's drive away, and the hazards of Prohibition gin in a speakeasy in the adjoining industrial town of Lawrence. A classmate and I dramatized our distaste for long Sunday sermons by preparing an alarm clock in the stuck drawer of the preacher's lectern so it went off twenty minutes after he started speaking and continued to ring until it wound down. And I was a leader of an expedition that broke into the sacrosanct premises of an undergraduate secret society and caused a photograph of its arcane mantelpiece and motto to appear on the front page of the *Phillipian*.

After four years I appeared rather prominently, if not altogether honorably, in the "Class of 1932 Statistics." I was voted first place in "Wittiest," "Most Original" and "Biggest Bluffer in Classroom," second by very close votes in "Laziest" and "Hardest to Rattle," and by a more comfortable margin in "Windiest," and scored a tie for fourth place in "Brightest."

David was more sociable than his brothers outside the home environment, possibly because within it he found it hard to assert himself. The occasions when he did, however, were apt to be notable. My cousin Richard L. Tobin, son of Anne and Richard G., recalls a time at our house in East Hampton the summer he became twenty-one. John was nineteen, and Jim and I, at seventeen and sixteen, also took part in the adult conversation, but David, at twelve, didn't try—most of the time. Except on this one occasion, when he broke a lull abruptly with "What's the absence-of-desire railroad?" That brought him stares from us all while he answered his own question: "The Lackawanna."

He entered Andover the fall after I graduated and thus had no brother to help him adjust, but Dye wrote Ellis early in the semester: "David has made what appears to me to be a much easier start than the other boys made." He went on to report that

David had fallen into the routine with an ease he had rarely seen bettered and that he had heard a number of comments on his attractiveness, always with the comment that he combined Jim's appeal with my ability to say what I thought. "He is excellent company and is always amusing and entertaining."

Another thing that impressed Dye was David's healthy and well-balanced interest in school life and his work. This embraced all student activities, including some his brothers had been inclined to regard comtemptuously at times, which I take to be a reference to major athletic events like the Andover-Exeter football game. "He has a spontaneity and naturalness quite in keeping with his age and his little sudden breaking into song or giggles delights me when I hear it."

Dye's analysis seems to conform with what I said previously about David's relative maturity and assurance at all ages. The fact that he had already been a boarder for two years in a much smaller school close to home was certainly also a factor in the way he took to Andover. Why, then, did he alone, out of the four of us, run into such trouble his second year that he couldn't be promoted from lower to upper middler?

I couldn't figure it out then, when I rushed up to Andover that fall of 1934 and arranged, in telephonic consultation with Ellis, for his orderly transfer to Taft. And the only explanation I have in retrospect is that he followed the family pattern of giving priority to his own reading and other interests, but somehow lacked the facility to fake it in classroom or on paper. Whatever it was, after he decided to apply himself, in another first-rate school half the size, he won higher marks and more academic distinction than the rest of us ever achieved at that level.

Outside his studies he played soccer without making the team, served as a cheerleader, and belonged to the debating club, the glee club, the choir and the editorial board of the *Taft Annual.* In the "senior voting" he was named "Wittiest," running up as many votes as the next three contenders combined. In the entry under his name in the *Annual,* emphasis was laid on his practice of saying exactly what he thought, but only when his opinion was solicited.

To my knowledge and best belief, none of Ring's hospital stays in the last three years of his life was the result of a drinking bout. When he was in Tucson that difficult spring of 1931, he did make an unauthorized excursion to Phoenix to see an ex-Chicago newspaperwoman and former colleague, and drank some whiskey before he returned to the sanitarium, but by this time he was getting such symptoms as stomach pains and swollen ankles without the aid of alcohol. Even when he almost burned himself to death in the East End Avenue apartment as a result of a lighted cigarette dropping or blowing out of an ashtray, I think he was unconscious from paraldehyde or chloroform, both of which he took for insomnia, rather than liquor, though the occurrence is a common one in alcoholism.

In March, 1932, he went back to Doctors Hospital, Ellis gave up the apartment and returned to the Croydon on Eighty-sixth Street, and John moved into a place of his own until June, when Dick Tobin graduated from Michigan and joined him on the *Herald Tribune* and as a roommate. Every check Jim and I got for our allowances and special expenses was accompanied by a warning about how short of money the family was. Ring was still in the hospital when Ellis went to Andover for my graduation in June, and he didn't join us in East Hampton until later that month.

In spite of his ailments he turned out a good deal of prose that year, but magazine rates had dropped so much he wasn't making enough to meet expenses. Monthly subsidies he had been sending for years to a brother and a sister had to be cut from a hundred to seventy-five dollars a month apiece. In the early part of the year he wrote a series of autobiographical pieces, largely about Chicago and baseball, for the *Saturday Evening Post,* and then he began a new fiction series for the same market. In the sense that it was the story of a baseball player told in the form of letters, the fiction series (soon to become the book *Lose with a Smile*) was a return to *You Know Me Al,* but it was significantly different in form and content. Readers of the magazine reacted quite favorably to it.

While still in the hospital, where he spent a lot of time listening to the radio, he conceived and proposed to a most receptive Harold Ross the idea of doing a radio column for *The New Yorker,* and that turned out to be practically all his published writing until he died. But he also did two or three short stories that appeared posthumously, and at some point before the end of 1932 he turned his main attention to the new play on which he was supposed to collaborate with George. Jean Dixon remembers visiting him in a Times Square area hotel and finding him enthused about the project. He wanted to live and he wanted to work, he told her, and both impulses were an encouraging switch from what she had previously heard from him.

The two main complaints I remember hearing him voice that summer in East Hampton were about the radio reception, which could be pretty rough in bad weather, and his insomnia, which had taken a diabolical turn. Unable to sleep, he would get up and try to work, and quickly become so drowsy he couldn't keep his eyes open . . . until he lay down, at which point he would be wide awake again. Even the powerful drugs he was taking ceased to perform their functions and eventually appeared to be achieving the opposite effect instead. At that stage, countering perversity with perversity, he began to take the sedative when he wanted to stay awake and caffein for sleep. For a brief while he claimed he was getting positive results from the switch.

That fall, after Jim had returned to Harvard and David and I had started our first years at Andover and Princeton respectively, Ellis wrote Jim that "Dad was very sick—couldn't keep anything on his stomach and had awful pains in both his knees." She took him to the hospital and reported a month later, "Dad is better but Dr. Tyson thinks he was worse this time than ever before and we have persuaded him to stay at the hospital another two or three weeks." In the same letter from East Hampton she wrote:

I am going to stay here until next Wednesday so I can vote here. I sent in an application for an absentee vote on the grounds that your father was ill and I had to go to town to take care of him but they sent back word that my reasons were insufficient and illegal and refused my application. I think Mr. Roosevelt [as Governor of New York] was behind it so I am going to stay here and vote for Mr. Hoover.

Ring meanwhile, at the urging of Heywood Broun, had announced his support for the Socialist Party candidate, Norman Thomas, but he made it clear that it was purely a protest occasioned by the two major parties' having so little to offer. I was the only one of the boys who expressed any interest in politics that year, and my views were changing rapidly. In June, 1931, on my way home from Andover, I had made an impromptu speech from the top of the bus I was traveling on, promoting the still unannounced candidacy of Franklin Roosevelt to a captive audience during a toilet and refreshment stop. It was the last time I ever supported or voted for a major party candidate until George McGovern in 1972. By the fall of 1932, when Roosevelt was running against Hoover, I was an active member of the Princeton Socialist Club touring eastern New Jersey weekends and taking my turn on a soapbox to solicit votes for Thomas (a Princeton alumnus and semiannual chapel preacher) from whoever would listen.

Ring couldn't quite disapprove since he was on record in favor of the same candidate, but he was much more impressed by the unusual number of by-lines John was getting in his first year as a reporter and Jim's new interest in songwriting. Regarding the latter he was willing to go into more detailed criticism than he ever did with a piece of prose from any of us:

As I said in my telegram, I think your refrain begins on the wrong word and on the wrong beat—anyway, it's unsingable as you have it, as you will find out if you try. Your music demands a two-syllable rhyme scheme (except in the middle eight bars, where you have written "ritardo"—incidentally, you don't want any ritard; it ruins the number as a dance tune). If I were you, I'd rewrite the music to those middle eight bars, simplifying it: you can almost do it with a couple of monotones, allowing the harmony to embellish it, or you can go into an entirely different key—A flat for instance.

That winter Ring's doctor strongly advised a desert climate for him; he and Ellis raised money for the trip by negotiating an advance from Scribner's and borrowing on his insurance, and left by boat at the beginning of February. The immediate financial pressure was intensified because Ring had written a short story that for the first time in his career had been turned down by all his regular outlets, *Cosmopolitan, Saturday Evening Post* and *Collier's.* The story, eventually published in a magazine called *Delineator,* was the only one he ever wrote concerned with the Depression and its effect on people's lives. It was called "Poodle" and it was, for him, a quite serious treatment of the subject.

There was no doubt in anyone's mind that Ellis was indispensable to him; the only problem about her going along was that for the first time we would have a spring vacation without a parent to come home to. This was solved by David going to Ellis's sister Jane and her family in South Byfield, Massachusetts, and Jim and me sharing a room in New York at the Peter Stuyvesant Hotel, where John and Dick Tobin were living. We didn't do anything to worry our parents while they were gone except that Jim, who had developed boils on the freshman wrestling team, worked his way off probation and onto the varsity team at Harvard, which brought on a case of the contagious skin disease, impetigo.

All these family events are tied up in my memory with the momentous ones taking place that year in the nation and abroad, especially in Germany, where Hitler became chancellor in January. After the inauguration of President Roosevelt at the beginning of March and before that spring vacation, came the day the banks were closed. Our economics professor at Princeton began a session by announcing: "Gentlemen, I have been teaching for fifteen years that a bank crisis was impossible under the Federal Reserve System. I will never again represent any opinion of mine as a dogmatic fact."

It was also a time of lively debate over whether men should be allowed topless on New York beaches.

From Los Angeles, where their boat landed, Ellis and Ring went to La Quinta, an isolated desert resort southeast of Palm Springs. Ring was now working exclusively on his play with an alcoholic protagonist, preparing an act for George Kaufman "to tear apart." He wrote letters jointly addressed to "Bill, John (and Dickie), David, James," which order, he said, was "probably the best from a standpoint of speed in transmission. When Bill has read and, perhaps, memorized these words, he is supposed to send them on to John, who, after mumbling them to Dickie, will forward them to David, and the last-named (in every way) will mail them to Jim or, as some call him, the dead letter office."

In his first letter, reporting on the boat trip, he said it was all right except for the way his feet had swollen up as a result of wearing shoes after a long unshod period. He said a deck steward, after noting that he was reading *Van Loon's Geography* and being told it was a present from one of Ring's sons, said, "Isn't that queer, Mr. Lardner? Because I was planning to give it to one of my sons for his birthday. That's a paradox." Ring wrote it was a revelation to discover the real meaning of a word he had always thought meant two consulting physicians. A fellow passenger was Warner Baxter, a movie star, who walked around the deck every night before dinner. "Mrs. L. pretended she didn't know who he was, but she followed him with her eyes every time we turned our Baxter."

He also analyzed the prospects for the baseball pennant races that would end the week of his death. Jack Doyle had sent him the preseason odds, and he had decided to play the Yankees straight despite their being an odds-on favorite, and also to make two parlay bets combining the Yankees with Pittsburgh and Brooklyn at three to one and eight to one respectively. "If the Yankees lose," he said, "you will find my body in a sour apple tree." In a later letter to Dick Tobin he stated that he had "a yard and a half" on the Yankees. The World Series that year was between the Washington Senators and the New York Giants.

Ring and Ellis started home in mid-April, stopping in Niles to visit various Lardners and Tobins there, and in Detroit to see Ellis's sister Ruby and her family. When they arrived in New York, they checked in at the Biltmore because Ring had "to see Dr. Gerber [his dentist], Dr. Tyson [his physician] and Dr. Kaufman [his collaborator]." He had a second draft of his first act, which, he had reported to us from La Quinta, "is nearly an hour and a half long in its present plight, which will give Mr. Kaufman the opportunity he lacked in *June Moon* of masticating and spitting out five and six pages at a time."

At the beginning of May Ellis went on to East Hampton to stay and Ring moved over to the Hotel Edison either to be nearer George's base of operations or just because he preferred the Times Square area. His enthusiasm for the play kept growing:

> I only hope I can stay well enough to work. If I can, I promise you and the rest of the world one thing: that never again will I take a vacation when I am through with a job, I think it is the biggest mistake a person can make—not to keep on going. I never felt better in my life than when I was working twenty hours a day, trying to get *June Moon* into shape, and never felt worse than afterwards, when it was in shape and I treated myself to a "layoff," which was mostly spent in the lovely atmosphere of hospitals.

In June the family was reunited in East Hampton except for John, who came down every other week on his days off. Ring spent most of the time upstairs, where he had his workroom and a sleeping porch leading off it from which he could see and fret over our riding the waves when the ocean was rough. Sometimes, when we were close to the house, his voice would break into what we were doing, as once when he suddenly called to me in a surprised tone: "Do you know, you'd really have a nice singing voice . . . if you could only carry a tune?"

He worried that that same lack of an ear would be a handicap in my first attempt at a musical comedy book, though he was pleased that I as a freshman had come out cowinner with a junior in the competition to determine who would write the annual show of the Princeton Triangle Club. It had been decided the two of us would collaborate and we began the process by mail that summer.

Some evenings he felt well enough to join us downstairs for dinner, though he didn't want to see anyone else except the Rices; sometimes we would set up a card table next to his bed, and Jim and I, who were learning to play bridge together, would play against him and a partner who might be Ellis or Kate Rice or Kate's visiting sister, Lizabeth Vereen.

When John's vacation came at the end of July, Ring was well enough to be left alone with the two women servants (Danish at the time, if I remember rightly; at various times we also had a Finnish pair and a Swedish one and a Japanese married couple) while the rest of the family set out by car for Chicago and the "Century of Progress" World's Fair. John was twenty-one, Jim and I had driver's licenses, and we all took over the wheel at times, but Ellis still didn't trust us with the more difficult driving, so the party also included Albert Mayer, who had worked for the family several years in Great Neck and then returned to us in East Hampton after an interval with two other chauffeur-gardeners. He stayed on with Ellis for another twenty years after Ring died.

Six of us with our luggage was not too great a burden for the car; it was a sixteen-cylinder Cadillac, a model the company abandoned after a year or two. No matter how often somebody had to go to the bathroom, it was always time to stop for gas anyway. Other than that extravagance, we tried, as Ring said in a letter to Kate's sister Mildred, "to see how cheaply they can make the trip, for two reasons—the 'fun' of the experiment and the fact that they won't have anything to spend."

Between seeing the fair and visiting relatives, I detached myself in Chicago for a mission I was still keeping secret from my family, proceeding to the modest offices of a new magazine that was to have its first quarterly issue that fall. The venture was *Esquire* (soon to convert to a monthly), and its founder, Arnold

Lake Wawasee, Indiana, 1933:
John, Ellis, David, Ring, Jr.
and Jim

The last picture of Ring, about
two years before his death

Gingrich, had asked Alexander Woollcott to nominate a candidate to represent the college generation. Woollcott had suggested me, I had written the desired article and it had been accepted, and now I had to meet the editor and arrange to be photographed. Before I rejoined my family on one of the hottest days I can remember, a photographer, Gilbert Seehausen, took a picture that filled a page of the magazine when it came out in October.

What I didn't know was that the enterprising Mr. Gingrich had persuaded an astonishing number of prominent writers to contribute to his project for much less than their normal fees. (My name on the cover was in the distinguished company of Hemingway, Hammett, Dos Passos, Vincent Starrett, Morley Callaghan, Erskine Caldwell, William McFee, Gilbert Seldes and Nicholas Murray Butler.) Among those who had succumbed was my father and he had sent in a story that didn't make the deadline for that inaugural issue and eventually appeared in the third one.

Shortly after we got back home in time for my eighteenth birthday in August, Ring reacted indignantly to an item in the morning mail. In my presence as it happened, he denounced Gingrich because the man, after entreating him to accept a pittance of two hundred dollars, was now sending him only a hundred. It was one of my finest moments to date when I called his attention to the "Jr." on the check.

Although Ring had seemed in better shape and spirits ever since the trip to California, the recovery was short-lived. One night Ellis woke Jim and me because he had lost consciousness on the toilet seat and she could neither rouse nor move him. We carried him to bed without his awaking. Toward the end of the summer Miss Feldman came out from New York for a visit, and when she saw his condition, she offered to stay and take care of him. I was not party to the arrangement, but I think she did it for a good deal less than what she was then getting as a registered nurse going home from the hospital with maternity patients.

The last communication I know of he sent to anyone was a telegram to John on the occasion of a prominent by-line story on the front page of the *Herald Tribune.* The message was: "VERY PROUD OF MY SONS ECLIPSE OF SUNS ECLIPSE ON PAGE ONE."

By September 24 Jim had already gone off to Harvard and David to Andover, and I was due to leave for Princeton the next day. That night we had a bridge game on Ring's sleeping porch, with Ring, who had become terribly thin, sitting up in a padded chair. Kate Rice and I played against Ellis and Ring. The next morning, before Dr. Tyson arrived from New York on a periodic visit, Ring had a heart attack and became unconscious. John was summoned, I put off my departure, and when the doctor came he had no hope to offer us. Ring never came out of the coma and died the same day. He was forty-eight.

Elder's biography contains an improbable version of Heywood Broun's last words: "Ring Lardner died a happy man because he wrote what he wanted to." According to a letter to me in 1959 from Broun's friend, Morris Ernst, the actual words were quite the opposite: ". . . He asked about his chances of recovery and then in effect said to the doctor: If I live I will never forget Ring Lardner. The doctor asked why. Heywood replied: If Ring had written only what he wanted to write, he would have lived fifteen years longer."

11

To students of the New York press it was an accepted fact, in the years following the demise of the *World,* that the *Herald Tribune* was the best-written paper, and that its pre-eminence was largely due to the standards of its city editor, a slight, sharp-featured Texan named Stanley Walker. The stately *Times* was the newspaper of record, but it was the feature stories in the *Trib* that people in and around the writing business talked about. Walker, who had met Ring a few times, regarded him as a major influence in the history of journalism because of his revolutionary innovation of reporting what people actually said. Before that you put quotation marks around what a person might have said if he had had the time and talent to present his best-written case.

Accordingly, Walker was receptive when James M. Cain proposed that he consider John Lardner as a candidate for his staff. This came about after John submitted his first piece to *The New Yorker* and Cain, then managing editor, responded with the kind of rejection a writer likes to get, if any: "Everybody, however, looks forward to your next piece and believes that you ought to do well." John did indeed succeed with his second effort and it was published before the end of the year.

Cain went on to say he had spoken about him to Walker, and Walker would like to see him. Two months later John went to work for the paper and Ring wrote Walker a letter of thanks: "You will find him a little reticent at times, but personally I never felt this was a great handicap." Walker, who eventually reached the verdict that John "came close to being the perfect all-around journalist," realized what Ring meant when John came back from one of his first assignments. He had been sent up to Rye in Westchester County for a birthday interview with Simeon Ford, an almost forgotten wit, hotel proprietor and after-dinner speaker.

"Did you get an interview?" the city editor asked.

"I'm afraid not," John said. "He died while I was there."

John was two months past his nineteenth birthday and just returned from his final year of schooling in Paris and a short stint on the European edition of the paper when he went to work on the *Trib* in New York in 1931. He took readily to a routine in which almost as many hours were spent in the speakeasy downstairs as in the city room or out on assignments.

The speakeasy and the legal establishment that succeeded it were always known to the customers as Bleeck's (pronounced "Blake's"), but when a sign went up after Repeal, it bore the more official name of the place. The sign said on the top line "Artist and Writers Restaurant" and on the bottom "formerly Club." Whether the singular form "Artist" was a sign painter's mistake, as maintained by one school of thought, or sprang, in the opposing view, from the fact that Jack Bleeck knew many writers but acknowledged only one artist, the cartoonist Clare Briggs, it is retained to this day on the sign and in the phone directory listing. Twenty years later a group of habitués, John among them, in a delayed reaction to the second line of the sign, decided to justify it by organizing on the premises a social institution called the Formerly Club.

John resembled Ring, or patterned his life after Ring's, to a greater extent than any of his brothers. The same words come up in descriptions of them: dignity, reserve, standards, taciturnity, subtle influence. They both sought company but not companionship. They avidly gathered and stored information in a variety of fields that interested them but left whole areas of practical living to wives, servants, accountants, building superintendents and other specialists.

In many respects John was a survivor from the middle-class America that all but expired in 1929. Writing, not for publication, of the speakeasies in his *Herald Tribune* days, he wound up with "best of all, Bleeck's, with its floors never profaned by the foot of a woman." He didn't deliberately refrain from housekeeping, cooking and mechanics beyond changing light bulbs and typewriter ribbons; it just never occurred to him that he could or should intrude on the people who performed these functions.

I am dealing here with a distinction that may not be readily clear to present-day readers but which existed to a certain extent even between John and me although we were only three years apart. That could be attributed to certain small environmental influences like my getting married nearly two years before he did and living, on a smaller income, in a house in California rather than an apartment in New York. In any case, while his enormous accumulation of facts covered even subjects like the plundering of the planet years before ecology became a familiar word, there were certain actual practices I indulged in, though never to excess, like raising chickens or camellias, building barbecues or bookshelves, that were as alien to him as they would have been to our father.

Filling out a questionnaire for *Newsweek* in 1944, he described his hobbies as "playing the typewriter, piano and races" and his idiosyncrasies as "excessive shyness—can't get drunk—mental age 7 financially." The second-to-last item was only a slight exaggeration. He drank regularly and sometimes, during his twenties and thirties, a great deal, without displaying much evidence of it. He had Ring's impulse to do his drinking in public places, where he could see and hear other people and even exchange an occasional word with them. But he never became addicted to alcohol and found it no struggle to cut way down on it during the last decade of his life.

Sports, theater, books, music, gambling, movies and popular history were his main interests, and he wrote about all of them although he was primarily known as a sportswriter. This came about, after he had worked two and a half years on the *Trib,* when John Wheeler offered him a syndicated sports column for the North American Newspaper Alliance (NANA) at a hundred dollars a week, which was phenomenal for a twenty-one-year-old in the depths of the Depression.

Till then he had written general news stories for the city desk, though the Sunday book section, aware of his familiarity with sports, gave him a succession of books in that field to review. His skill as a reporter and writer was rewarded with a large number of by-lines, more often than not on stories of little news importance. During the months when Franklin Roosevelt and Adolf Hitler were rising to power in their respective countries, John Lardner leads reported such events as:

> A forty-year-old botanical argument, involving the violet and the sunflower, was revived yesterday at Center Moriches, L.I., by Frank N. Evanhoe, known in New York City half a century ago as one of the toughest and most astute detectives ever to dog the footsteps of a public enemy.

And:

> Gabong, Dohong and Dyak, three shrewd and vindictive inmates of the primate house at the New York Zoological Park, in the Bronx, entered yesterday upon the third act of a little melodrama entitled "Orang-utans Laugh at Locksmiths." They removed a six-inch spike from the skylight over their cage, jimmied open the cage door and were kept from escape only by a chain recently installed in front of the door.

In these feature stories John often departed from the literal accuracy of mechanically perfect journalism. When a fox escaped from its owner's yard in Brooklyn, he fantasized that in the heat of the chase its pursuers cried "Yercks!" in place of "Yoicks!" the traditional cry of English fox hunters. And he assisted another restless resident of that borough named Harry Gerguson to assume the character of Prince Michael Romanoff, heir presumptive to the Russian imperial crown, by attributing grander and funnier statements to him than Mike was capable of improvising. Later in Mike's highly successful Beverly Hills restaurant, Romanoff's, the displaced autocrat bestowed a number of free drinks on me because of my kinship to his cocreator.

What John started with was a delicate instinct for the difference between stories that had to be recorded faithfully and those that permitted some creative license. It is a nicety largely undiscovered by the "new journalism" of today.

Communication with him was sometimes difficult but often rewarding, the more so if you shared the special knowledge to interpret his more succinct comments. When Stanley Walker fell on bad times and had to undertake a job beneath his merits, John could characterize him to Joseph Mitchell in the word "Beauregard" because they both knew the Confederate hero had lived through three decades of post-Shiloh anticlimax, including a long period as manager of the Louisiana lottery.

One of the closest friends he made in Bleeck's was Don Skene, whose reputation in his early thirties as a drinking man began to outdistance his considerable one as a sportswriter. While he was still employable Don guided John with his knowledge and experience when John was getting started in sports. Then came a stage in which Don, unable to hold a regular job, divided his time between doing legwork for John and writing a funny book about the boxing world called *The Red Tiger*. One night in 1935, John brought Don home from a night at Bleeck's to the apartment in Greenwich Village John shared with Jim and Dick Tobin. There Don remained, wasting away from alcoholism, until his death in 1938 at the age of forty. It was not entirely a coincidence that John was married a few months later: the custody of Don Skene was no longer an impediment.

In January, 1934, about two months after he became a sports columnist, John started a journal or diary. He kept it up for eight days, averaging an entry every other day; at least I think that was the total duration of it; the four entries are in a loose-leaf note-

Jim, Ellis and Ring, Jr. at
East Hampton, 1934

David around the same time

The match game at Bleeck's, 1936 *(left to right):* Don Skene, John Lardner, Walter Kerr, Bruce Pinter, Stanley Walker, Alva Johnston, Jack Bleeck and Fritz (the waiter)

book, followed by some notes on a baseball story and then by a few dozen blank pages. The urge for self-revelation had apparently run out.

One entry begins: "Mother said at Kate Rice's that John Wheeler told her he was amazed by the number of papers that take my column. I'm amazed by the number that don't."

And another:

Tonight Mother talked to me about Jim. She says he's really unhappy, desperate to leave Harvard. At nineteen it's hard to understand, for me, anyway. But it's possible to be depressed in school or college. I was more deeply unhappy my first year at Andover than I've ever been since.

Jim's case is difficult to analyze. His unhappiness may be compounded of loneliness, shyness, inarticulateness. More likely he's mentally restless and afraid of the future. His insistence on leaving school may be a sort of resolve to plunge into work at once and see what happens.

I'm always more nervous for someone I like than for myself. I'm afraid for Jim as a reporter or writer, afraid he'll be licked and suffer. I was afraid for Dickie [Tobin] when he came on the *Herald Tribune*. Then when he seemed to be doing well, I got spasms of jealousy. And now it's anxiety again.

If Jim is unhappy from loneliness he's not like me. Anywhere, at grade school, Andover, Harvard, Paris, working, I had a few friends who satisfied me for quality. . . .

John Homer Dye, still at Andover but in touch with Jim at Harvard, wrote Ellis his views on the same crisis. He said he had not tried to dissuade Jim for the same reason she had not. He also shared the feeling she must have expressed to him that Jim's chances of success in his coming job were unpredictable. "I know," Dye said, "he has the capacity to succeed somewhere and somehow but I know he has a certain perversity of temperament which does not function well in a group." That was something Jim would have to learn by experience to modify and curb if he was going to accomplish much in the competitive world. But

Dye thought he was wise enough to absorb that lesson without too much delay. He hoped Jim realized he didn't have to follow the pattern set by his brothers but was and must remain an individual. He thought Jim felt that John and I had somehow gotten "the jump" on him.

The inclusion of me here when I was still in my sophomore year at college indicates Dye's knowledge that I had already been published in *Esquire*. What he concluded about Jim was that "He will have plenty of energy and determination and certainly has the brain power if only he can get the capacity for adjustment and compromise of his own stubbornness."

None of us knew at the time of another element that contributed to some indeterminate extent to how Jim was feeling in the fourth month after his father's death. The previous summer in East Hampton, having been cast for a Broadway play that required her to play jazz on the piano without benefit of sheet music, Floncy Rice decided to take lessons. Jim, still in his songwriting period, felt he needed the same technique, and a teacher was found who could park on the joint driveway, give one lesson and cross the hundred feet of lawn for another. Between lessons his two students listened to each other practice.

Floncy was twenty-six that year and Jim was nineteen. I have mentioned her sensational beauty, which combined with an appealing personality to produce an almost unanimously stunning effect on males from puberty to dotage. In the eight years since Ring had based "I Can't Breathe" on her inability to decide among the men in figurative prostration at her feet, we Lardner boys had observed, often at close range, a long succession of suitors and one fleeting husband, and regarded them all with subjective disfavor. Since her debut in *June Moon* she had also tried to further a theatrical career based more on beauty than on talent, but the part she was now preparing for, in Edward Hope's *She Loves Me Not* directed by Howard Lindsay, was the first really good one that had come her way. (It led to a ten-year career of low-budget stardom at MGM.)

She and Jim saw a lot of each other that summer, but I think it was in the few days after Ring's death that their emotions over that event led to an expression of feeling for each other. Jim never said anything to me about it, and I was the closest to him in the family, so all I have to go on are the few letters and telegrams from her to him I found in his effects many years later.

A week after he returned to Harvard, she wired him:

NO REHEARSALS YET WHAT WOULD HAPPEN IF I TOOK ONE OCLOCK FOR BOSTON SATURDAY NOT SURE IT IS POSSIBLE BUT IF SO WOULD IT BE CONVENIENT PLEASE BE TRUTHFUL WILL UNDERSTAND PERFECTLY IF NOT WIRE AS SOON AS POSSIBLE TO 1158 FIFTH BE SURE TELEGRAM IS DELIVERED NOT TELE-PHONED LOVE

FLONCY

The last instruction was so her parents, with whom she was again living, would not be aware of the rendezvous and, presumably, reproach her for "cradle-robbing." Back in New York that Sunday night, she wrote:

Jimmy Dear,
    Just a note to say that I've already realized I was wrong. At least I know that right or wrong, it can't be done. Not seeing you will be awfully hard, but after all, the times won't be so terribly far between.
    I'm dead tired so I'll say no more at present.
    Everything is all right, and needless to say I shall never forget these last two days.

Love, darling—
Floncy

Her letters and telegrams over the next couple of months are concerned with the play, including a crisis in which she was briefly out of the cast, and arrangements for weekend meetings in New York. It is evidence of Jim's devotion that he managed to make it there two weekends between her visit on October 9 and the Thanksgiving break. Our modest allowances weren't designed to cover all that train travel.

There are no surviving communications after that until the final one, a telegram on January twenty-fifth. My guess is that he had told her during Christmas vacation of his intention to leave college. That last wire read:

DONT KNOW WHAT YOU MEAN HAVE HAD NO PREVIOUS WORD FROM YOU PHIL IS HERE SO CANNOT PLAN ANYTHING ARE YOU STILL LEAVING IF SO WHEN LOVE

FLONCY

The only supplement I can provide to the documentary evidence is that "Phil" was almost certainly the actor Phillips Holmes, a swain of long standing.

Five years later in Hollywood, Floncy came at my invitation to the organizing meeting of the James Lardner Memorial Fund, set up to aid the Lincoln vets who returned from Spain.

Jim's love life didn't last long enough to set much of a pattern, but he did become involved the following year in New York and again in Paris with women several years older than he.

John, who had started his daily syndicated sports column that fall, was living in the Peter Stuyvesant Hotel with Dick Tobin and a third newspaperman named Thomas Sugrue. Sugrue persuaded *American* magazine to pay his expenses for a year of travel while Jim was finishing that final semester at Harvard, and Jim moved into the vacancy he left in the apartment. He also moved into a job on the *Trib* with little more expenditure of effort on his part. Stanley Walker was willing to gamble on another Lardner to replace the one he had lost to Wheeler.

Jim performed his job on the paper competently for the next three years. His father's and his brother's names were powerful factors in getting him on the payroll, but after that he was on his own and had to satisfy his bosses every week to remain there, especially in an unemployment situation that seemed immune to all the New Deal programs to improve it. He was bright and literate enough to carry out all the jobs assigned him, but not nearly aggressive enough to make a name for himself in the competition of a New York press corps recruited from the country's best. He won himself few by-lines and spent most of his time on the monotonous round of funerals, banquets, strikes, accidents and minor crimes that a young reporter habitually had to cover. Occasionally he would fill in for his friend Robert Neville on the daily column "The Bridge Table," and during one Neville leave of absence, took over the feature for an extended period.

I left college four months after Jim did, at the end of the academic year. I had enjoyed myself in the fall during the preparation and rehearsals of the Triangle show. It was the last one before the direction passed from Dr. Donald Stuart of the French Department to Joshua Logan, and the star of the previous year, José Ferrer, would drop by from his architectural studies at the graduate school to lend a hand. One evening he found Dr. Stuart watching one of our scenes with a frown of deep concern.

"Joe," said the middle-aged scholar, "is that scene dirty?"

"No," said Joe, "but I'll show you how you can make it dirty."

But during the winter and spring I became increasingly dissatisfied with what I personally, at the age of eighteen, was making of my life there that could justify the cost to my mother, who had invested the proceeds of Ring's insurance and was trying to operate on the income plus the dwindling earnings from his copyrights. Like Jim I was anxious to get on to the next stage of life, which, of course, was service as a newspaper reporter, and see if I could handle the challenge. Even though I had represented my university in a radio debate with Smith College on the proposition "Resolved, that a woman's place is in the home," and served as an alternate on the Princeton bridge team, I didn't feel I was accomplishing anything, certainly not scholastically. Only in bridge, to which I devoted five or six hours a day, and poker, which consumed an evening or two a week, was I making any real progress, and I was able to figure out, all by myself, that you could play cards in a nonacademic setting.

John had had both parents to consult on the question of curtailing his formal education, but Ellis had to face on her own similar ultimatums from Jim and me in the roughest year of her life to date. She had gone on functioning after Ring died simply because there were so many responsibilities no one else could meet. Within weeks she had closed the East Hampton house for the winter and rented a two-room suite in a New York hotel. One of her first visitors there was her youngest sister, Dorothy Kitchell, who reported to the oldest one, Ruby Hendry:

Ellis is certainly lonely. She has adopted a way of living which would kill me in less than a week. However, she seems to find merit in it. The hotel is clean and adequate in every physical way. Ellis does not accumulate things as you know and even after two weeks the rooms seem very bare to me. She reads about eight hours a day and eats sufficient food, I'm sure. She hates so to go out that that is where she will go bad unless she gets an urge to go out more. She and I went to the Rices' Sun. afternoon. We walked about twenty of the short blocks up to their house and that was the first time Ellis had been in anyone else's house since she had come in. Kate had taken her out in the car but that was all. We stopped on our walk home at the Wheelers' and had a nice visit. Then Mon. eve we went to the movies, John and Ellis and I. I think that was a mistake as Ellis had seen some of the movies and the rest were sad. I told her that much before we went but I think she wanted to get the first time behind her. Letters I know will help.

Ellis doesn't seem to me to be brooding unduly and she has Ring's picture on her dresser and talks of him and of the last week with him as though it were a treasure. I think it will always be the same grief to her but she may be able to find some comfort outside. John is simply adorable to her. I believe I shall always love him, no matter what comes up or if I shouldn't know him better than I do now, I'd love him for the sweet way he has with Ellis and the care he takes of her and the thought he gives her.

241

I can't say that I think she ought to live with him. I know she is lonely but I think she has a joy from having him come to see her which wouldn't be the same as it would if they were always together.

Ellis was talking about the boys, what fine boys they were and how happy she was in them. She had read an article where the women in like circumstances said My children are fine but they are another generation from me and my husband and there isn't any intimacy. As Ellis repeated it she said, "You see, that is what you miss, that intimacy which you can't have with anyone else and which nothing ever replaces."

All Ellis's sisters were concerned about her that fall. Florence Torrence also made a trip to New York to see her, and Jane Kitchell (she and Dorothy were married to brothers) persuaded her to come up to Massachusetts for a visit and a look at Noah Webster Kitchell, the fourth son on whose arrival Ellis had consoled Jane that summer.

Kate and Granny Rice prevailed on her to spend the month of February with them on vacation in Phoenix, and Ellis timed her departure so she could have a day with Jim on his final return from Harvard, and a couple of days each in Detroit and Chicago to visit family. When she came back east, it was with the program of finding herself a new place to live. The house she had built on the dunes with Ring was too grand and too full of memories, and with only her own taste to consider, the ocean had no special appeal. Since the East Hampton property was a good summer rental if left furnished, she would be able to take only her best eighteenth-century pieces and start with them in the sort of early American house where they belonged.

It had to be close enough to New York and large enough for all her sons to visit at once, along with the families they might have. And it had to be isolated, not only from all the friends she knew but from the threat of new ones. She found what she was looking for eighty miles north of the city in New Milford, Connecticut—a two-hundred-acre dairy-and-tobacco farm with a pre-Revolutionary house in a valley all its own without a neighbor in sight. The house, which had been known a generation before as "the place with eight rooms and eight fireplaces," was without running water or electricity, and in that Depression year the farm, with all that land, two other houses and three barns, cost her seventeen thousand dollars. She spent about the same amount more to modernize the house and add a kitchen, a porch and two servants' rooms for Albert and a housekeeper.

Many people, including a few men with matrimonial intent, tried to coax her out of that isolation during her first decade there, but each time she began to emerge into a social existence, another death in the family sent her back to seclusion. After David was killed in 1944, nobody tried very hard to change her ways any more, and she went on another fifteen years after that, most of the time with no one else in the house with whom she could have any significant communication. She did spend the majority of winters in New York, but the life she led in a mid-town hotel was as uneventfully antisocial as her regime in the country. Reading, knitting and doing her puzzles (jigsaws, cross-words, double crostics, letter divisions, cryptograms) and, in New Milford, tending her flower garden—those were her activities, day after day, year after year. Her last three baseball seasons she watched Brooklyn Dodger games on a television set John and I sneaked into the house when she wasn't there.

She had been forty-six when Ring died—an unusually attractive, smart-looking forty-six, with unfailing good humor and an infectious laugh. And though she developed an increasingly gloomy attitude toward life in her remaining twenty-six years, that emerged only on rare occasions with intimates. Her personality and outward manner remained as convivial as before and she could always manage to be playful and funny with her grandchildren in particular.

I don't think she made much of an effort to keep Jim in college; she wrote Jane Kitchell:

> He is so discontented there that I haven't the heart to make him go on. He has a newspaper job promised for around March 1 and we don't want to start the new term as we would have to pay for it all.

She did, however, try to persuade me to stay at Princeton when I expressed what she probably regarded as an imitative urge only a few months later. She pointed out that I had spoken quite recently of possible careers as a lawyer or history teacher and she recalled Ring's semiserious complaint the summer before: "Isn't somebody in this family going to do something else [besides writing]?" But my various writing activities in the preceding year had strengthened my confidence in that direction. And the prospect of not only two more years of marking time but graduate study beyond that had all at once become intolerable. So I persuaded her instead that I would be saving her so much money she could afford a few hundred dollars to send me abroad that summer before I set about finding myself a job.

12

I sailed (third class) to Hamburg on a German ship and proceeded by train to Leningrad, the starting point of my travels (third class) in the Soviet Union. Although I had remained a member of the Socialist Club, I had been considerably impressed by a Communist candidate for mayor of Princeton, and some things I had read made me more curious about Russia than any other country. Soviet-American diplomatic relations had just been established, and unilateral tourist travel along with them. The University of Moscow had marked the new era by inaugurating an Anglo-American Institute for summer study, and the left-wing National Students League had organized delegations to attend it from a number of American campuses. One of the students registered there was the former president of the Princeton Socialist Club, and I called on him at the institute the day I reached Moscow. The day after that I canceled the rest of my program with Intourist, moved into a dormitory at the university and enrolled myself in Sociology II or "Crime and Punishment in the Soviet Union."

I never regretted that decision even though a measure of disagreement I had with the orthodox majority at the school almost got me expelled from the country. A Canadian student from McGill and I found the official wall newspaper produced by the NSL group (Budd Schulberg from Dartmouth among them) rather dull and sycophantic, and we put together and hung a parody version of it. We ended up in a disciplinary session with Professor Pinkevich, who ran the institute for the Commissariat of Education with an American associate. When I tried to explain our intentions, the professor said he knew the English word "satire" but not "parody." When I ventured a definition, he questioned a phrase of mine. "Humor for the sake of humor?" he said. "We do not have that in the Soviet Union."

From Russia I went to have a look at Germany just after the S.A. purge and the death of Hindenburg. Everything I saw there, including a glimpse of Hitler and William Randolph Hearst in the back seat of a car in Munich, strengthened my impression that the best hope for mankind lay with the Soviets. Only in Russia were massive construction and planning for the future going on at a time when the West was either locked in stagnant depression or, like Germany, headed resolutely backward to barbarism.

It was probably also a factor in my political development that I enjoyed myself in Moscow, welcoming such diversions as mixed nude bathing in the Moscow River and sitting around a heaping plate of caviar and a carafe of vodka at the university at a cost to the group of less than fifty cents.

On my return I went back to East Hampton, where Ellis, having rented the big house, had taken a smaller one till New Milford was ready for her, which turned out to be early November. It was that fall she dispatched me to Andover, after David failed his Greek exam, and I helped him transfer to Taft School in Watertown, which had the great virtue in Ellis's eyes of being only twenty-five miles from New Milford.

I moved into her new home with her, but I had already been to see Stanley Walker at the *Trib.* All he could do for me there, he told me, was give me a little work at space rates, which meant I would be paid by the line if and when my stories appeared. But he promised he would have a job for me early in 1935 and that I would be surprised to find out what it was.

In January came the news that Walker was taking over as managing editor of the *Daily Mirror,* the Hearst tabloid which competed for many years with the *Daily News,* mainly on the strength of Walter Winchell's column. Walker's contributions to the paper were not impressive; they consisted for the most part of his secretary from the *Trib,* Hazel Hairston, later Mrs. John Lardner, and me as a reporter. He found himself in a typical Hearst quagmire of conflicting authority and went on after a few frustrating months to an equally frustrating period as managing editor of *The New Yorker.* Hazel went with him.

I remained, but there was never a time during my brief career with the paper that I didn't have my antennae up for other opportunities. There was very little connection between working for the *Mirror* in 1935 and the great newspaper tradition of the 1920s that persisted into the thirties on the *Trib* under Walker and to a lesser extent on the other nontabloid papers.

It was not enough, in that tradition, to get the facts straight and relate them coherently under a lead that stated the essence of the story in a provocative way. The best reporters were also literate, entertaining and so individual that devotees could recognize their style without a by-line. They brought knowledge and values of their own to the material they covered, and they included in their numbers at one time or another most of the worthwhile writers of all kinds in the decades that followed.

Talent like that would have been wasted on the *Mirror.* Although I got four or five by-lines during my ten-month stint, most of the time I phoned in the facts I had gathered to the rewrite men who wrote the bulk of the paper. Two of these, Gordon Kahn and John McNulty, became good friends and continued as such in their later careers in Hollywood and on *The New Yorker* respectively. Another friend was Sam Boal, who spoke the purest cynicism I ever heard but organized the Newspaper Guild on the *Mirror,* a risky enterprise in Hearstdom. Sam wrote photo captions, an important job on a tabloid, along with Jim Bishop, who later discovered the knack of devoting more words to a single day in time than any writer since Joyce.

The firmest tie that began there was with Ian McLellan Hunter, who became in Hollywood my closest friend and sometime collaborator. For most of the forty years since we met on the *Mirror,* we have been in geographical proximity, shared our creative problems, both formally and informally, and competed on the tennis court and at the poker table.

One of the satisfactions of that year in New York was that I saw a lot of Jim. There wasn't room for me in the apartment on Eighth Street to which he and John and Dick had moved from the Stuyvesant. I shared a couple of rooms in Tudor City, within walking distance of the office, with a *Trib* reporter and a friend of his, but we all worked different hours and our contacts were minimal. John and Jim and I all went to New Milford when we could on our days off and sometimes they coincided or over-lapped. Otherwise I didn't see John often. He was concerned almost wholly with sports now, for a national rather than a local readership (his New York outlet in those days was the *Post*) and that meant traveling a good deal. Then and most years for the rest of his life he would go to Florida for up to two months of baseball spring training and to Saratoga Springs, New York, for part of the summer racing season there, besides many other quick trips all over the country for specific sporting events. Occasion-ally I would go across town to Bleeck's in the evening, rather than to our neighborhood resort, Tim Costello's, hoping to find him there, but it had to be by chance; unless I had something specific to discuss, I would have felt it violated some kind of code to seek a prearranged meeting.

Jim and I sometimes found ourselves covering the same story, especially after I became the *Mirror*'s bridge specialist (tourna-ments only; there was no daily feature on the subject). At a couple of these events there was a separate newspapermen's tournament, and Jim and I made up a team with two other *Trib* reporters. I discovered a bridge club in my area and, with it, the fact that I could raise my twenty-five-dollar-a-week income an average of ten dollars by two or three evenings' diligent applica-tion to the game. I got Jim to join me in these sessions whenever I could, and we always functioned more effectively as a team than the sum of our separate skills would warrant.

We also shot dice and played poker and made bets on a variety of sports contests. Ring's fondness for gambling was shared by all his sons, but in those years only Jim approached it with a degree of scientific precision. Like Ellis he loved puzzles and calculations of all kinds, and he could figure out in his head astonishing things like the odds against improving your hand with a three-card straight flush. On a subway ride, and in our business you might take ten of them a day, he would generally assign himself some kind of mathematical problem to solve. He had the most logical mind I have ever encountered; a few people were actually frightened by the coldness of his reasoning, his contempt for irrationalism in any form and his lack of any sign of emotion except occasional laughter.

One day in his teens Jim decided he didn't like his posture; he straightened himself up, sort of thrust out his chest, and held himself that way the rest of his life. Another time—I think it was his second winter on the *Trib*—he counted up the overcoats he had left various places, usually because he was working out something in his head, and concluded that the solution to that particular problem was to stop wearing one. He went coatless as well as hatless from then on, no matter how cold it was.

Except for the nearsightedness we all derived from Abbott genes, he was always in fine physical condition and beautifully coordinated. Besides phone-book-rending he caught flies (insect variety) by hand.

As a man of logic he was strongly against superstition but was able to treat the subject in a lighthearted way. In one of his bridge columns he said he had "come to the conclusion that we are the only person alive today who not only publicly disavows all superstitious beliefs but disregards them in practice."

Then he went on to describe a hand he claimed to have witnessed in which South had thirteen clubs, West thirteen diamonds, North thirteen hearts, and East, as one might expect, thirteen spades. (He could have told his readers, but refrained, that the odds against even one such hand being dealt were one hundred and fifty-nine billion to one.)

The hand looked promising and South was about to mention clubs, which looked like his best suit, when he remembered suddenly that he had neglected to walk around his chair before the hand began. Knowing that he would probably go down about six tricks if he opened his mouth, he played safe and passed. . . .

West had never made a contract in diamonds since the day in 1913 when he had sold thirteen acres of land in South Africa from which $13,000,000 worth of diamonds were taken in the next thirteen weeks. He shuddered when he saw all the diamonds in his hand, and when he realized that there were thirteen of them he dropped his cards as if he had been bitten by a fer-de-lance.

After West's pass there was a slight pause. North was debating with himself. He had shuffled the red deck five times, according to his regular formula, but that could hardly have any effect on the play until the following hand, and he remembered distinctly that West had shuffled the blue deck only twice. North's thirteen hearts looked very pretty, but he resisted the temptation and passed also.

The players then looked expectantly at the chair where East had been sitting, but it was no longer occupied. East was not in the room. This baffled the rest of us, until someone remembered that East had once been told by a medium that when he looked at his hand and saw thirteen spades he would vanish into thin air. East had always been very superstitious.

John, Jim and I were all backward in the area of sex, as I take it Ring had been in his day. (David was more normal.) We had our first experiences rather late in our teens and, more significantly, devoted very little of our time and attention to the pursuit of girls. I don't think any of us, once initiated, went any long period without sex; we just didn't, for the most part, make the overtures. As the fat one I didn't get as many approaches as the others, but there were enough to make me realize that some percentage of women are attracted to men who appear to be uninterested, whether genuinely or out of shyness, and seek them out in preference to more aggressive types. Later on, after I shed forty pounds at the age of twenty-three, I found what it was like to confront about the same number of advances as my brothers, but the timing was a bit off: I had already been married for two years.

I had roomed my second year at college with my former neighbor, Herbert Bayard Swope, Jr., and continued to see a good deal of him when I worked on the *Mirror,* usually at his parents' apartment or their summer home in Sands Point, Long Island. The senior Swope recommended me to David O. Selznick, who was launching his own independent movie company, and we had some correspondence about a job in which I would learn the business under his tutelage. But it didn't become a definite offer until his secretary, Silvia Schulman, who became my wife fifteen months after I went to work for her boss, told him I was a good bet because she had seen me in the RKO office in New York the previous year and thought I was good-looking enough to be an acting as well as a writing possibility. Her opinions carried some weight with Selznick as I was to discover a year later when he, lacking the time for such diversions himself, asked both of us to read the novel *Gone With the Wind* in typescript and advise him whether or not to buy the film rights. Her vote then was yes and mine no. But in the earlier instance she was embarrassed when I reported for work in Culver City and she realized it had been my brother John who had so caught her fancy in New York.

Selznick assigned me to assist his publicity director, Joseph Shea, who was faithfully trying to carry out his instruction to promote not the man, David Selznick, but the company, Selznick International, and its productions. Shea was summarily replaced after a couple of months of this effort by Russell Birdwell, who was given the same instruction and made a smashing success by executing it in reverse. (He also proved to be a master of his tawdry profession.) I became his assistant for a year until Selznick assigned Budd Schulberg, a reader in his story department, and me to rewrite some of the scenes in *A Star Is Born* despite the fact that there were four writers already involved, all of them at hand. It was his habit, when the flavor of a script didn't satisfy him, to keep throwing more writers into the mix until it did; there were nearly twenty, most of them well known, on *Gone With the Wind*. In our case when our work pleased him, he decreed that we were now screenwriters. Having taken him at his word for four decades now, I have a sporting chance to make dean of the profession if I survive a few more years and some of my colleagues don't.

We began the painful process of learning, as in the armed forces, to "hurry up and wait." There was always a deadline, always pressure to get the job finished at the earliest possible moment, and then you sat around endlessly while somebody— a producer or a director or a star—avoided reading your work. No one had mastered the knack of nonreading better than Selznick himself—no one, that is, with a valid claim to literacy, and he had that. There was clear evidence, in fact, that he had read a number of books in his childhood, and some reason to believe that he eventually made movies of them all: *Little Women, David Copperfield, Little Lord Fauntleroy, Anna Karenina, A Tale of Two Cities, Tom Sawyer, The Prisoner of Zenda, The Garden of Allah*. But he didn't read the material Budd and I turned out with such a sense of urgency. Once, after I left his employ and Budd was collaborating on a project with the old silent film director, Marshall Neilan, a motorcyclist was engaged to gather their hot copy from the typist and speed it to Palm Springs, where Selznick was spending the weekend, because he couldn't wait till Monday morning. Two years later Budd ascertained that the pages were still unread.

He didn't even have time to look over his own work. "Dictated but not read by" was the printed caption over the lengthy memos which Silvia and her coworkers transcribed in such profusion that a magazine profile of Selznick bore the title "The Great Dictator." Perhaps "transcribed" isn't quite the right word in Silvia's case, for she had never taken the time to learn shorthand properly, and the only way she could keep up with the man was to summarize his thoughts and later paraphrase them in his distinctive prose style. When she and a friend, Jane Shore, produced

252

a book, *I Lost My Girlish Laughter* (published under the pseudonym of Jane Allen), which consisted to a large extent of just such memos in that familiar style, Selznick, who was infuriated and tried unsuccessfully to prevent Orson Welles from doing a dramatic version on his *Mercury Theater on the Air,* took it for granted I had had a hand in the enterprise. He didn't see how a mere scribe could be that creative.

He did read, assiduously, questioning the minutest details, every line of a screenplay he was actually producing. When he again faced an ending problem on the picture *Nothing Sacred,* he sent Ben Hecht's script to a half-dozen leading craftsmen— George Kaufman, Moss Hart, Robert Sherwood among them— putting them all on salary to devise an alternative. Then, recalling that Budd and I had come through on *A Star Is Born,* he commanded us to apply all our energy to the same task, a pressing one since the picture was almost through shooting. Budd took sick and I was assigned to work instead with George Oppenheimer, on loan from MGM for the purpose. George and I devised the idea that appealed to Selznick the most and wrote what became the final scene of the film.

In return for such services, our employer, patriarchal at thirty-five, was willing to take responsibility for our private lives. Budd and I both distressed him by undertaking mixed marriages. David, who had once been assistant to Budd's father, B. P. Schulberg, called Budd to his office and lectured him on the inadvisability of marrying a gentile, especially in view of the future career David had in mind for him as an executive. When Budd protested that his only ambition was to be a writer, David reproached him for being untrue to his "producer's blood."

He didn't think he could speak that directly to either Silvia or me. Instead, he called Herbert Swope in New York and told him to warn my mother I was making a hasty and ill-advised match. I had given Ellis a choice between attending the actual ceremony in a judge's office or waiting a month and paying us a more extended visit. After hearing from Swope she selected the first option and Jim rescheduled an already planned vacation to come with her. Her effort to dissuade me never got beyond the standard admonition about being sure you know what you're doing before doing it.

Budd gave me a bachelor party that developed into a poker game which his father joined, raising the stakes higher and higher as he lost. Jim and I won more than a thousand dollars between us, and he wired Dick Tobin on the desk of the *Trib* for an unpaid extension of his vacation. It was granted and he stayed about a week after Ellis went home. Since my honeymoon with Silvia was only a weekend affair, both of us returning to the studio Monday morning, I had my first chance in almost a year and a half for a number of long talks with Jim. The content was almost entirely political.

For a whole year after I arrived in Hollywood, my days and nights had been filled with work, drinking, reading, movie-going, bridge, tennis, swimming, one sustained affair with a colleague's wife, and occasional dates, mostly with Floncy and Silvia. Floncy and I may have gone as far as to hold hands, but it seemed a bit farfetched, after we had been photographed together in the forecourt of Grauman's Chinese Theatre at a Selznick premiere, for a wire service caption all over the country to report our engagement just because the name combination was newsworthy. Silvia and I also pursued various social activities together without any real romantic involvement until a few weeks before we decided to marry.

I thought of myself as a socialist, with the conviction that for Russia at least, the Communist variety of the doctrine was the most appropriate. In my first election a few months after my twenty-first birthday, I voted for the Communist Presidential candidate and felt the privacy of my ballot had been violated. Outside my polling place there was a list of registered voters according to party affiliation: Democrats, a long list of names; Republicans, a somewhat lesser number; and "Declines to State —Ring W. Lardner, Jr." The day after the election the results were posted alongside the list of voters: Roosevelt, so many;

254

Landon, so many; and "Browder—1."

That same autumn *Time* magazine ran a story about the Stalin-Trotsky split, which I found biased in favor of Trotsky. I wrote a letter on Selznick International stationery, which was published, propounding a close approximation of the orthodox Stalinist point of view. It attracted little attention anywhere except in the nascent Communist Party of Hollywood, where Budd was prodded for his failure to report such a politically developed coworker. We had actually begun our collaboration on *A Star Is Born,* but because of our somewhat strained relations in Moscow, we had had only the most gingerly exchanges on political issues. Now he set out to recruit me, a process that took him all of five minutes.

By the time of my marriage and reunion with Jim (in February, 1937), my way of life had changed drastically. Every week I went to a Marxist study group one night, a meeting of the newly formed youth unit in the party on another, and some other meeting of a political nature on a third or even a fourth. My very brief exposure two years earlier to Communist Russia and Nazi Germany had left me strongly partial to the one and antagonistic to the other. The main thing I thought the trip had accomplished for me was that by being able to check in person the accuracy of some reports on some aspects of the societies observed, I could determine which sources of further enlightenment were to be trusted and which dismissed as unreliable. It seemed to me by this gauge that most of the favorable accounts of the Soviet Union confirmed my own observations and were therefore trustworthy. It didn't occur to me that all accounts, the pro and the anti (there were almost literally none in between), were partisan and highly subjective. And though I frequently asserted the principle that advocating Communism for America didn't mean you had to defend everything that happened in Russia, in practice that's what the preponderant majority of arguments came down to.

Another influential factor was the quality of the people I met in the party. Budd and his bride, Virginia, known as "Jigee," seemed to me just about the ideal representatives of our generation, and most of the other people I came to know as Communists were brighter and more admirable and more likable than other people. (I once proposed the slogan "The most beautiful girls in Hollywood belong to the Communist Party," but it wasn't taken seriously, even by me.) A distinct few of them I found objectionable, but that fact just seemed to sustain Bernard Shaw's thesis that revolutionary movements always attract the very best and the very worst elements in the existing society. The Schulbergs I have cited by name because their membership became a matter of public record when both of them, divorced and married to other people, testified, to my dismay, as cooperating witnesses before the House Un-American Activities Committee. But even after all these years I don't feel free to identify other comrades, alive or dead.

It seemed quite clear to me at the time that my conversion to Marxism-Leninism was a purely intellectual process, with my affiliation growing stronger as I learned more facts and analyzed them in the cold light of reason. I realized there were people as bright as I and brighter, as well and better informed, who reached quite opposite conclusions about the merits of Communism. But that could be explained by the overriding influence of their class or economic interest on what they kidded themselves was objective thought. The same factor didn't apply in my case because my ideology was actually contrary to my class interest.

For all its simple beauty that logic doesn't stand up as well now that I realize I was deluding myself on a number of points. I am not speaking of the basic tenets of socialist doctrine, which seem as plausible to me today as they ever did. Nor am I admitting my mistakes with any sense of guilt or remorse. You can't feel remorseful about theoretical delusions that were never translated into significant action, and mine weren't. Which is distinctly different from, say, "The Best and the Brightest," who guided American policy in Vietnam, with all the consequences that flowed from their utter, fact-defying wrongheadedness.

But they do indicate to me now that there must have been some emotional and psychological content to my political thinking in my twenties. In one sense I think I was fulfilling my lifelong defiant impulse, the urge to be different, to call attention to myself. And I'm sure I found ego satisfaction in the image of myself as a revolutionary, a fighter for the underprivileged and the downtrodden. But was there anything special in my inheritance or environment that spurred me to rebellion generally and this manifestation in particular? I don't know. The case for saying there was is clearly strengthened by the fact that Jim later turned to Communism, too.

John and David never even came close. They were both left of center; John once told a man who claimed to be an honest conservative to have himself stuffed because he was one of a kind. But Communism had no appeal for them; for one reason because politics just didn't play that important a part in their lives. It could be said that both of them fit more readily into journalism than Jim or I did, that they eased into a life pattern established by our father and therefore had less reason to look around for an alternate system of values. Possibly Jim and I felt a need to separate ourselves from that pattern by some drastic assertion of independence. Those things could be said. But I don't find I can say them with any assurance.

Ellis and I had political debates by mail in those days. The argument in my letters stuck pretty close to dogma:

The only "intolerance" of Communism is that Communists refuse to tolerate the elements which decline to recognize the will of the majority, including those so-called "radicals" who do not understand Lenin's principle that without majority support there can be no revolution. Indeed, it is certainly obvious that with all the money and the resources on the other side you would need a very considerable majority before attempting to seize power. That is why Communists are not making a specious argument when they say they do not advocate overthrow of the present regime by force and violence. Marx taught ninety years ago that the task of socialists was to win

257

over the oppressed classes by education, but he warned that, as they did so, force and violence would be used *against* the workers in ever-increasing measure and that they would have to be prepared and organized to fight back. . . .

Spain is a classic example of this process because the whole transition from virtual feudalism has taken place in such a short time and because the struggle is still going on and the outcome in doubt. There you see the ruling class in 1931 forced to consent to the abdication of their puppet king and grant a democratic government to the people. It took only five years before the people had developed to the point where they were actually beginning to vote capitalism out of office. The government elected in February, 1936 (by almost exactly the same percentage as Roosevelt over Landon), threatened the Old Guard with extinction. They couldn't get much support within the country (very few Landon voters, believing in the democratic process, would have rallied to an army intended to throw Roosevelt out by force) so they got it outside by pledging the major portion of the national resources of the country.

That is what Marx meant in his analysis of the course of a decaying capitalism. That is why the Communist Party of Spain as students of Marx called on the other parties in the Spanish People's Front to replace the Fascist-minded army officers—advice that was unheeded until too late. That is what Fascism is—the last refuge of a minority intent on maintaining a system which has collapsed and which can no longer provide enough work and enough bread for the people.

That was the position I tried to sell Jim the last time we were ever together. It was hard to tell whether I was making any progress or not. He wasn't as interested at the time as I was in political doctrines or as concerned about international affairs. I don't mean that he wasn't well informed in these areas, just not emotionally involved. He absorbed and retained a lot of facts on a lot of subjects, but he would analyze an election campaign for the same purpose as analyzing a baseball pennant race: to figure out where to place his money. He had recently done well by backing up his precise prediction that Roosevelt would win 523 electoral votes to Landon's 8.

Despite being a year younger, I had quite an influence on him and I was aware of it, but it seems unlikely I was more than a minor factor in all that happened to him during the remaining year and a half of his life. When he was killed, there was certainly no conscious guilt in my grief. Yet for twenty-five years afterward I dreamed over and over again that I had murdered someone and was trying to escape the consequences. Sometimes the identity of my victim was obscure; sometimes it was clear enough to be recognizable as Jim.

13

Two months after his trip to California, Jim switched to the European edition of the *Herald Tribune,* published in Paris. Hazel Hairston, who was closer to him than to John at the time (although she had dated both, and me as well during the months we were on the *Mirror* together), came to see him off and met her future mother-in-law. On the boat going over he noted that the "horse races," in which each entry had an equal chance since their progress was dice-controlled, paid off by a pari-mutuel system, which meant that by waiting till all other bets were placed, he could buy a ticket from the largest pile remaining and get about seven-to-one odds on a five-to-one shot.

Having spent a week in London en route, he observed his second day on the job in Paris that people there understood his French better than the English did his English. He found it in most ways a pleasant place to live, but the paper itself was depressing because of its subservience to its advertisers. It was a relief to be sent for two weeks to Tours, where the Duke of Windsor and Mrs. Simpson were in a château laying their wedding plans, and again to cover the actual ceremony, the only time he ever led a newspaper with a two-column by-line. The story had to be written at second hand because he was not one of the five reporters admitted to the wedding. Instead, it fell on him to wait in the lodge at the château gate for a telephone flash from inside, and to announce, in English and French, to the throng of newspapermen and curiosity-seekers, that Wally had attained duchesshood at 11:47 A.M.

Late that summer Dottie Parker and Alan Campbell arrived from Hollywood with Lillian Hellman, who was on her way to a theater festival in Moscow and, it has now been revealed in the chapter called "Julia" in *Pentimento,* a dangerous en-route mission in Germany. They reported to Jim my triumph on *Nothing Sacred* and my elevation to the executive board of the Screen Writers Guild as the representative of the so-called "junior writers." (It was rather intimidating, while I was still only twenty-one, to find myself part of a group that included Dottie herself, Dashiell Hammett, Donald Ogden Stewart, Dudley Nichols and Charles Brackett).

Through Dottie Jim met a French Communist who had worked eight years in Hollywood and was seeking a collaborator on an idea he had for a Marx Brothers picture. Jim wrote a screen treatment with him despite Lillian's sound advice that it was an unsound project. The Frenchman later disappeared with Jim's typewriter and two hundred borrowed francs.

Lillian recalls a discussion with Jim after her month in Moscow in which he spoke of enlisting in the Lincoln-Washington Battalion (as it was then generally known) of the International Brigades fighting with the Spanish government. She told him she felt it was a losing cause as a result of the embargo against Spain by England, France and the United States, and started to make the argument that he and others should save themselves for coming struggles with a better chance of success. But Jim broke off the discussion by taking out a mathematical puzzle of some sort and asking her if she could solve it, which she couldn't.

No one else I have spoken to recalls his expressing such an intention that early, and I think it must have been quite a tentative one. But at least Lillian's account of the conversation and of its ending in particular has a ring of authenticity. A story that does not is the one reported by Burton Bernstein in his biography *Thurber* on the authority of both James and Helen Thurber.

An improbable scene is presented of a mass argument at the Deux Magots in which "Lardner was agonizing over going to Spain to fight, and Thurber was about the only person present who tried to talk him out of it." According to Thurber in a letter to Stanley Walker, ". . . he just gave me the old Lardner smile. Hemingway and Jimmy Sheean were pulling against me."

It would have been so unlike Jim to instigate or permit such a discussion that I would disbelieve the story for that reason alone. It is also disproved by the written accounts of Sheean, Hemingway and Jim himself, all of which establish that Sheean had no knowledge of Jim's existence until the three of them departed for Spain together, and that neither Sheean nor Hemingway had any reason to suspect he intended to enlist. His closest friend in Paris, Walter Kerr, said afterward he *thought* the idea might have been in Jim's mind before he left, but even he didn't recall Jim actually speaking about it.

What is apparent from his letters in late 1937 and early 1938 is that he was restless on what he called "this chamberofcommercistic sheet" but the efforts he reported were all directed at preferable jobs with the Paris bureau of the *Trib* proper or with *Time* or the United Press. As late as February 18, he wrote Ellis he was taking German lessons at Berlitz against the possibility of going to work for the U.P. in Berlin. He couldn't contemplate that prospect with unreserved enthusiasm because, as he had written me three weeks earlier:

Waverly Root, who is a good friend of mine, and whose wife is a very good friend of mine, was fired last week by the U.P. (it is not his job that I am considering) for sending out a story that François-Poncet had said there would be trouble started by Germany in the spring. . . . Waverly was fired because the U.P. lost its only two customers in Berlin as a result of the story. . . . The Roots may be in Hollywood next summer in which case they will call on you. Joanne, who is a French girl, born in Nice, is my most consistent drinking companion. At least she was while Waverly was working from midnight to 8 A.M. for the U.P.

That letter and one to Ellis were mailed in New York a week later by Root himself, who also delivered to the NANA (John's employer) office a late Christmas package for Ellis and some photographs of Jim taken by a semiprofessional photographer who described him as the hardest male subject he had ever encountered.

In the same letter to me he also wrote:

A couple of times I have almost gone down to Spain, but I couldn't quite swing it. I know the head of foreign propaganda for the government, a German exile who makes his headquarters here, but he thinks I couldn't do much good there unless I could persuade the HT or some agency to use my stuff regularly. The HT is not interested in covering the war first hand. There is an opening now for a U.P. correspondent with Franco, but I don't think I will ask for it. I don't know enough Spanish anyway.

In the February 18 letter to Ellis, this project had become "a series of pieces on the Americans in the International Brigade . . . for magazine appearance first and then for publication as a book. . . . I hope to persuade him [the foreign propaganda chief] to finance me, which is not as unlikely as it sounds."

On March 23 he wrote both of us that he was definitely going to Spain for his vacation about three weeks hence, and that he had made tentative arrangements for a short book on the American volunteers. He had started Spanish lessons that day but was continuing his German ones because "the U.P. job is fairly certain eventually." His editor had agreed to take any stories he mailed out or wrote on his return, and to give him "a letter enabling me to fix up my passport as a Herald Tribune representative." He promised his mother that "I shall be very careful and not get mixed up in any fighting, as most of what I want to do is behind-the-lines research." To me he said, "I am planning to go to Barcelona, unless it looks entirely impracticable, and to Valencia and Madrid."

He also commented to me on the events which had so dramatically fulfilled the prediction reported by Root:

Europe is always much closer to war in America than it is in Europe, but it certainly was uncomfortable for a few days. Not so much after the Polish ultimatum as during the Austrian business. Now I don't think there will be a general war for some time. It all depends on how cleverly Hitler works in Czechoslovakia. If he stops short of actual invasion, and I think he will find some way of doing it, France will jump at the opportunity of staying out. The Czechs are in for a tough time, though. . . .

I have been working very hard of late, both in the office and out. With John Elliott in Spain and Walter Kerr in Vienna, I had to handle the Austrian story locally, writing the lead and several other angles every night. It is almost three weeks since I have had a day off. John and Walter are back now, and things are easing up.

Kerr, who had been on the *Trib* in New York with him, was one of Jim's roommates. Another one, Jim wrote, was getting married and had asked Jim to stand up for him. "People are beginning to whisper behind my back: 'Toujours le garçon d'honneur, jamais le marié.'"

His plans developed more quickly than he had figured. On March 31, he wrote Ellis a briefer and brisker letter than usual:

Dear Mother,

I have only a few minutes to write you, as I am taking a train at 8:20 P.M., and I still have to pack. The train goes to Perpignan and from there I am going to be driven to Barcelona tomorrow, which should be a beautiful ride. Ernest Hemingway is going with me.

While it is in a way my vacation, I am pretty well fixed up with things to do. I am the accredited correspondent of the Copenhagen "Politiken," the International News Service and the Herald Tribune. If things get any more exciting in Catalonia, the HT will undoubtedly want direct coverage and since I will be there they will probably have me take care of it. This is what Mr. Hills thinks, and he is nominally in charge. If the paper doesn't come through, then I will do some pieces for the I.N.S. There are a couple of other angles, too, which I haven't time to explain. One of them may be for Newsweek.

The trip down is not costing me anything, as a result of my friend in the loyalist propaganda machine, but don't say anything about this, because if the vacation from the Herald Tribune turns retroactively into an assignment, all my expenses will be paid by the paper.

I shall be staying at the Majestic Hotel, but owing to the censorship do not think I shall be able to send any personal letters out.

Love,
Jim

At the Gare d'Orsay, Hemingway, an old hand in Spain, introduced Jim to Vincent ("Jimmy") Sheean, who was also going down for the first time in the war. At that time Hemingway and Sheean ranked about equal as celebrities; in later years the familiarity of their names proceeded in opposite directions. *Personal History,* Sheean's 1935 account of his experiences as a foreign correspondent, had been a runaway best-seller, a distinction Hemingway had yet to achieve. Both men were thirty-nine years old. Jim was not yet twenty-four.

"One of you has to decide which is the chef de bureau," Hemingway said, "since you're both from the *Herald Tribune.*" Actually, Sheean's arrangement with the paper had been negotiated quite suddenly with the New York office and was something of a blow to Jim's plans. For his part Sheean was impressed by the fact that Jim had more information than he did about the geography, politics and recent history of Spain, and very decided opinions about what was going on there.

Their train ride ended next morning at Perpignan, where Hemingway secured a car through the Spanish consulate. He had brought with him large quantities of food, whiskey and cigarettes, two big cans of gasoline, and a customs pass that covered all three of them, so all they had to do at the Spanish border high in the Pyrenees was change drivers. They reached Barcelona late in the day and checked in with Constancia de la Mora, the aristocrat in charge of press and propaganda. Jim and Sheean had dinner and spent the evening together, and their friendship progressed.

Jim was given a room without a bath at the Majestic Hotel and

Sheean invited him to make use of his. They both had to wait some days before getting passes and transportation to the front. Jim finally drove with two other correspondents out to the Tortosa area, where a battle was in progress between the Internationals and a division of Italian regulars. They were on a bridge across the Ebro River when it was bombed and slightly damaged, they had a chance to talk to General Lister under shellfire at the village of Chert, and they saw how truly desperate the Republican situation was. Jim showed up in Sheean's room for a bath and then wrote his story. It was a long and thorough account of what he had observed, and the Paris desk cut it to a few negligible paragraphs on an inside page. The dispatches under Sheean's famous by-line were carried prominently and in full in the Paris and the New York editions. Both men understood the cause-and-effect involved, but it didn't strain their personal relationship.

In Sheean's opinion, while Jim might have considered the idea of volunteering during the preceding months, he made up his mind in the days after that first visit to the front and the mutilation of his story. About ten days after their arrival in Spain he came to his older friend's room and revealed that he wanted to join the Internationals. The man who had been closest to him during that time was taken completely by surprise and tried, at considerable length and out of strong personal feeling, to persuade him he could do more good with a typewriter, but Jim said there were too many war correspondents already.

He went through a briefer version of the same argument with Hemingway. Both men finally realized Jim was consulting them not about whether he should enlist but simply about how to accomplish it.

And that, it turned out, was not an easy matter. The government forces had just suffered a disastrous defeat in Aragon; the International Brigades no longer had any facilities for training recruits; there was already talk of withdrawing all foreign volunteers in order to put pressure on Hitler and Mussolini to pull out their regular army and air force units; and in any case Jim's eyesight wouldn't have met the normal requirement in any man's army. He was told he wasn't wanted and when he persisted he was shunted from one person to another for twelve days before somebody decided on a compromise: they would accept his enlistment for its propaganda value (Ring's name made it a big news story) but they would put him somewhere behind the lines where he wouldn't be in any danger.

In Sheean's words in a chapter called "The Last Volunteer" in his book *Not Peace But a Sword:*

> Hemingway, as a matter of fact, did make a last-minute effort to dissuade Jim from enlisting. . . . Lardner's enlistment came so late that it seemed sheer waste; and at that time he did not strike any of us as being military material. That is why we (and in a general way all the colleagues of the press) tried to stop him or divert his determination into another channel.
>
> On the next day (April 25) we went to the first showing of the Spanish version of Hemingway's and Ivens' film, *Spanish Earth.* . . . I was with Lardner and Marty Hourihan, a brigade man who had been badly wounded at Brunete. Marty also did his best to change Jim's mind at the last minute, but Lardner was in high spirits again by this time and only laughed at him. When the film was over he went off into the town somewhere to complete the acquisition of his outfit, which was khaki trousers and a leather windbreaker and some heavy shoes. He signed up sometime that afternoon.

We already had the news before Jim's first letter reached Ellis. The papers quoted him as saying, "I think somebody has to do something. I've seen the front and I know what I'm going into. This is a fight that will have to be won sooner or later and I'm in favor of doing it here and now."

His letter went into considerably more detail:

Mother, darling,

This is a letter which I started to write on April 10. At that time I thought I was going to have to break the news to you gently, but you seem to have heard it before I had the chance. I have kept putting off writing you because each day it seemed as if on the next

I would know what I was going to do and where I would be stationed. I still don't know exactly what the situation is, but I am leaving in half an hour for Badalona, about seven miles up the coast, where I will learn the rudiments of artillery in company with a new mixed international unit. It looks as if French will be the medium of instruction. I shall let you know more as soon as I can.

This is a most exclusive army. It has taken me twelve days of going from person to person and office to get where I am. I have listened to advice of all varieties, a large part of it against my enlisting at all. The decision has been very much my own, and I took it after a great deal of consideration. My closest friend and principal adviser here has been Vincent (Jimmy) Sheean, who told me not to join, which shows you how stubborn I am, if you didn't know. Ernest Hemingway's advice was that it was a very fine thing if I wanted to fight against fascism, but that it was a personal matter that could only be decided by me.

I don't know how closely you have followed the war, but I imagine you must have an exaggerated idea of the danger of our position. On the map it looks as if Catalonia were a small fragment of territory about to be pushed into the Mediterranean, but in reality it is a lot of country, and I don't think it will ever be conquered. There are too many people here who are fighting for things they believe in, and too few on the other side.

My views on the whole question are too complicated for me to try to explain here. I hope you are on our side and will try to convince your friends that I am not just being foolish. Not that I mind being thought foolish, but American opinion is a very important factor.

I have made up a list of reasons why I am enlisting in the International Brigade, which is fairly accurate, as I did it for my own information. I am copying it here so that you may see for yourself which are the real ones. Some of them are picayune and most of them would have been insufficient in themselves, but all have something to do with it.

Because I believe that fascism is wrong and must be exterminated, and that liberal democracy or more probably communism is right.

Because my joining the I.B. might have an effect on the amendment of the neutrality act in the United States.

Because after the war is over I shall be a more effective anti-fascist.

Because in my ambitious quest for knowledge in all fields, I cannot afford in this age to overlook war.

Because I shall come into contact with a lot of communists, who are very good company and from whom I expect to learn things.

Because I am mentally lazy and should like to do some physical work for a change.

Because I need something remarkable in my background to make up for my unfortunate self-consciousness in social relations.

Because I am tired of working for the Herald Tribune in particular and newspapers in general.

Because I think it will be good for my soul.

Because there is a girl in Paris who will have to learn that my presence is not necessary to her existence. [Despite his candor to his mother, Jim refrained from saying that the girl was married.]

Because I want to impress various people, Bill for one. [By this time Jim generally called me "Ring" but not to Ellis.]

Because I hope to find material for some writing, probably a play.

Because I want to improve my Spanish as well as my French.

Because I want to know what it is like to be afraid of something and I want to see how other people react to danger.

Because there may be a chance to do some reading and I won't have to wear a necktie.

Because I should like once more to get in good physical condition.

The first four reasons and the ninth, especially the first, are the most important ones in my opinion, but you may decide for yourself. I have also considered a few reasons why I should not join the army, such as that I might get seriously wounded or killed and that I shall cause you many weeks of worry. I am sorry for your sake that they are not enough to dissuade me. If it is any comfort to you at all, I still hate violence and cruelty and suffering and if I survive this war do not expect to take any dangerous part in the next.

If you still consider me one of your sons, you can send me an occasional letter and possibly a package now and then. My address here, I think, will be in care of the Brigadas Internacionales, but for a while I think it will be simpler to communicate through the

Sheeans. Anything edible would be appreciated, milk chocolate or raisins, or anything in cans that does not require preparation.

Love,
Jim

The next stage of Jim's story was told in Sheean's book:

One morning early in May I struggled out of sleep in my bed at the Majestic, vaguely conscious that somebody was talking to me. When I got my eyes open I saw that it was Jim; he was demanding a bath, as usual. This time he looked as if he needed it; he was very dirty and unshaven and looked tired.

"What the hell are you doing here?" I inquired. "I thought you enlisted in the army."

"I did," he said, "but I'm a deserter now. Can I take that bath right away?"

After he had had his bath and a shave he came back into the bedroom and woke me up again. We got some coffee and I made some inquiries.

"How come you have deserted so quick?" I asked. "Don't you like the army?"

"Not that army out at Badalona," he said. "I came in to see if I can't get transferred somewhere else. I don't see why I can't join the Lincoln battalion."

"You have to get some kind of training somewhere," I pointed out. "Do you know how to handle a machine gun?"

"No," he admitted, "but I'll never learn out there at Badalona. All we do is lie around on some dirty straw all day long, and answer a roll call twice a day. I don't know what kind of outfit it is, but it seems to be mostly deserters and soreheads. Or maybe prisoners. It's pretty hard to tell."

I found out afterward what this mysterious encampment at Badalona was. It was a group of the so-called "inutiles de guerra," men judged unfit for war by reason of their incorrigible lack of discipline, their bad spirit, their demoralizing influence on others, their cowardice or their doubtful loyalty. . . .

Jim wrote Ellis before he left Barcelona again:

270

Tomorrow morning I am going to Mora-la-Nueva, on the Ebro River, where the Lincoln-Washington Battalion of the Fifteenth Brigade of the Thirty-fifth Division is stationed. There I shall confer with Johnny Gates, political commissar of the brigade. He will probably send me to a training base. . . . Gates is a quiet, honest and very brave former steel organizer from Ohio, about twenty-six years old.

Although my present course of action is on the advice of Lieutenant Al Cohen, who has some sort of a mysterious liaison job and is highly thought of in the Communist party, and I have a pass to the front signed by an I.B. executive, it is nevertheless a more or less independent move, which some small-minded persons at Badalona might describe as desertion. . . .

This letter and a previous one, which should arrive at the same time, I am giving to Jimmy Sheean to mail in Paris when he gets there Tuesday morning. They are therefore uncensored. Most of the letters I write you will be censored, but I think that the only taboo subjects will be military information and hypercriticism. . . .

He showed up on foot on the ninth of May at the battalion headquarters near the village of D'Armos on the east bank of the Ebro. A correspondent there described him as "neat, clean, his khaki clothes almost spotless, with a brand new rucksack in which he carried, among other things, a French grammar, a Spanish grammar and a copy of *Red Star Over China.*" He found he had a certain amount of antagonism to overcome. The men at the front had reacted sourly to the publicity surrounding his enlistment and were prepared to haze him out of any concept he might have of himself as a celebrity. On top of that, since we all patterned our values on Ring's and he had such a marked distaste for vulgar language, Jim had trouble adjusting to the obscene lyrics of a popular marching song in the battalion. He tried to explain to some of his new comrades that he had realized soldiers talked rough, but thought it might be different in this very special army.

Both problems worked themselves out in a short time. The men of the Third Company discovered Jim had no affectations and accepted him as one of them. For his part Jim entered into

271

the spirit of their obscenities and within two weeks, elevated to the rank of corporal, was marching at the head of his squad, singing the very song that had disconcerted him.

At the beginning of June, a trio of correspondents—Sheean, Joseph North of the *Daily Worker* and Leigh White, an American friend of Jim's working for a London paper—visited the battalion and found it quartered in some stables near the village of Cervera on the Barcelona-Lérida road. The men had been pulled back from the front lines for a rest. Jim reported the visit to Ellis, saying it was especially welcome because they brought his first two letters, one from her and one from Walter Kerr. He didn't mention, presumably because she would know how deprived he had been, that before he could read the letters he had to put on the new glasses Sheean delivered to him. His had been broken some weeks before, probably at Badalona, and the optician in Barcelona had been dilatory about making him new ones. Somehow he had made it through rifle and machine-gun training and secured his promotion with unaided 20/200 vision.

According to Sheean both of them had trouble recognizing the other, Jim because he was without glasses and Sheean because Jim kept his eyes half-closed in the glaring sun, and was bearded and unkempt. "I asked him what had become of all his fine clothes from Barcelona. It was impossible that they could have been worn to rags so quickly. He said—rather shamefaced—that he had given them away piecemeal; they were a little too fine, and so on." Sheean also asked if Jim wanted anything from Paris and Jim, unable to think of anything, had to consult a friend, who said, "I think you need some chocolate, don't you?" and Jim said yes, he guessed he did.

In her letter Ellis asked a question she probably knew was a foolish one but couldn't have resisted asking even if she were 95 percent sure of the answer. He wrote back:

> You asked me how long I enlisted for. There is only one way of enlisting: for the duration of the war. Sometimes Americans are sent home, but it is only if they are incapacitated, or for propaganda

purposes if they have been in the lines for many months. Don't pay any attention to the plans of the non-intervention committee. There is no chance of Hitler or Mussolini's withdrawing support from Franco before it is all over, and the government has no intention of being tricked into weakening its forces. These are facts. What the committee announces are just words.

I don't mean to be cruel. But it is better that you should resign yourself to my being in Spain indefinitely. A good soldier is hard to hit and I am going to be a good soldier.

It was Ellis's first summer in New Milford without David. She had promised him what had become the standard trip to Europe the year a son reached nineteen, and she couldn't renege on it, much as she would have liked to have him with her during those trying months, in which, as she wrote Jane Kitchell, "I get through the days but the nights are awful."

In the same letter she said of Jim: "He is a strange combination of ruthless logic and romantic idealism and after spending four weeks reporting from the Loyalist camp I know what he did was inevitable. I don't think anything justifies fighting but I am proud of him for doing what he thinks right."

For David to get a proper birth certificate in order to secure his passport, it was necessary for Ellis to attest to the Cook County, Illinois, authorities that his name had been changed from Henry (after his grandfather) to David Ellis (after some thought). She and Ring had had difficulties with male names after John because each of the other three was Barbara right up to his birth.

Kate Rice knew what Ellis was going through and called her the day before the second Louis-Schmeling fight to invite her to use "an extra ticket." After that brief but exciting entertainment they went to the Stork Club, which, coincidentally, was the place to see Hemingway if he happened to be in New York, which he did. He told her, Ellis wrote Jane Kitchell, that Jim "is in the anti-aircraft division and will probably never be in the front ranks as they always stay behind the lines." This was inaccurate information, perhaps deliberately so; the Fifteenth was an infantry brigade preparing for the Ebro offensive launched that July. It consisted of four battalions, one American, one English, one Canadian and one made up of volunteers from Cuba, Mexico, Puerto Rico and South America.

Sheean, too, felt the impulse to reassure her. He wrote her long letters from Paris each time he returned from Spain. In them he told her how good the weather was at the front, that the food was superior to that in Barcelona hotels, and that the Republican position on a high plateau on the east bank of the Ebro was the quietest part of the front. The only danger in the immediate future was that of bombing from the air, and the troops had good refuges to take cover in whenever the alarm was sounded. Jim would probably have a couple of months of alternate training and idleness before he even saw a Fascist operation. And in his letter a few days after he saw Jim on the Lérida road, he said there was a real possibility the British-French proposals for the withdrawal of volunteers would be accepted, the battalion repatriated and Jim never see any action at all. "This would disappoint him, but not you, I imagine!"

John was also at Yankee Stadium to watch Louis flatten the symbol of the master race. I don't know quite what occasioned it but Jim sent him a taunt via Ellis: "How many times has John changed his mind since picking the Cardinals? Why doesn't he bolster up his reputation by picking the Loyalists and the Chinese?"

David heard the fight on the radio in Killarney, winning five shillings from a stranger, in the course of a bicycle tour of the British Isles with a couple of other American youths. After Ireland they crossed to Holyhead, Wales, cycled to Liverpool and then through the lake district to the Scottish border. During that last part of the trip it rained every day and David wrote Ellis he didn't know what Wordsworth, whose house they visited, meant by "I wandered lonely as a cloud." He also reported that they stayed at youth hostels at one shilling for bed and a shilling threepence for breakfast. They sold their bikes in Carlisle and took the train to London. David went on to France and Germany in July, but, of course, there was no way he and Jim could make contact.

In Hollywood, meanwhile, Silvia and I were awaiting the first of a new generation of Lardners. Her book had appeared in *Cosmopolitan* and I was unsuccessfully trying to make a play of it during a layoff period in my contract with Warner Brothers, where, after leaving Selznick, I was learning about the Bryan Foy method of making B-pictures.

In mid-June, with the Fifteenth Brigade still getting set for the offensive, about a hundred of its corporals were sent to a school for corporals. They all lived together in a large house and Jim edited the wall newspaper on top of a tight schedule of curricular activity. They rose at six-fifteen, marched across town for exercises, returned at seven for breakfast and rifle-cleaning, had theoretical and practical instruction from eight till noon, lunched at twelve-thirty, did political or language work from two to three, had another instruction session from three to six-thirty, and ended up the day with roll call at nine-thirty. The course wound up on the eleventh day with tests, on which, Jim reported, he did "pretty well."

All his best friends, he wrote Ellis, were Communists. "They are the best soldiers as well as the best men." At some point that summer Jim became a Communist himself. Like other Lincolns who took the same step, he joined the Communist Party, not of the United States, but of Spain.

He wrote me in July that while there was more to infantry technique than I might think, he was getting a bit bored with it and anxious to see some action. "Two or three times we have set off with full equipment, presumably headed for the front, but each time it has been a false alarm for one reason or another." Because the U.S. Post Office was not accepting packages for Spain (a quirk of the so-called Neutrality Act, I assume) he asked us to send him one in care of Walter Kerr in Paris:

275

Don't spend much, as there is a good chance of its not arriving. Several chocolate bars, a few small tins of meat and something to spread on bread, or something like plum cake or cookies if fixed so that they wouldn't get too stale, would be fine.

Give my love to Silvia and let me know about the child.

The day after that was written, on Bastille Day, Peter James Lardner was born.

Ellis must have expressed some of her reservations about Communism in one of her letters, for she was treated to the kind of polemic she had been getting from me. After making more or less the same points about the C.P.U.S. and the Soviet Union, he went on:

And the U.S.S.R. today has one tremendous item on the credit side. It is always ready to swing its weight on the side of peace, whether through total disarmament, the League of Nations, economic boycott, mutual assistance pacts against aggressors or anything else. It wants peace not only for the reasons that all normal people want it, but also because the Russians believe that given a sufficient period of peace they can show the rest of the world by their example the superiority of socialism.

To his way of thinking, and mine and that of most of the coalition behind the New Deal, this Soviet attitude was in sharp contrast to American "neutrality." We were appalled by Roosevelt's fear of the Catholic vote and consequent refusal to sell arms to a friendly democratic government.

In the same letter he told her it was a good season for eating where he was. They were getting fresh potatoes, string beans, tomatoes, onions, carrots, plums, peaches, cherries and olives, along with bread, meat, fish, wine, coffee and hot chocolate. "The grapes will be ripe soon, which will be a big help when we are advancing and there is trouble bringing the food up on time."

On July 27, more than three months after his enlistment, Jim finally had his first experience of battle and was wounded. The Lincolns had crossed the Ebro and after two days of forced marching encountered the enemy near Gandesa. Two hundred prisoners were taken in a short time, and Jim was one of the guard that ferried them back across the river. Then, in his words to Ellis on August 2:

I heard a rumor that there was an orchard 200 yards away and, not having eaten all day, got excused and headed for it. There were some unripe pears and apples and peaches, which were better than nothing, but my attention was soon distracted by one of the frequent duels between anti-aircraft guns and bombing planes. The small round white puffs of smoke where the shells explode keep appearing all around the bombers until either one of them lands and a plane comes down or, much more often, the planes fly away after dropping their loads.

This time the bombers were coming directly overhead. I began to wonder what were the chances of my being hit by one of the anti-aircraft shell fragments. It didn't occur to me that there was any danger of being bombed all by myself until a munitions truck 300 yards away burst into flames with the explosion of a bomb.

I was lying on my stomach when the planes passed over, but the bomb was a little too close. The explosion and concussion were terrific, but I didn't discover I was hit right away. In fact, I walked over to where my rifle, munition belt and canteen of water were lying, picked them up and started back. Then I began to notice that my left calf and the left side of my behind were hurting. I felt them and found my trousers were covered with blood. A little further on I found several soldiers waiting in a trench for all the planes to go. I joined them, and one, a Negro friend of mine, went for a stretcher. The stretcher-bearers dressed my wounds and took me to an ambulance. Since entering the trench I haven't been able to put my weight on my left leg. It seems the flying shrapnel hit me in the flesh and muscle, picking very soft and fortunate spots. It will be about ten days more, I think, before I shall be considered cured. I hope to get a few days in Barcelona before returning to the front.

This hospital is clean and sunny, but nothing to read. I am going to write a piece on my recent adventures, which I shall retail through Walter.

Medical aid to Spain was all that was permissible for Americans to promote, and we had concentrated in Hollywood on raising money for ambulances, which were in short supply there. Since I had already antagonized Jack Warner by organizing a demonstration during a visit to the studio by Vittorio Mussolini, I was cautious about soliciting contributions during working hours, but lunch, even if eaten in the studio restaurant, was considered our own time. With help from John Huston, still three years short of becoming a director, in persuading such rising stars as Bette Davis, Humphrey Bogart and John Garfield to listen to our appeal, I had chaired a campaign on the lot earlier that year that had sent an ambulance to Spain.

The news of our son's arrival had reached Jim and he wrote me from a second hospital (he spent time in three):

> While you are doing your best to increase the tribe of Lardners, there seems to be a counterrevolutionary plot here to thwart your work. They missed me this time, fortunately for the People's Army, although I did stop a little flying iron in my eagerness to pick up the bomb and throw it back at the wop pilot. Now I am sating myself with reading, mostly Marxist.

It was actually more than a month before he was released, and another week at a convalescent base before he returned to the brigade, which had meanwhile been involved in two severe actions near Gandesa. He had heard of a Heywood Broun column about him and asked to see it. What it said in part was:

> I have not seen James Lardner since he was one of four chubby children who all looked exactly alike. They lived in a big house in Great Neck across the lawn from the Swopes. I saw a lot of Ring in those days, and I try to grab back things he said or did, because I imagine he was the only man of genius I ever met.
>
> It would interest me enormously to know just how Ring would have reacted to Jim's enlistment with the Loyalists. For the life of me I can't remember Ring's ever saying a word about politics or economics or world affairs. . . . But I think that in a way which is curiously remote Jim has carried on the tradition of his father.

Jim, just out of the hospital, Spain, 1938

Under an insulation of isolation and indifference Ring boiled with a passion against smugness and hypocrisy and the hard heart of the world. . . .

You may agree or disagree with the decision at which Ring's son arrived. But nobody can justly say that he was put up to it by "subversive influences." He saw with his own eyes, and he made his own choice. Ring and the rest of the Lardners always did run without blinkers.

Jim's two best friends in the Third Company, John Murra and Elman Service, were wounded shortly after he was, both seriously enough so they were still in the hospital when the Internationals were pulled out of the lines. The first thing Jim did when he got to Barcelona from the convalescent base was visit Murra, who had taken a bullet through his lung. Both men, two or three years younger than Jim, who had his twenty-fourth birthday in Spain, wrote Ellis after he was killed, and Service came to see her. Murra wrote:

In the months preceding our Ebro campaign, we got to be friends. We talked and we read each other's letters and Jim kind of worried along about our troubles. Journalism interested Service and even me. He used to talk about his newspaper work, about Paris—he was older than both of us and had seen more. Just before we went into action we planned in a jocular sort of way the publishing of some magazine when we got back. Before going into action, one always seems to be making plans, one really tries to conjure fortune.

Service, saving his recollections for his visit, just introduced himself in his letter:

Jim and I were in the same platoon and for some time shared our blankets. In this close association I came to like and admire Jim more than anyone I knew.

Jim returned to his outfit in the rocky Sierra Pandols region on the sixth of September, and was almost immediately involved in heavy fighting. Wherever they moved now the shelling and the bombing made it necessary to dig trenches and foxholes in almost shovelproof terrain. In a letter on September 19 Jim told Ellis how he and three others had dug in stony ground with pick and shovel for seven nighttime hours until, just after daybreak and just before the mortar shells began to land, they had a trench deep enough to sit in with their heads below the surface. "I never was so well paid for hard labor as by that feeling of comparative safety. This is not a very cheerful letter, but I will do better next time."

There was no next time. On September 21, the Spanish Government announced its decision to withdraw all foreign volunteers immediately. To maintain morale, however, the news was not officially communicated to the men concerned until they were pulled out two days later. Meanwhile, during the late afternoon of September 22, it became necessary for the Lincolns to relieve a badly battered unit of the Eleventh or Ernst Thälmann Brigade of anti-Nazi Germans. The Americans moved into the trenches dug by the Germans in a river bed a quarter of a mile behind the front.

The American command anticipated an enemy attack in the morning and it was imperative to know what lay on their apparently wide-open right flank. At about eleven o'clock at night Jim was sent out in charge of a small patrol to contact a Spanish unit supposed to be occupying a nearby hill to the right rear of the battalion. It was very dark and he and his two men, an American and a Spaniard, may have lost their way. At the foot of what they thought was the right hill, they heard digging, and Jim instructed the others to wait while he investigated.

As he neared the top of the slope, his men heard a shout in Spanish and Jim's voice challenging in the same language. The enemy on the hill replied with enough machine-gun fire and hand grenades to repel a full-scale attack. Hearing this barrage to the right front, the officers awaiting the patrol's return suspected it had run into a Fascist position and been wiped out. Actually, the Spaniard at the bottom of the hill was killed, but the American, Anthony Nowakowsky, was not hit. After remaining under cover for two hours, he made his way back to the battalion. Early the next morning Moorish troops attacked the American position in force from the direction of that hill, inflicting severe casualties.

Although his superiors were quite sure Jim had been killed instantly, it was not an absolute certainty and somehow the first news stories reported he had been taken prisoner. Then there was "an unconfirmed report" that he had been killed after capture by the Moorish outfit. This account was widely circulated and has been repeated as fact in at least two books. But it probably came from that mixture of rumor and deliberately contrived atrocity propaganda that is always circulating in war situations. It is quite unlikely that Fascist sources would have put out such a story and there is no way anyone on the Loyalist side could have acquired the information. The Internationals were being withdrawn and no Republican force ever regained that piece of territory.

As long as there was the slightest chance of his being held prisoner, that was what we tried hard to believe. We sought information from every source we could think of. There was even an exchange of letters between Ellis and the Franco representative in New York. On October 7 Hemingway cabled Ellis from Paris that he was taking all steps with Premier Negrín and Foreign Minister Del Vayo of the Republican government to arrange an exchange, and that she should inform Herbert Matthews of the *New York Times* in Madrid as soon as she had any definite word where Jim was being held. It was another couple of weeks after that before he heard through a correspondent with the Fascists that a corpse had been found with press credentials. But Jim's body was never recovered.

Milton Wolff, commander of the Lincolns, said later:

> You have no idea how keenly the men felt about him. In the short time he was with us, and despite his extreme natural shyness, he won the friendship and respect of everyone in the battalion. He was looked up to both as a man and as a soldier and he won his rank of corporal quickly by hard work and courage.

What he did was an unusually courageous thing—going ahead alone in no-man's-land in the middle of the night and leaving his two men behind because he did not want to risk the safety of anyone but himself.

He was the last American volunteer to join the Republican army and one of the last to be killed.

14

Hazel and John were married one week before Jim was killed. She had gone out with three different Lardners over a five-year period, but there is no doubt John was her major objective from their first meeting. I'm not positive when that was because I don't know whether she came to work for Stanley Walker on the *Trib* just before or just after John left to do sports for NANA. John quit the paper in the fall of 1933 and Jim joined it the following spring, so either of them could have been the Lardner she laid eyes on first.

Born Hazel Bell Jean Cannan in southeast Texas with a father named after Jefferson Davis, she was a graduate of Rice University. After a few years on the Houston *Chronicle,* and marrying and divorcing a fellow reporter there, she came to New York about 1930. She worked as a reporter for the *Daily News* and the *Telegram* before she took the job as private secretary to her fellow Texan.

Whether or not that was during John's service on the *Trib,* she and he had reached a point by December, 1934, where he left her a scrawled note beginning "You insulted me by falling to sleep" and she responded with "I'm suffering the most horrible pangs of remorse or something like that today. You were sweet." And there were many contacts by mail, phone and in person over the next several years, even though there was a time, before Jim left the country for good in the spring of 1937, when people thought of her as his girl. A year or so after that she started dating John again.

There must have been enough similarity among all four of us for more than one of us to like, and be liked by, the same women. My dating Floncy in Hollywood is a not very significant example because it never reached a romantic stage except in the newspapers. But Bruce Barton's daughter Betsey corresponded with and dated both Jim and me before an automobile accident wrecked her life at the age of seventeen. John Wheeler's daughter Liz, who saw Lardner boys en masse throughout her childhood and was once quoted as saying she was fourteen years old before she realized small boys could talk, had her closest and longest relationship with David, but also went through a time when she thought she might be in love with Jim. The same married woman whose demands Jim cited as one of his reasons for going to Spain later discovered David and was his major attachment at the time he first met his wife, Frances. Silvia was so smitten by her first sight of John that she mistakenly encouraged Selznick to bring me to Hollywood, and I always felt she continued to have what we used to call a crush on him. As a matter of fact, I came, in a later decade, to wonder if the same thing wasn't true of Frances, whom I had married two years after David left her a widow.

It was while we were all still clinging to the rumor that Jim was merely a prisoner that John had to leave his bride of less than three weeks to cover the start of the World Series between the New York Yankees and the Chicago Cubs in the latter city. He wrote her from there that he had bet twenty-five against a hundred and twenty-five dollars that the Yankees would take it in four straight, entirely, he claimed, so he could concentrate on her instead of "my favorite sporting event of all the world." Whatever his motive, it was one of those five-to-one shots that paid off, a phenomenon, the best statisticians report, that occurs just under 17 percent of the time.

John was already beginning to make the transition from newspaperman to magazine writer, which he didn't complete until after the war. He had sold his first article to the *Saturday Evening Post,* about the "Black Sox" scandal of 1919, in March of that year for seven hundred and fifty dollars, and the magazine took a second one in December. To further supplement his syndicate salary, he soon began talking to *Newsweek* about a column called "Sport Week," which began on March 13, 1939. That first column was a prognosis of the coming baseball season, as was his final one in mid-March twenty-one years later, and it set the style ("literate, informed and pleasantly skeptical" in Stanley Walker's words) he maintained throughout that period:

> Frank Menke, the Gibbon of sports, says in his new "Encyclopedia" that the Doubleday legend and the date (1839) are all wrong and morally misleading, but baseball executives are going to celebrate their centennial just the same, and if they have to do so over Menke's dead body, they are confident that this can be arranged as part of the regular ceremonies.

Because I was in California and David had started his third year at Yale (which, true to family tradition, he never completed), John had the double burden of his own grief about Jim and the same kind of care of his mother her sister had observed after Ring's death. It was mid-January before he and Hazel could manage a sort of delayed honeymoon cruise to Havana, and even then there was a third party along, Bruce Pinter of the *Herald Tribune,* with whom I had shared an apartment. John and Bruce had some sort of project in work over which they spent many shipboard hours.

Even the parties to a marriage don't always have a clear image of it, and outsiders generally see the more superficial symptoms. The fact that Hazel was a good bit older than John didn't seem to make much difference one way or another, and was not even particularly noticeable during the early years in which she bore three children, Susan, Mary Jane and John Nicholas, by Caesarean section, at regular two-year intervals. They appeared to be happy together despite or even because of his frequent absences. He regularly went to Florida for about six weeks of preseason baseball activity, traveled a good many other places in the course of his work, and from February, 1942, until June, 1945, was abroad as a war correspondent more than half the time.

They wrote each other often and at length, especially during his extended wartime tours. The expressions of devotion in these letters, John's in particular, were intense and unceasing. This is one of those symptoms that can be deceptive. The Western concept of romantic marriage doesn't really allow for much middle ground between undying love and outright hostility, especially when the spouses are separated and addressing each other on paper. What came to be known during the war as the "Dear John" letters announcing that the wife or sweetheart at home had found a new love were all the more startling to the distant serviceman because her last previous message had probably been about how fervently she awaited his return.

The evidence in John's case, however, is pretty strong that he believed as Ring had in monogamous bliss and felt as Ring had that it was his. When the news reached him in Italy at the end of 1943 that Silvia and I were living apart, he wrote Hazel:

It made me feel bad—and more than a little astonished, it almost seems sometimes like I don't know everything—to hear about Bill and Silvia. How do such things develop? I mean, how do you go about falling out of love with someone you love? The joker is, I guess, that you don't really love the character to begin with. Fortunately we will both be dead long before I can fall out of love with you, being in it very deep. Did I tell you that I love you? It is absolutely the fact, and I do not see what can be done about it. I don't quite understand this jockeying for position in the matter of who is dropping who in Bill's case, but he is a very good guy and has a good mind to know and knows it, and he can't be very far wrong in anything he decides to do.

I wouldn't have been much help explaining to him how such things develop. After our first three years and with our second child, Ann, on the way, the modest progression of my career in Hollywood was reversed. In 1939 I had finally achieved screen credit with two small-budget pictures I wrote in collaboration with Ian Hunter, but then suddenly there were no jobs to be had. Part of the trouble was that the outbreak of war in Europe had created a general unemployment crisis because the companies were uncertain about future prospects. I was looked on with particular disfavor because I had been too prominently associated with radical causes and the emerging Screen Writers Guild for one on so low an echelon of achievement. And this at a time when the Nazi-Soviet Nonaggression Pact and the Russo-Finnish War had made Communists and "fellow travelers" the target of liberal as well as conservative opprobrium.

In this situation the only possible way to make money as a screenwriter was to create and sell projects of my own. Carole Lombard, whom I had known since *Nothing Sacred,* became enthusiastic about a story I wrote in which she would play an alcoholic, but all the producers she approached said it was an unacceptable subject. (*The Lost Weekend* came five years later.) An Austrian writer, Fritz Rotter, and I actually sold a story to MGM, accepting a low price of five thousand dollars because of the opportunity to develop the screenplay at two hundred and fifty a week apiece. We thought the quality of our work would overcome the drawback that they would guarantee us only two weeks at this figure. But they simply paid us the two weeks' salary, told us not to bother to come to work and gave our story to a contract writer to develop. The story editor congratulated himself on acquiring the property for a mere six thousand and remarked in the hearing of someone who reported it to me that he wouldn't have "that Commie Lardner" on the lot.

The only reason Silvia and I and our babies didn't actually go hungry during this bleak period of about eighteen months was that we borrowed money from Ellis and a little from Silvia's family. Handouts rarely come unaccompanied by advice and it was suggested to me with varying degrees of subtlety that I should acknowledge failure in the movie field and return east, possibly to a job in a business in which a prosperous aunt of Silvia's had an influential position.

This time of stress, with no clear beginning and no foreseeable ending, brought out some incompatibilities we might have overcome in more pleasant circumstances. Then our fortunes changed dramatically when Garson Kanin gave Katharine Hepburn a story his brother Michael and I had written. Kate liked it so much she took over the whole operation, removing our names in order to jack up the price and demanding two hundred and eleven thousand dollars from MGM for the script and her services. A hundred thousand was for the screenplay, she explained, a hundred thousand for herself, ten for her agent and the remaining thousand to cover her round-trip expenses from Hartford to Hollywood.

Louis B. Mayer accepted her terms. It was the highest price paid to date for an original screenplay. The picture, *Woman of the Year,* brought her together with Spencer Tracy, whom she had never met, and won us an Academy Award for the screenplay. And that same story editor offered Kanin and me a choice of assignments at two thousand dollars a week for the team.

Couples with two young children can be pretty rough on each other when they're out of work and living on borrowed money, but one option clearly not available to them is separation. Now at least it had become a physical possibility, though neither of us was yet ready to consider it seriously. Instead, we concentrated on buying a new house and some of the other possessions we had been coveting.

Meanwhile world events were moving from one climax to another. During screenplay conferences Kate and I would sometimes change the subject to our sharply conflicting views about the war. We were actually in the midst of one of these arguments when word came over the radio that Germany had invaded the Soviet Union, and we suddenly agreed that our differences had become academic. At the end of the year, after Pearl Harbor, I became increasingly affected by the feeling that the war was too vital a part of our times for anyone, especially a writer, to miss out on. Not draftable because of my eyesight and my dependents, I set about a program of putting aside enough more money

Ring, Jr. on the set with Katharine Hepburn, 1941

Arriving in Rome with Otto Preminger, 1963

to take care of the family, and then finding a place in the war effort that could be of some value to me and vice versa.

Silvia was not wholly wrong in thinking some part of this impulse was simply a desire to get away from the domestic responsibilities I had taken on so young. But whatever the balance of my motives, it turned out I was wanted wherever I applied, and then again, on second thought, I wasn't. The Office of War Information (OWI) was ready to send me to the Russian front to work on a film; the Marine Corps thought I could be part of their film unit in the Pacific; the Office of Strategic Services (OSS) had a job for me to do in Washington. But then they ran a security check and said never mind. I was labeled, and it was the first time I or anyone I knew had heard the phrase, "a premature anti-Fascist."

The only outfit that would have me was the Army Signal Corps, which was hiring "civilian technical experts" to work with uniformed personnel on its training-film program in Astoria, Long Island. I signed up, but soon the only question in my mind was whether I was less valuable to the operation than it was to me. When the chance came after a few months of it to go back to Hollywood and work with Otto Preminger on a script about the rise of the Nazi Party and the Reichstag Trial, that seemed by comparison to be a genuine contribution to the United Nations cause.

Otto was shooting the picture *Laura* at the time, and at his request I took time off to rewrite the dialogue, with special emphasis on the character played by Clifton Webb, but that seemed trivial beside the story of the Nazis. I returned to the latter with renewed enthusiasm and the resulting screenplay was one of my best, producing in Darryl Zanuck and the management of 20th Century–Fox a curious but not unprecedented reaction: they raised my salary and shelved the project.

During that year (1943) I learned that Jigee and Budd Schulberg had separated, and the revelation helped me admit to myself that I had been in love with her for some time. This was by no means a rare condition; among writers in particular it approached epidemic status. The one she decided to marry was Peter Viertel, and my rather strenuous efforts to persuade her otherwise had more effect on Silvia than anyone else. At her request I moved out. Some months later we were reconciled on the familiar and generally shaky grounds of the children's welfare, but it was this separation John heard about in Italy.

David stayed at Yale through the fall term after Jim's death, but instead of returning from the Christmas vacation, he drove to California with Ellis to see us and the country. Sixteen when I had left New York, he was on the verge of twenty now, and I was confronted with a fellow adult I didn't know very well. Broad-shouldered and strong-looking, he was a shade under my six feet, a distinctly larger man than Jim and a distinctly smaller one than John. He had the family nearsightedness at its worst, finally registering about 20/800 in the last vision test he took. David's eyesight and John's proportions can be illustrated in a single incident. Leaving a fight at Madison Square Garden or one of the outdoor stadiums, David came up behind Joe Louis and tapped him on the back under the impression he was John.

For a Lardner he was positively gregarious. He brooded less than the rest and enjoyed himself more and didn't mind revealing it. He could be funny himself, but more of the time he seemed to be looking for and appreciating humor in other people. He laughed a lot and sang, among other places, in the shower. And the forthrightness noted in the Taft yearbook was still a noteworthy characteristic: he was willing and able to say exactly what he thought about something whenever his opinion was solicited and sometimes when it wasn't.

We couldn't and didn't have the same feeling of closeness that had existed between Jim and me, but I developed a warm affection for him and I got the feeling he enjoyed the visit with us. It was before the bad times started for Silvia and me, and we provided a number of diversions for him and Ellis, who was trying hard to be cheerful and not quite making it. The main diversion and best possible therapy for her was her first contact with her first grandchild.

I didn't see David again for nearly three years. Silvia and I went to New York for a vacation after shooting ended on *Woman of the Year,* returning with Ellis just before Pearl Harbor. In New York we saw quite a bit of David and of Frances, to whom he had become engaged. Then there was a gap of more than a year until my service with the Signal Corps began just in time for me to go to the hospital for a look at Katharine, their first child. He and Frances hadn't reached a final decision on her name yet, and when a head nurse tried to corner him to say they couldn't leave the space blank any longer, David just pointed at me and continued on out. She was pretty indignant when I said I was a mere uncle with no authority in the matter.

That was the only time I saw him over a sustained period after he grew up, and we became much better friends than ever before by the time I went back to the coast. We found ourselves in pretty close harmony in most areas, but he resisted my efforts, abetted occasionally by Frances, to politicize him, especially when they conflicted with his sense of his responsibilities as movie reviewer for *The New Yorker.* I would suggest, for instance, that a picture like *Mission to Moscow* should be treated more tolerantly because of the importance of the message it sought to convey. David's judgments remained steadfastly independent of such factors.

Once he had to review a war picture, *The Cross of Lorraine,* on which my name and Mike Kanin's appeared along with another team of writers who had succeeded us on the script. David sidestepped the issue by saying there were too many names on the screenplay to justify recording them.

Finally, in the spring of 1944, I made a quick trip east to see the play *Tomorrow the World,* which I was adapting, and had my last glimpse of David just after Joe, his second child, was born and three months before he left for Europe and the war.

On the staff of America's most sophisticated popular magazine at the age of twenty, David had quickly found favor with as singular a group of editors and writers as was ever assembled on one publication. He soon attained the magazine's informal equivalent of academic tenure, though most of the work he did during his first two years there was not in the area where, in the opinion of William Shawn, then managing editor and since Ross's death editor-in-chief, his special talents lay. As an anonymous reporter and interviewer for "The Talk of the Town," he satisfied his editors, but it was only after they began to assign him to signed opinion-writing in fields in which he was knowledgeable but not expert that he became one of the valued regulars who turned out the bulk of the magazine's nonfiction content.

This development started near the end of his second year there when he began to take over some of the sporadic sports departments: "The Oarsmen," "Yachts and Yachtsmen" and "The Tennis Courts." That same summer of 1941, when E. J. Kahn, Jr. was drafted into the army, David inherited not only the department "Tables for Two" but one of Kahn's more frequent companions on his nightclub tours, a successful young radio and stage actress named Frances Chaney. When he announced to his bosses that fall that he and Frances were going to be married, their image of him changed abruptly from a bright boy to an adult writer whose responsibilities and income needed to be increased. First they devised a whole new department for him, "Notes on Sports," which he conducted intermittently for more than two years and which was discontinued permanently when he left for London.

The thinking behind this innovation, according to Shawn, was that David's stuff would have more individuality and therefore reader interest if he himself chose the sports events he wanted to cover. He had been doing the new feature for only a couple of months when John Mosher, the movie critic, died, and it was decided that David had the capacity to assume that function without abandoning his nightclub and sports coverage. "The Current Cinema" appeared with his by-line in a hundred and one of the next hundred and four issues. And he also filled in as substitute theater critic a few times and managed to do one long piece under the heading "A Reporter at Large."

Editorial policy decreed that the same by-line should not appear in different departments and accordingly the movie reviews were by David Lardner, "Notes on Sports" by D. L., and "Tables for Two" by D.E.L. The first of these might cover as many as half a dozen films in one column, the second three or four different sports and the third perhaps eight night spots, so even though it was a rare issue that contained all three features, David, and Frances when her own working hours permitted it, spent a great many hours a week in projection rooms, sports arenas and cafés. Evenings that weren't taken up by duties in one of these places were apt to be spent at the theater, at a poker game in John's apartment, or at Bleeck's or Costello's playing a guessing contest called the match game for rounds of drinks. As a result, during a period when she had both a morning and an early-evening radio show, Frances would often have to work in a few hours sleep between the two.

There were nearly three years between the start of David's job on *The New Yorker* in 1939 and John's departure as a war correspondent in 1942. For that length of time and during John's periods at home between wartime assignments, they saw a lot more of each other than I did of either of them, and the seven-year gap between them became an increasingly irrelevant factor. They occasionally covered the same sports events, they played in the same poker game, they often sat at the same table in Bleeck's playing matches, they relaxed together at our mother's house in New Milford, and there were family gatherings at Thanksgiving and Christmas. A firm bond of unspoken affection grew up between them. There were to me at least some distinct personality differences, but outsiders were more aware of the similarities, the Lardner pattern they shared. And certainly they had in common an easy adjustment neither Jim nor I ever found to a kind of life that was pretty close to Ring's as a young man.

Both Frances and David had been earning enough to live comfortably alone, and since they both did better after their marriage, they managed to stay much freer of domestic tasks than most young couples. He continued to bank his own paychecks and she hers, and questions of who paid which bills were resolved without discussion by one of them performing the act. They had a cook-housekeeper and later on a baby nurse besides. Almost never did any of their hands come in contact with a pot, a dishrag, a broom or a diaper.

John, who had been a rare contributor before the war, did an increasing amount of his writing for *The New Yorker* during and after the war years. Shawn feels there were some distinct resemblances in the two men's writing: discipline, tautness, control and a general similarity of humor, but also some differences. David's style was more open, airier; he wasn't as frugal about the space it took to express his thought. John's writing was denser; he seemed to feel an obligation to create an effect, usually comic, with each line. But any comparison needs the qualification that David died at twenty-five. Unusually mature he was, but still developing as a writer and a person.

What he had to a remarkable degree for his age were firm opinions in a variety of fields and an easy assurance about expressing them. He told you the facts you needed to know, but he was functioning as a critic in all three of his departments and that meant equal attention to his personal views. When a number of people, including the formidable columnist and opinion-maker, Dorothy Thompson, protested that the movie *Lifeboat* presented a too sympathetic portrait of a Nazi, David took issue with them:

> . . . reluctantly because I have already reviewed the picture, and a reviewer likes to think that a picture, once reviewed, will lie down. . . .
>
> Although they have not clearly expressed it, I think I know what is bothering the opponents of this film. They would like to see the case against the Nazis not merely stated but overstated. They would like to see more of the same exaggerated super-salesmanship which the movies have often used during this war and which, I think, may be a perilous thing. It's my belief that many people in this country

have actually met Germans and are aware that they do not tip their mitt by walking right up and biting you in the ankle. . . .

One of his "Tables for Two" columns led off:

> Something kind of deplorable happens to comedians who get too giddily popular, and it becomes most evident when such a comedian goes to work in a night club. The trouble lies in the fact that he has built up too big a circle of acquaintance, a good part of which is apt to be on hand wherever he performs . . . there are incomprehensible gags flying back and forth which apparently mean something to their authors, who often threaten to faint dead away from sheer hilarity. The rest of the audience, confident that something pretty comical is afoot, joins in the merriment, but its laughter tends to be short and puzzled.

And a sports story began:

> As often happens when tennis is suffering from a general shortage of talent, the doubles was better to watch than the singles . . . It's almost bound to happen anyway when Pancho Segura is still in the doubles and has been eliminated from the singles. The young two-hander from Guayaquil was beaten as a onesome by E. Victor Seixas. . . . Teamed with Alejo Russell, of Argentina, however, Segura lasted longer, reaching the semifinals, and there continued to last, along with Russell and their two opponents, just about as long as any player in a championship tournament ever lasted before. The score was 6–4, 8–6, 18–20, 2–6, 7–5 in favor of Charles Mattman and William Talbert, the two other fellows. This total of eighty-two games took in the neighborhood of four hours to play, and both North and South Americans were ready to knock off for the summer when they were through.

Easy assurance is an effect; in David's case at least it was by no means easily produced. Shawn says they never had a department writer who worked so close to deadline, revising until he had to surrender the copy from his typewriter.

15

In July, 1941, John Lardner wrote a letter to John Wheeler, recalling that:

A year or so ago you suggested—not at all in a definite way, but simply as something to think about—that in case of real action abroad, perhaps involving this country, you might consider sending me to do some work there instead of, or in addition to, the people that usually do the stuff of that kind for you and the Times. The idea stuck in my mind, naturally, but I haven't given it any serious thought till recently, because I take a certain pride in doing my column consistently and doing it well.

That still holds true of the column. I think that it is, thanks to the chance you gave me, the best of its kind in the country. But I also think I can do other work as well as or better than most newspaper men and writers, and that a time may be coming shortly when that work will be more important and valuable both to you and to me. This sounds swellheaded—but if I didn't feel the way I do about writing, I wouldn't give a damn about being a writer.

The following February, two months after Pearl Harbor, John was on his way to the war. A box appeared alongside his final "Sport Week" announcing: "John Lardner left last week for an undisclosed war front and new duties as a war correspondent. On arrival, he will begin a NEWSWEEK feature, to be called 'Under Fire,' on his experiences with United Nations forces overseas. . . ." By the time his first column, from Melbourne, appeared five weeks later, there had been some editorial reconsideration and the revised title was "Lardner Goes to the Wars."

It was accompanied by a new photograph of him in his war correspondent's uniform and I was the photographer. Silvia and I had driven up to San Francisco to spend a couple of days with him while he was waiting for passage to Australia, and when he mentioned that he had left New York in too much of a hurry for picture-taking, I shot a whole roll of film of him. Another one of my pictures served the same function for his newspaper stories syndicated by NANA.

During the long trip on a Matson liner converted to a troop ship, he was invited to disclose his sports predictions for 1942 in the ship's newspaper. He picked, correctly, the Yankees and Cardinals to meet in the World Series. He said Billy Conn had the best chance among Joe Louis's prospective opponents for the year but "it's my guess that Joe will cut Billy down in less time than it took him before." As it turned out, more than four years elapsed before that second fight in which Louis knocked out Conn five rounds earlier than the first time. John also wrote that the two best lighter fighters he'd seen recently were Ray Robinson and Young Kid McCoy. It was five years later that Sugar Ray won the welterweight title.

He arrived in Australia the same week General MacArthur did from the Philippines vowing, "I shall return." Singapore had fallen the previous month and it seemed more than likely the Japanese would soon invade the island-continent itself. John remained in the area for three months, reporting on the gradual change from defensive to offensive planning. He traveled more than ten thousand miles, visiting United Nations installations, mainly American ones, in Australia and New Guinea, sending stories to his two regular employers and also gathering material for longer articles that appeared in the *Saturday Evening Post* and formed the basis of his book *Southwest Passage: The Yanks in the Pacific*.

That trip was the beginning of John's attachments to Australia generally and to a young newspaperwoman named Mary Coles,

John in San Francisco, on his way to the Southwest Pacific, 1942

David and Frances, 1942

Hazel Lardner with Susan, John Nicholas and Mary Jane

both of which deepened on further visits thirteen and fourteen years later.

At the beginning of summer *Newsweek* told its readers that "Our roving correspondent has returned from Australia and, after a short rest, will head for the fighting fronts beyond the Atlantic." Actually, he did a few more columns about the war in the Pacific, then took some time off to get his book in shape, and in late September resumed the sports column although the masthead still listed him as "John Lardner, War Correspondence." In mid-October this was changed to "John Lardner, Sport Week." The listing remained the same through February 15, 1943, but there was no column of any kind in that issue. The next week there was again no column but the masthead listing was back to "War Correspondence." Two weeks after that came his first wireless dispatch from Allied Headquarters in North Africa.

He remained in that theater of operations until the beginning of June, reporting the American side of the Anglo-American squeeze on General Rommel's Afrika Korps. One day in Algiers he found himself surrounded by "twelve Arab boys all four feet tall" who relieved him of a wallet containing his five hundred dollars in expense money. John maintained afterward that they had been trained by his friend A. J. Liebling, *The New Yorker*'s war correspondent in that area, "the Fagin of Algiers." It was Joe Liebling who eventually wrote John's obituary in the magazine and said in reference to their African experience: "John was naturally brave; when he saw blinding bomb flashes by night, he used to walk *toward* them to see better."

He tried to time his return to New York to be with Hazel when John, their third child, was born, but actually arrived about ten days after the event. Two months later he was back in North Africa and a month after that he landed on the Italian mainland with the British Eighth Army. He and two other correspondents, one Australian and one Scottish, with an English captain in charge of them, set out in a jeep and a run-down British staff car to cover the fifty miles to the American Fifth Army's beachhead at Salerno. Italy had surrendered and there were no substantial

German units south of where the Americans confronted most of the Germans in Italy in the Salerno-Naples area. At town after town along their route, the four men were the first Allied invaders the civilians had seen and they were welcomed as liberators.

In each locality, however, the same problem of communication arose. Neither the Englishman, Captain Mike Davis of the London Irish Regiment, nor the three correspondents spoke any Italian, and Davis had questions to ask about German outposts and roving patrols. To his relief, however, there was always at least one Italian who claimed to speak English as a result of having lived some years in America. Then, to his dismay, Davis found he couldn't understand a word the man said. Neither could the Australian or the Scotsman. And the American-speaking Italians couldn't understand any of them. But John understood their dialect and they understood his familiar intonation. Thus he served as interpreter in a series of conversations in which all parties professed to be speaking the same language.

Among the many American-speaking Italians he encountered was one

named Cimini in Positano, a little resort town near Amalfi, who said that he was glad to leave America, that he had to, that for medical reasons he could not afford to go back. "I was sick to my stomach all the time there," he said. I asked him why. "I drank too much," explained the fugitive.

John remained in Italy for nine months, more than two of them spent on the Anzio beachhead south of Rome. He landed there, as was customary for correspondents, with a back-up unit after the first assault wave had established a hold on the beachhead. They were able, therefore, to move rapidly inland without encountering any resistance until they overran a farmhouse not realizing there were three sleeping Germans inside it. For their part the Germans had no idea there had been an invasion and that in the harbor there were hundreds of ships that hadn't been there when they went to bed. One man was captured in his underwear, but the other two managed to put their pants on and get out a back door into an armored car, shooting wildly at the Americans as they rode off.

John and some other correspondents, mainly British, shared a seaside house at Anzio, with an Italian manservant to cook and clean for them. Although the small, heavily populated beachhead was under constant bombardment and was the first target of the Nazi "V-1" (secret victory weapon), the robot or "buzz" bomb, the only casualty he suffered was when his jeep hit a deep rut while he was carrying two sixty-liter demijohns of wine. One vessel shattered, its contents filling and running over the sides of the jeep.

While there he acquired a new outlet for his war stories. The brief weekly column he did for *Newsweek* was necessarily a quite different form of writing from the daily dispatches he did for NANA. But he was also running across feature material that didn't suit either medium—material that should be treated at greater length and that had no deadline urgency about it. He wrote one four-thousand-word piece for *The New Yorker* in February and it was quickly bought with a request for more. This created no conflict that John could see and he was startled to get a long cabled complaint signed by both the publisher and the editor of *Newsweek,* "offering," he wrote Hazel, "to fire me." There were references in the cable to "divided sovereignty," "part-time correspondent" and "sharply contrasting" material. Without understanding what had gone wrong, he managed to appease them enough so the discussion of his future relations with the magazine was postponed until his return home in the spring. During the rest of his stay in Italy and in the Pacific the following year, he appeared increasingly in *The New Yorker* with war correspondence that was clearly inappropriate for a newspaper or news magazine.

Back in New York in May, he discovered why *Newsweek* had reacted so intensely. He had written about the "buzz" bombs for both magazines, but one dispatch had passed through an army censor, the other a navy one. Whichever one had handled the *Newsweek* story had cut out all reference to the new weapon; the other had let *The New Yorker* account go through intact.

After that was cleared up *Newsweek* devoted two full pages to his description and analysis of the war in Italy to date. Then he took a two months' vacation from that job before resuming "Sport Week" for six months. It wasn't much of a vacation as it turned out: he had a couple of *New Yorker* pieces to finish and at the end of June that magazine asked him to fill a post that had abruptly become vacant. John accepted on a temporary basis; all his employers understood that he would eventually return to the fighting fronts if the war lasted much longer.

The job he took over was writing "The Current Cinema." David, whose vision disqualified him for the armed forces, had been after his editors to send him to the war. Bill Shawn says a partial reason for turning him down was that after Jim's death in action, the dangers John was risking almost constantly seemed enough for one family. The official reason was that the services restricted the number of correspondents a publication could have in any theater of operations, and the magazine had its full quota in all of them. Affected by much the same impulse that moved me in my fruitless efforts to get involved in the war, David applied to the OWI and was accepted as a "senior field representative" assigned to the London office.

The New Yorker gave him a leave of absence and apparently promised him he could switch to war correspondence if he somehow managed to secure accreditation on his own.

He arrived in London a month after the Normandy invasion and soon went to work on a pamphlet, to be translated into French, that would acquaint the newly liberated with developments during the past four years in American, British and Russian films. He wrote in a letter to Ellis: "I haven't seen any of John's thoughts on the movies and probably won't for some time, but if they happen to be particularly good, don't let me hear about it or I'll write damaging anonymous letters to the editors."

In the same letter he wrote of the "buzz" bombs, which the Nazis had just begun to shower on London after the Anzio tryout: "I've seen a few of the things in flight, and they are curious objects. They're smaller and faster than a plane, and they make a bumbling, dishonest sort of noise."

Ellis passed on some of what David reported in a letter to her sisters and told them she had his two babies and their nurse for a visit because:

> Frances is trying to get all the radio work she can to make up for the small pay the O.W.I. gives out. . . .
>
> What a wonderful day it will be when all our sons are home safe: Helen Stilwell and I have a date to get drunk in New York the day of the armistice.

The five Abbott sisters had eleven male children of military age, but only four of them were overseas at that particular moment.

After starting in a borrowed flat David managed to find one of his own. A number of his magazine and newspaper friends from New York were in London, including the man he had been closest to on *The New Yorker,* Sanderson Vanderbilt, now a sergeant working for the army weekly, *Yank.* David seems to have begun almost immediately to go to work on U.S. Army authorities and after ten weeks his efforts bore fruit. On September 24 he wrote Frances he was officially resigning from the OWI the next day. He also said: "I'm getting as bald as an egg, or at least as I dimly remember an egg to be." This was considerably exaggerated, but he was the only one of us to inherit the tendency, which Ring had had to a marked degree.

The next time she heard from him he was writing from Paris, and then on October 3, with a return address in care of the First Army, he explained to Ellis:

> I've been back on the payroll a little less than a week, and I think Shawn is still trying to figure out how I got there. Somebody in Washington kept telling him the Army wouldn't accredit another New Yorker correspondent, and in the meantime somebody in London was giving me an accreditation. This puzzled both of us, but in any event I'm here, and a bizarre place it is.

He couldn't, of course, say where the place was, just that he was "living in a hotel in a town that's a little short of food. At lunch it was liver and squash and the devil take the hindmost." He did report that he had ridden "over three hundred miles in cold jeeps in the last few days" and that the jeep that had taken him most of the way was driven by Jim's old friend, Walter Kerr of the *Herald Tribune.* He had found another friend from Bleeck's, war correspondent Joseph Driscoll, in the hotel dining room and they started playing the match game almost immediately.

The hotel was the Brasseur in the city of Luxemburg. David arrived there shivering because he had no heavy clothing with him. Driscoll warmed him and Kerr up with some captured German rum. David wrote Frances:

> I guess I won't be through in these parts as soon as I told you I might in earlier letters, in case you got them. At the time I thought I'd be here for the end of the war in October, do a couple of pieces on Germany afterward, and go home. It took me a little longer to get here than I figured, though, and anyhow it doesn't look as if the war will be over tomorrow or maybe even next week. However, I'll see what can be done.

At that time, before the last German counterattack and the Battle of the Bulge, it was still generally felt that the war in Europe was all but finished. David told Driscoll he figured on going to Hollywood for the winter, having arranged with *The New Yorker* to do a series of pieces on the picture business.

He stayed about ten days in Luxemburg, walking all over the city and interviewing people. Before he left town he wrote a piece for the magazine which appeared in the October 21 issue under the title "Letter from Luxemburg." He wrote it in his chilly hotel room, with a bath towel wrapped around his shoulders.

Driscoll had a jeep and driver at his disposal and was able to send David's story and personal messages to Mackay Radio for transmission to the United States. He also drove David to Arlon so he could get a lift by light airplane to Aachen, where the first major battle on German soil was still in progress. Two planes were warming up on the airfield at Arlon, but it was late in the day and poor flying weather. David was anxious, however, to get to First Army Headquarters and then to the front so he could write more stories, and he persuaded one of the pilots to take off. David was wearing a light field jacket and the hotel towel around his neck and carrying very little else. The pilot joked that if they couldn't carry all his baggage, he would come back for another load. David told Driscoll, who was wearing a captured sheepskin greatcoat, he would try to promote himself some cold-weather clothing in the Aachen area.

There was a delay before he could get to the front and he had a chance for a last all-night poker game with Kerr, Russell Hill, also a correspondent, two lieutenant colonels and a captain. Kerr won heavily, David a little.

On October 19, 1944, he drove with Hill and a driver in a jeep to Aachen, which was, as Kerr described it a few days later, "a shambles—windows gone, floors and furniture crashed down into the cellars, the streets covered with twisted wire and rubble, and the outside walls of the buildings pitted with rifle, machine gun and shellfire."

In Hill's words to Frances when he was able to write:

The awful thing is that it would never have happened if I had not suggested going home a shorter way instead of taking the road by which we had come.

We had been looking at the Cathedral in Aachen and were rather late starting back. I suggested the short cut and Dave naturally agreed, since I had been doing this sort of thing much longer than he had, and he trusted my judgment. It was a surfaced road, but one we had not been over before. It all happened very quickly. We were driving along when suddenly I saw a blinding flash.

What happened was that American engineers had cleared a minefield near a railroad underpass but had not yet removed the mines, piling them instead at the side of the road. Driving with blackout lights, on a dark night, the jeep swerved off the road and hit a pile of mines. The driver was killed almost immediately. When Hill came to, he saw David lying in a field, still unconscious with a head wound. The two of them were rushed to an evacuation hospital by ambulance. Hill escaped without serious injury but David, after a blood transfusion, died under the X-ray machine as surgeons were preparing to operate on him. He had not regained consciousness.

The last paragraph in *The New Yorker* the issue after that single piece from Luxemburg was an obituary notice signed by "The Editors" and ending: "We liked and admired him as much as any man we have known, and we have never printed a paragraph with deeper sorrow than we print this one."

John got the news first by phone in New York two days later, on a Saturday. He went to the Beverly Hotel, where Ellis was staying, to break it to her while Hazel got a message to Frances's answering service asking her to come to their apartment as soon as possible. John also called my house in the Westwood section of Los Angeles and Silvia told him I was visiting a friend, Dalton Trumbo, at whose house he reached me. We agreed I should make every effort to fly east to be with our mother and Frances, even though wartime travel was strictly rationed according to priorities. I was on a plane the next day solely because of the influence of James Cagney, for whose company I was working, and Abe Lastfogel of the William Morris Agency, which represented both Cagney and me. It was Lastfogel's volunteer responsibility to decide which Hollywood personalities got what priorities on their troop-entertaining tours.

Frances's children, Katharine and Joe, were twenty-one months and six months old, much too young even to be told what had happened. Because of them and her work, which she deliberately didn't interrupt, Frances began a surface recovery from the shock within hours, though her deeper emotions remained in a kind of frozen animation for a very long time.

For Ellis the cumulative effect of this third blow on top of the others was devastating. She had been doing volunteer war work, filling in as a nurse's aid, first at the New Milford Hospital and then in a New York hospital ward full of terminal-cancer patients, thus releasing more highly trained nurses for war-related duty, but it was some while after the news about David before she could return to work. She also knew that John was planning to cover the war against Japan and that she couldn't dissuade him from it even if she tried.

He left right after Christmas, embarking once more from the port of San Francisco. He stopped off in Honolulu to do stories from there for all his employers, including a long one for *The New Yorker* about the phenomenon of Japanese-Americans pitching into the war effort there, while their counterparts on the mainland were in internment camps.

In Honolulu one night he sat in a taproom with two other correspondents, Ernie Pyle of the Scripps-Howard chain and Fred Painton of the *Reader's Digest.* They had covered various fronts together for about three years, but that night Pyle found himself slightly irritated by John's cheerfulness. Finally he said, "I know I'm going to get mine on this trip, and you're going to get yours, too." He was right about himself, but the other one of the trio to meet sudden death in the next three months was Painton.

John went by way of Guam and Saipan to the landing on Iwo Jima. From Saipan he wrote Hazel:

> The peaceful side of this trip is going to end very shortly, but I don't want you to worry about me—I will take better care of myself than I ever have before, for you and the kids and for me as well. I haven't got the old drive and incentive and curiosity I used to have on some of these operations. I don't see how anybody can. You get to know all there is about them, and after three years you begin to think about your own skin. Mine is slightly darker than it was when I left home, but just as beautiful as ever.

A few days later he reported that he had sent a long story to *The New Yorker* and worried for days because he didn't get the usual cable from Shawn. Then the officer who handled radio communications at the base on Saipan told him it had been returned, in John's words "rejected by the New Yorker Hotel, which does not seem to have a very good taste in literature. I guess I will have to start writing for the pulp hotels. . . . The boys around here seem to consider the whole episode very comical."

He went ashore at Iwo two hours after the first wave of Marines, whose survivors were now in safer locations than the beach, which was under heavy and continuous Japanese mortar fire from the heights of the volcanic mountain, Suribachi, that dominated the tiny island. The unit he was with was completely pinned down for forty-five minutes. But eventually it moved forward, proving, he wrote, that "an irresistible force has a slight edge over an immovable object." When he and another correspondent returned to the flagship that night to file their stories, as they were transferring from an LCT (Landing Craft, Tank) to a smaller boat that could go alongside the flagship gangplank, John's typewriter sank irretrievably to the ocean bottom.

A week after the invasion he received "personal evidence of the boorish behavior of bypassed Japs." He and Robert Sherrod of *Time* magazine were walking across an airstrip that had been in undisputed American possession for several days when a sniper hidden in the wreckage of a Japanese plane opened fire on them. John said the man scored with "a carom shot" that lighted in a pile of stones, causing one of them to fly up and catch him in the groin. Actually it wasn't a stone at all, but John didn't realize that till months later when he was taking a shower in New York and a small-caliber machine-gun bullet worked its way out of a testicle and struck the tile floor.

At the time, since it was general knowledge among his colleagues where he had been hit and one of them might report the fact in a story, he sent Hazel a cable of reassurance:

The invasion of Okinawa, the largest amphibious operation of the Pacific War, took place on Easter Sunday, April 1, 1945. Again John was in on the landing itself and he remained on the island for the three weeks it took before the last significant resistance had been overcome. From there he wrote for *Newsweek* about the "weird orgy of Japanese self-destruction." He and other correspondents had been aware previously of the limited use of "kamikaze" weapons, but they couldn't write about them until Admiral Nimitz made the facts public in the second week of the operation on Okinawa. There were suicide swimmers (Okinawa was their training base) carrying grenades and suicide small boats packed with explosives that tried to ram American naval vessels, but the most spectacular weapon was described by John as follows:

> It's a long way from Anzio to Okinawa but it can now be reported that the cycle of Japanese imitation of German military ingenuity has been completed with the use by the Japs in the East China Sea area of a rocket bomb greatly resembling the German "buzz" or flying bomb with one typically daffy Japanese "improvement"—their bomb is a suicide bomb. It has a tenant. He rides along in the little cockpit and when he hits something he blows up with the bomb.

In a long, two-part "Letter from Okinawa" for *The New Yorker* he reported two incidents, one personal, one of world-wide significance. The first:

> After a few minutes I was jarred by a sort of clout like a hand being dropped heavily on my shoulder. The thud was loud enough to make everybody look at me and I in turn looked guiltily at my shoulder. A fragment of a shell about the size of a small spool of thread had ripped the left sleeve of my field jacket but failed to penetrate my heavy shirt inside though it left a small burn and bruise. I picked up the fragment, found it too hot to handle and quickly threw it in front of me.

And the second:

I was with the Thirty-second Regiment on the morning of April thirteenth, Okinawa time, when Colonel Finn got the news over the telephone—at our early breakfast—of the death of President Roosevelt. There were men near the table and more men out in front of the tent so that within twenty minutes the news was all over the command post, but it spread quietly and the reaction was quiet. Some men were nonplussed or helpless to put thoughts into words; others were shocked into stillness and went about their work in a sort of walking reverie. Now and then when two men met they would stop to speak of what had happened but they spoke in a slow way with long pauses between their sentences and when the pauses grew into a silence they would part and move on as though it were impossible now to understand the event and therefore to discuss it. I had never seen any effect of news quite like this one. Finn, after exchanging fragments of low-voiced, half-unbelieving conversation with his staff, lapsed into the same sort of brown daydream. Along about the middle of the morning he suddenly said, "Well, damn it, the sooner we attack again, the better it will be for everybody."

A few days after that morning he wrote Hazel:

Yesterday I sent a message to Shawn telling him to let you know I had put Okinawa and all combat operations behind me. That was the last one, baby. . . . During the last few days I was there, I got one or two small and gentle hints, much more gentle than the one at Iwo Jima, that my luck was beginning to run out and I had better quit while I was still in one handsome, symmetrical piece. By the time I get home it will be practically three and a half years since I started covering the war, which I guess will be enough. It has all been very fine, even fun, but I love you the best. Naturally, as always happens, I left stuff all over the ocean and the air and got back here [Saipan] with nothing but a typewriter and a jacket, so this morning I went shopping. . . .

I wish you would let mother know, if she doesn't already, that Okinawa was my last operation and that I am clean away from there. Then she won't have to worry any more either. Dames are always worrying, but they are nice people, and I love you. . . .

313

In the latter part of June, six weeks after V-E Day, "Sport Week" began appearing again. And by the time the Japanese surrendered in mid-August, John was sharing my bachelor apartment in West Hollywood and we were collaborating on a screenplay about the war in Italy.

16

Silvia and I had agreed on a divorce in June in the midst of an acute shortage of housing and hotel space. It took a week of following up various leads before I found a sublet, and a couple of months more before a property settlement was worked out and the papers filed. Hazel, separated from John once again by his work, wrote him at the end of August that "the papers this morning were alive with the Tokyo landings and the Ring Lardner divorce, plus pictures." That suggests more press attention to the latter story than it actually got, but there was enough to make us feel uncomfortable.

The screenplay collaboration was based on *Up Front,* a collection of Bill Mauldin's cartoons. We had Mauldin's characters and his vision of the war to work from, and such of his jokes as could be worked in, but we had to devise a structure and almost every detail of sight and sound that went into that structure. It had seemed when the deal was set in July that the time was fast growing ripe for what would be the first comedy treatment of the war, but by the time we finished the script in November, the prevailing view in Hollywood was that the public wanted to forget the war entirely. Our employers said they found our script both hilarious and moving, but that they would have to wait to see how peacetime box-office trends developed. A version of *Up Front* was produced years later, but it wasn't ours.

All we gained from our labor was the money and three months

of very close association. Hazel came out toward the end of it and John moved into a hotel with her, but except for that the two of us were together day and night. Not even whiskey, generously applied, served to break down the reserve, even stronger in him than in me, about discussing anything personal or emotional, but there was enough unarticulated communication to bring us closer than we had ever been. Since we hadn't seen nearly that much of each other since I was about fifteen, it was at this time that I finally overcame my childhood awe of him and related to him on a more or less equal basis.

Working together was an interesting process. John had no background in movies except as a critic and I had never been in Italy or in a war zone anywhere. We found we could talk out a general continuity for the picture as a whole and for each se-quence as we came to it, and also which of Bill's cartoons could be incorporated most effectively into our structure. But if we tried to go into more detail than that, we seemed to run out of creative fuel. The only method that worked was for John to start writing with no concept coherent enough for him to convey orally. When he had a version of a scene done, I would get a lot of ideas for variations on it, but the only way I could express them satisfactorily was to write the whole scene over again. Next John would fix the things I had got wrong through not knowing the background, and add any new jokes my draft made him think of. Then we would both worry it a bit and turn it over to a secretary to make a clean copy we could start marking up all over again.

What we each found out about the other and the way he functioned in those months of working and living together did a lot for our relationship. Over the next fifteen years we were a good deal closer geographically and emotionally than we had been the previous fifteen, and each of us knew he could rely on the trust, understanding and affection of the other.

Whether I specifically said so or not, John certainly knew that on most of the occasions when I went out by myself in the evening, it was to attend a Communist meeting of one sort or another. And I made clear to him what my quite sharply defined views were on the world situation at the end of the war. John's own views were much looser and more open-minded. He didn't reject the possibility that my friends and I might be right; he just didn't feel the compulsion we did to be so positive about it.

The party had just been through a painful crisis. Its national leader, Earl Browder, had developed over the war years a theory that was especially easy for his middle-class and more comfortably fixed followers to embrace. The harmony between the Soviet Union and its Western allies, forged in common struggle and at the Teheran and Yalta conferences, would endure throughout the foreseeable future and even make possible a peaceful evolution to a socialist world. In 1944 Browder presided at the formal dissolution of the Communist Party of the United States and the establishment in its place of the Communist Political Association, with claims of greater internal democracy and potential mass membership.

A year later, as the war in Europe ended, a dissenting minority, fortified into a majority by an open letter from Jacques Duclos, the leading theoretician of the French party, rallied around William Z. Foster and tossed out Browder, his Association and all his heresies.

The membership of the Hollywood section emerged more or less intact from this ferment. We were flattered that the leadership in New York considered us important enough for Foster himself to give us his view of the future and our role in it at a private meeting in a member's home. And any lingering sentiment for Browder and his idyllic vision was soon dispelled by Harry Truman's headlong retreat from the policies of Franklin Roosevelt. Rejected by his voters at home, Winston Churchill took ideological command of America's cold war against Russia.

Frances and I began to write each other and talk over the long-distance phone, and while we both felt free to pursue our own affairs, and did, an understanding gradually developed that

317

we might find enough in common after a suitable interval to put our futures together. One area of almost total harmony was politics. When in the spring of 1946, eighteen months after David's death, I flew to New York to see her, I joined her in an ill-fated effort to broaden the May Day observance by involving some of her *New Yorker* friends in the preparations. We were still clinging nostalgically to the fleeting dream of a popular front.

We made better progress by far in our personal relationship, though we each had at least one serious adjustment to make. Frances's whole life was in New York, and a major part of it, her identity as an actress, with firm roots in the radio and theater worlds there, would be jeopardized if she moved elsewhere. She had just aroused some attention with an ingénue role on Broadway and that could mean realizing her desire to work mainly on the stage. Yet she had to face the economic fact that I had no earning power outside Hollywood to meet my obligation to Silvia and our children.

For my part I regretted that my marriage had failed but not that it had taken place at all, for not only were the children of it an enormous satisfaction but I was glad I had had them so young. I liked the projected image of myself in my forties, children grown up and hence less pressure to make money and more freedom to live and work as I pleased. Acquiring a pair of younger children in a new marriage was a distinct threat to that image.

Along with these considerations we had the skepticism of my mother to face. She had come to doubt whether I was capable of making a sound decision in personal affairs, and she was much too fond of Frances to see her victimized by my capacity for self-delusion. She was openly relieved that my divorce wouldn't be final till the end of summer.

We were quite willing to move slowly ourselves. I returned to California and took a furnished house in Beverly Hills with Ian and Alice Hunter, and an assignment at 20th Century–Fox with Otto Preminger. In July Frances arranged some time for herself and flew out for a two-week visit that gave us a chance to know each other better. We set a date for her return with her children and their nurse in September, at which time the Hunters yielded us the house and Otto gave us a premarital dinner that is memorable because the ladies were requested to leave the gentlemen to their brandy and cigars. The way we were sitting, on a dais with our backs to the wall, Frances's most direct exit route was under the table. She took it.

By early October, toward the end of our brief honeymoon, cold war politics had developed so ominously that I got a message saying maybe we should remain out of town awhile. There was a rumor in the Hollywood party that subpoenas were out from the California State Committee on Un-American Activities. This wasn't so, but an investigation was soon under way by the main committee in Washington that led to preliminary hearings in Los Angeles the following spring and full-dress ones in Washington in mid-October.

We knew there was a cloud on the horizon, but we also knew there wasn't much we could do to prevent more from gathering. So we concentrated on other things. Frances played Lady Macbeth in a local stage production. I responded to an offer from Fox by signing a contract at two thousand dollars a week, with the number of weeks I worked each year pretty much up to me. After nine months in the furnished rental we bought a large house with a tennis court near the beach in Santa Monica. We were still in escrow when a United States marshal came to the door of the old house with a subpoena from the House committee.

It developed that there were nineteen of us who came to be known as "unfriendly witnesses" as opposed to those who were willing and eager to tell the world what they knew about Communist subversion of the movie business. There were many meetings over the next few weeks among the large number of liberals who felt the scheduled hearings were a threat to the freedom of the screen generally, and among the small group in more immediate peril. From the first category came a broad Committee for the First Amendment, which used the cumulative prestige of its members (Humphrey Bogart, John Garfield, Fredric March, Rita Hayworth, Groucho Marx, Katharine Hepburn, John Huston and William Wyler among them) to expose the House committee's purposes to the public. From our more private meetings, generally with two or more lawyers present, agreement finally emerged, after considerable debate, on the best general approach to take at the hearings.

One of the nineteen, Bertolt Brecht, did not attend those meetings or subscribe to that approach because of his special status as an alien and his anxiety to get to East Germany without delay after making his required appearance.

The policy we finally adopted was proposed by Dalton Trumbo and me. The first thing to recognize, we felt, was that the committee had you in a rather tight bind, with strictly limited choices, none of them pleasant to contemplate, especially if you were indeed a member of the Communist Party.

If you weren't, you could say so and concede the right of Congress to go into such matters, and also help isolate those who had exercised their perfectly legal right to be Communists. If you told the Congressmen it was none of their business, you faced the possibility of prosecution for contempt.

Some of the subpoenaed men who were Communists wanted to say so, to proclaim proudly an affiliation they had been reluctantly concealing because it was party policy in Hollywood and certain other vulnerable sections across the country to do so. It had to be pointed out that the next question put to them would be to name all the other members they knew. If, having conceded the committee's right to ask the first question, they then balked at informing on other people, they would be in the quixotic position of exposing themselves to contempt prosecution without any Constitutional grounds for a defense.

Others, including a couple of men who had already denied membership, falsely, before the California committee, wanted to do the same in Washington. Trumbo and I persuaded them that there were most probably informers in our ranks and even if real ones were lacking, the synthetic variety would do the job just as

320

effectively. If we were going to risk prison sentences, it was a lot better to be sent up for contempt than for perjury.

There was another conceivable choice, a tricky one. We could decline to answer on the basis of our Fifth Amendment privilege against self-incrimination, which is what scores of witnesses did at the next round of hearings in 1951. But in the three and a half years between our appearance and theirs, the national leaders of the Communist Party were convicted under the Smith Act of 1940 and lost their appeal in the Supreme Court. If we had taken the Fifth before those events, we would have had to argue that there was a law on the books saying it was a crime to advocate the overthrow of the government by force and violence, that we believed the Communist Party practiced such advocacy, and that therefore we were liable to prosecution under that law. But we all maintained the contrary: that Communists did not teach force and violence and were as legal as any other political party. And there was no instance we could point to of a single indictment of a Communist in the seven years the law had been in effect.

It was more reasonable, more principled and legally sounder, we argued, to refrain from answering questions or cooperating with the committee in any way on the grounds that the First Amendment made the whole investigation unconstitutional. Judicial precedents had established that where Congress was forbidden to legislate, Congress was forbidden to investigate. The committee hearings, we would maintain, had no valid purpose.

The group and its attorneys, who had been dubious to begin with, finally agreed on the idea of challenging the committee in this way. And the broader Committee for the First Amendment asserted the same principle in its public relations campaign.

After those of the group who were called to the witness stand took this position and became known as the "Hollywood Ten," there were many people who considered our behavior disgraceful and possibly treasonable. There were many others, then and since, who seemed to think we had committed an act of great heroism and, in going to prison, sacrificed our personal freedom in the defense of the Constitution. This second view is just as subjectively weighted as the first. Once we were the targets chosen, by what seems to have been a rather haphazard process, we had no acceptable alternative to doing what we did.

The unacceptable one (for Communists) was to tell the Congressmen you had been a member of the party, that you had been deluded and sorely regretted it, and that you were willing to show your remorse by giving them as many names as you could think of and sometimes, as happened with a number of ultracooperative witnesses, some you didn't remember at all. These were cheerfully provided by the committee staff, for their own purposes, to be read back to them.

A number of people who did take that road genuinely felt they had been deluded and even that they were performing some kind of vaguely patriotic service, though they had to be pretty insensitive not to feel some distaste in doing it under those auspices. (One of our inquisitors was Richard Nixon.) But most of the stool pigeons were terrorized into it, by economic and other pressures, went through the ritual with self-loathing, and sooner or later came to wish they hadn't done it. Trumbo had them in mind when he said, in accepting an award from the Writers Guild of America a few years ago, that there were no villains or heroes, "only victims."

I particularly aggravated the committee chairman, J. Parnell Thomas, Republican, of New Jersey, by saying, "I could answer the way you want, Mr. Chairman, but I'd hate myself in the morning." He started pounding his gavel wildly and ordered the sergeant-at-arms to remove me forcibly from the witness chair. When I arrived at the Federal Correctional Institution in Danbury, Connecticut, to serve my sentence thirty-three months later, Thomas was already an inmate there, having meanwhile been found guilty of padding his payroll and receiving kickbacks. Neither of us made any social overtures to the other.

The entire proceedings were given an enormous amount of publicity, which was presumably the reason the committee decided to go after Hollywood in the first place. When during the

Ring, Jr. and Frances at the House Un-American Activities Committee
Hearings, 1947

first week such "friendly" witnesses as Robert Taylor, Gary Cooper, Ronald Reagan, George Murphy, Robert Montgomery, Louis B. Mayer, Adolphe Menjou and Jack Warner gave their testimony, it was front-page news everywhere, every day. And at the beginning of the second and final week, when the big names from the First Amendment Committee flew in to show the glamour was not all on one side, their pictures as spectators in the hearing room helped keep the story going.

Among the ten of us my inherited name was the only one that was widely known and stayed in people's minds after they read the stories and heard the radio bulletins. To most of Ellis's friends and relatives, publicity in this particular context was virtually a crime in itself. It seemed inconceivable that anyone connected with them could respond to the question of whether he was a Communist with anything but a resounding denial. Ellis avoided discussing the subject whenever that was possible; when it wasn't, she defended my position with more conviction than she felt.

When Frances, who made the trip to Washington with me, and I went to New York afterward, Ellis expressed her real feeling of deep concern about the consequences of what I had done. By that time she had gone most of the way in her extended conversion from optimist to pessimist, and she could see only the direst trouble ahead for us.

In trying to reassure her, I naturally went a little overboard on the optimistic side, but the truth is, and this has been hard to explain ever since to people who invest us with something like martyrdom, the prevailing sentiment among the Hollywood Ten was that we had the better of the issue. What has to be realized now to appreciate our perspective then is that it was so much the beginning of the McCarthy era that McCarthy himself had not yet discovered the virtues of anti-Communism. Some of us were less serene than others, but not even the gloomiest of us (that sounds like a figure of speech, but his name was Alvah Bessie) foresaw the paranoia of the next seven years.

So we had two disqualifications from heroism: We weren't

volunteers and we thought we were winners. We didn't anticipate that our careers would be wrecked or that we would go to prison. On the first count we had the assurance of the head of the Motion Picture Producers Association to our lawyers, in Washington during the hearings, that there would never be a blacklist in Hollywood. On the second it seemed likely we might be indicted for contempt of Congress and lose at the trial level but we had reason to be confident of vindication by the Supreme Court. As it turned out only the deaths, in the summer of 1949, of two liberal justices, Murphy and Rutledge, and their replacement by two Truman-appointed reactionaries (one of them, in Truman's own words, "about the dumbest man I think I've ever run across") lost us the vote for a review of our case by the Court. And it was the kind of basic Constitutional question, most legal authorities agreed, that was easier for the justices to ignore than decide in favor of the prosecution. When a nearly identical case was finally reviewed by the Warren Court, the decision seemed to say we had been right all the time. For us it was quite a hollow victory because we had not only served our time but were at midpoint in a fifteen-year blacklist.

The blacklist came into effect quite suddenly a few weeks after the hearings were adjourned. The top men in the film companies, based in New York and traditionally more conservative than their associates in Hollywood, met at the Waldorf Astoria Hotel. Their reading, more accurate than ours, of the trend in the cold war and domestic reaction, led to a declaration that they would not employ any of the Ten or anyone else who took a similar position.

I was still getting along fine at Fox. I had agreed to do some revisions on a script during the weeks I was away for the hearings and I wasn't even taken off salary. When I came back with the job finished, I was asked by Otto and the studio hierarchy to undertake a new one. Darryl Zanuck, the executive in charge of production, announced after the Waldorf Astoria meeting that he would still respect my contract until commanded otherwise by his board of directors. His board promptly met in New York and so commanded him. I was reached at a meeting with Otto in his office and requested to leave the premises, which I did. It was nearly twenty-one years before I passed through that gate again, this time with Ingo Preminger, Otto's brother, to tell Richard Zanuck, Darryl's son, how I proposed to adapt a book called *MASH* into a movie that came to be called *M*A*S*H.*

We were eased into the full rigors of the blacklist by an intermediate stage that lasted until we went off to serve our prison terms. Before that there was enough feeling that we might be vindicated and restored to respectability for a number of independent and semi-independent producers to risk paying a quarter or even a third of our normal wages for our anonymous services.

The major studios stuck to the official policy but not too rigidly. Fox, for instance, went ahead and shot the screenplay I had revised during the hearings and released the picture the following year with my name on it. And after that, when Lazar Wechsler, the leading producer of Switzerland, borrowed Cornel Wilde from the studio for a film, it was part of the negotiations that I would return to Zurich with him and write "the English dialogues."

Frances and I continued to lead a pretty good life in our new home. We had to cut way down on our decorating plans, but within a few weeks of the blacklist declaration she became pregnant, by design, and our son Jim was born in September, 1948.

The tennis court got a good deal of use at this time. At a minimum I had a doubles game every Saturday afternoon with Ian Hunter, Hugo Butler and Michael Wilson, all screenwriters destined to join the Ten on the blacklist. For a period we made the court available mornings to Greta Garbo, a neighbor.

Trumbo and John Howard Lawson, whose appeals were by agreement to govern the cases of the others, had to surrender themselves several weeks before the rest of us came up for brief trials and sentencing. They had each been given one year in prison and a one-thousand-dollar fine and we expected to get the same. Six of us did, but a different judge decided six months and five hundred dollars were enough in the cases of Herbert Biberman and Edward Dmytryk, whose offenses were identical to ours in every significant detail.

Robert W. Kenny, one of our lawyers, had been Attorney General of California and was well acquainted in Washington. He asked the head of the Federal Bureau of Prisons, James Bennett, where we would be sent and was told we would be divided among several institutions—five as it turned out—none of them in the West, where our families lived, because bureau policy forbade the expense of sending us that far from Washington, the place of sentencing. Bennett didn't say what consequences the government feared from larger concentrations of us. But he took under advisement the information that two of us, Lester Cole and I, had mothers in Connecticut. And we were the two sent to Danbury.

All the one-year sentences were shortened by "good time" to ten months, but I alone was awarded an additional fifteen days off for "meritorious good time." My merits were typing, spelling and grammar. It was my job eight hours a day to transcribe the Dictaphone records dictated by the personnel of the Office of Classification and Parole. I felt freer as I settled into the job to improve the style of their correspondence and the lengthy reports they prepared on each of my fellow inmates, and the MGT, as it was known, was their way of expressing appreciation.

Ellis, who lived less than fifteen miles away, was my principal visitor. Albert, her German man-of-all-work, drove her to the prison, where she submitted to having her bag searched and was escorted to the visiting room. There was no barrier between us and we could embrace under supervision, but it was rigidly forbidden to pass anything from one to the other. On one of her first visits she brought my twelve-year-old son Peter, who was staying with her.

When I broke my glasses in a handball game and was told it would take weeks to get them replaced at the medical facility in Springfield, Missouri, I said my mother could take them into the town of Danbury and get it done right away. Absolutely not, I was told, strictly against regulations. But when I said I couldn't do my job without them, the matter was reconsidered and they let Ellis take care of it.

John drove up from New York when he could and so did a friend, Martin Popper, who as one of our lawyers didn't have to be a blood relative to qualify as a visitor. Frances made a quick trip east in the late fall and was granted a special dispensation of three visits within a week.

My considered advice to beginning criminals in this country is to commit only Federal offenses, simply because the accommodations are so much better than those in any of our state prisons or local jails, or at least they were twenty-five years ago. The only physical discomfort I experienced was insomnia while quartered in a dormitory cubicle. This, too, was solved by the threat that it affected my efficiency as a stenographer. I was transferred at my request to single-cell housing, which most inmates didn't care for because you were locked into it at night. But for me it not only made sleeping easier but also concentration for reading and writing.

As for the welfare of the spirit, I wouldn't go as far as to say incarceration is beneficial, but it does have one advantage: the serenity that comes with freedom from responsibility—the peace T. E. Lawrence found when he turned himself into Aircraftsman Shaw. You can't achieve it just by going into some kind of voluntary retreat because as long as you're free to leave the place, you worry about the things you should be taking care of. But once the element of choice is removed and you know there is nothing you can do about anything, then you can really open your mind to random contemplation or focus it on a single project with a degree of concentration that I at least have rarely been able to achieve outside.

At Danbury, despite a full-time job and a ban on personal use of my office typewriter, I made a good start on my only novel *The Ecstasy of Owen Muir.* The book deals in a light vein with the contradictions of Roman Catholicism in America, and as part of my preparation I studied books by Fulton J. Sheen and other conspicuously Catholic authors. These, sent me by Frances, had to go through censorship, and the Catholic chaplain was tipped off that one of the Red-hots was showing signs of going his way. As a result I received an invitation to midnight Mass on Christmas Eve, which I accepted so as not to make waves and because I had a midnight Mass scene in the book.

Whereupon both the chaplain and the Catholic civilian clerk who had spotted the trend in my reading tried to follow up on their promising missionary effort. I persuaded them a conversion as drastic as mine could be viewed with suspicion if it took place under conditions of duress.

There is a qualitative as well as quantitative difference between a prison term of less than a year and one that lasts, say, two years or more. When the time is comparatively short, you think of it as a temporary inconvenience and start counting the days till it is over. You never really make the adjustment to a drastically different way of life with all its deprivations, and thus escape much of the gloom and frustration that come with the prospect of sustained confinement. I found, for instance, at the age of thirty-five, that I was able to put sex out of my mind most of the time. But with a number of years of enforced celibacy to face, I might have succumbed to self-pity and brooded about what it would do to me or my marriage; perhaps about available substitutes.

Not only did I get out two weeks before Cole did; I was given an overcoat by my government and he wasn't, simply because between our releases came an arbitrary date—April 15, I think it was—on which it was considered warm enough for the departing graduate to do without. In the circumstances it was a memorable piece of altruism on Lester's part to take my measurements and pick out my coat for me, which he was able to do because of his job in the warehouse. It was a navy officer's black winter coat, with a detachable lining and some slight imperfection, and whenever I wore it over the next several years, I always remembered leaving that place.

Ellis and Albert were waiting at the gate. They drove me to John and Hazel's apartment in New York and after a while Ellis said she wanted to get back to New Milford and we said good-bye, not knowing how long it would be before we saw each other again. She was visibly happy for me that I was over that particular ordeal, and I thought about what a relief it must also be for her not to have the strain of those visits any more—driving through the gates and up the hill to the guard post to be challenged over a loudspeaker and have to identify herself, and then having the heavy metal door unlocked for her and her purse searched, and following a guard to the visiting room, where we sat, one couple among twenty under constant scrutiny and perhaps electronic eavesdropping.

From John's on West Twelfth Street I went over to East Tenth, where Trumbo and Cleo, his wife, were occupying half of Donald Ogden Stewart's house. He had been out a week and she had come from California to meet him, and we had some midday drinks together and talked about the uncertainties of the future. Later I went uptown to see my friends Sylvia and Julian Rochelle, and they bought me an early dinner and took me to the airport.

Frances and I had worked out by mail a plan founded on our urgent need of a new car. By turning in our old one in Los Angeles and arranging to pick up the new one at the factory in Detroit, she saved enough to cover her air fare there and our expenses driving it the rest of the way across the country and getting reacquainted in the process.

We didn't force the pace and it was a full week after I left Danbury when we stopped off in Newport Beach, California, where Silvia was living with Peter and Ann. We called our house from there and were told John had been trying to reach us. I called him and learned that the evening of my release, alone in her bedroom, Ellis had had her first stroke. The second occurred a few days later in a New York hospital.

17

We had had to sell our Santa Monica home for money to live on while I was away and the house I returned to with Frances was a rented one. The committee was out hunting again and the fearful uncertainty of the previous year had developed into panic. Even before I left Danbury a fellow inmate had called to me in my cell that they were talking about me on the radio. There were new hearings in Washington and later in the year there were extended ones in Los Angeles. The penitent were showing the depth of their remorse by naming other sinners, and once a name had been mentioned there was a tendency for it to be repeated: even in their anxiety to clear themselves some witnesses were reluctant to add another former friend to the roster of the damned. It grew nonetheless and the blacklist of ten became one of more than two hundred.

In this atmosphere of terror the kind of half-secret working arrangements we had made before were no longer thinkable. Even for Frances, who had had several small film parts while I was in prison, the demand vanished under the new gospel of guilt by association. Eight months after my return we became one of half a dozen similarly situated families who went to Mexico because of lower living costs there. Silvia, just starting to establish herself in the construction business in Orange County, simply waived all her legal claims on me and supported Peter and Ann by herself until I was earning enough money to help them through college.

On our way to Mexico City in the last days of 1951, we took a long route through Texas in order to see Ellis, who was visiting her sister Ruby, also a widow, in Fort Worth. Only a few slight effects of her illness remained and she was beginning to regain strength, but she didn't feel like living by herself any more and in the spring Ruby was going back to New Milford with her for a long visit.

By the end of that visit in mid-July, Frances and I and the three children had moved in on Ellis for what became a two-year stay. Mexico had been pleasant for six months but not as cheap as we had hoped; my novel was going to require more time and further subsidizing; and the New York area had the great asset that Frances had always been able to get plenty of work there.

Even after we moved again, into a New York apartment in 1954, we spent our summers and many weekends with Ellis for the remaining years of her life, and she came into New York every fall and spent five or six months in a hotel apartment.

John wrote me while we were still in Mexico that he had a diagnosis of active tuberculosis and passed on his doctor's suggestion that I have frequent chest X-rays. The infection, it appeared, could remain dormant for decades, and most adult TB is a recurrence of an earlier outbreak, often so minor a one as to go unnoticed. Sure enough, I had scar tissue from old lesions but no current manifestations.

John's condition was serious because he had neglected the symptoms so long. He needed outside agitation to make him take care of himself and it was provided not by Hazel, whose heavy drinking had become heavier, but by their old friend Ann Honeycutt, who observed him at poker and match-game sessions during a year in which he lost forty pounds and developed a racking cough. Honey went after him so insistently to do something about these symptoms that he finally agreed in the spring of 1952 to see an internist she knew. (Hazel had mixed feelings about this intervention and told a few people that Honey had sent him to an intern.) Afterward, when he called Honey, who hadn't told him quite how alarmed she was about him, to report he had TB, her reaction was "Thank God." After a moment John said, "Did you expect me to hold a higher hand than that?"

According to Dr. Louis Siltzbach, to whom Honey's friend referred John, the disease was quite far advanced, with four distinct cavities in his lungs, and would most likely have proved fatal if they had been limited to the standard remedies of only a few years before. But he responded so well to the new drugs P.A.S., streptomycin and isoniazid that his symptoms were practically gone by the end of the year. It was, Siltzbach felt, an extraordinary recovery.

John had dropped his syndicated sports column in 1948 and become a magazine writer only. In January, 1952, he started a feature page in the magazine *Look* called "John Lardner's New York." There he wrote on a number of subjects, most of all the theater, which he had covered occasionally for *The New Yorker* as a substitute for Wolcott Gibbs. After his first appearance in *Look* it was reported around *Newsweek* that he was leaving and a memo circulated: ". . . John told me that there is no truth in the rumor—that NEWSWEEK is his first love and that he will be continuing to write the Sports Column for NEWSWEEK as he has in the past."

He had to suspend both columns in May when Dr. Siltzbach insisted on a complete rest. He resumed the one for *Look* in September, but it was discontinued at the end of that year. The *Newsweek* people, however, got the message about diversification: in 1953 "Sport Week" became "Lardner's Week," though it continued to have some connection with sports more often than not.

His work appeared in more than twenty different magazines in the postwar years and there were three collections of it published: *It Beats Working, White Hopes and Other Tigers* and *Strong Cigars and Lovely Women.* A copy of the last-named is inscribed "To A. Honeycutt, the strongest cigar, etc., I've ever known—with love, John Lardner." (Honey also preserved a telegram from him after she had her gall bladder removed: "You look much better without it. Will call you in a day or two.")

The last two of these books reflected a growing interest of John's in informal history, the history of boxing in particular to begin with, and then of low life in general, especially as it was lived in nineteenth-century New York. After painstaking research he always presented the facts with his own distinctive slant. On the subject of the search for a "white hope" to capture the heavyweight crown from Jack Johnson, for instance:

Pseudo-physiology became fashionable while Johnson was champion and a quantity of homemade scientific and philosophical doctrine found its way into print. The purport of most of this was twofold: (1) that human intelligence increases in direct proportion to the amount of Caucasian blood, and (2) that Negroes have thicker skulls than white men. A newspaper writer, quoting a learned authority but not by name, put the average difference in skull thickness at one inch. The bearing of this argument on Johnson's case is obscure, since his chief asset in the ring was intelligence coupled with speed and an airtight defense, and practically no one hit him on the skull. . . .

Once they saw that race redemption was being taken seriously by the newspapers and the public, these men [the talented managers] leaped into the movement feet first. Some, like McCartney, who had a college-bred imagination, preferred to prospect in mines, on farms and in saloons for brand-new hopes—the crude, unsmelted ore. In the heat of the search, well-muscled white boys more than six feet two inches tall were not safe out of their mothers' sight. . . . The others were satisfied to work with the materials at hand, converting their regular heavyweights, or even their light heavyweights or middleweights, into white hopes overnight.

One of the ways in which he resembled Ring was in his keen attention to the uses, especially the abuses, of language:

It is in the time dimension, however, that radio-televese scores its most remarkable effects. Dizzy Dean's "The Yankees, as I told you later . . ." gives the idea. The insecurity of man is demonstrated regularly on the air by phrases like "Texas, the former birthplace of

334

President Eisenhower" and "Mickey Mantle, a former native of Spavinaw, Oklahoma." I'm indebted to Dan Parker, sports writer and philologist, for a particularly strong example of time adjustment from the sayings of Vic Marsillo, a boxing manager who occasionally speaks on radio and television: "Now, Jack, whaddya say we reminisce a little about tomorrow's fight?" These quotations show what can be done in the way of outguessing man's greatest enemy, but I think that all of them are excelled by a line of Mr. Gray's spoken four or five years ago: "What will our future forefathers say?"

It is occasionally argued in defense of broadcasters (though they need and ask for no defense) that they speak unorthodoxly because they must speak under pressure, hastily, spontaneously—that their eccentricities are unintentional. Nothing could be farther from the truth. Their language is proud and deliberate. The spirit that has created it is the spirit of ambition. Posterity would have liked it. In time to come, our forebears will be grateful.

John came home after the war with the idea of settling down to family life, a goal he never quite realized. One step in this program was the purchase of a summer home in Ocean Beach, Fire Island, an hour and a half from Manhattan. For about five years he spent the greater part of each summer there with Hazel, their daughters Susan and Mary Jane, and their son John. Then came the summer of 1952 when he was too sick to make it there. Somehow he never made it for any sustained period after that either, even when he was feeling better, during the seven summers he had left.

Contributing reasons were that he had to go to a number of sports and other events for his work, that he had a deadline every week at the *Newsweek* office in New York, and that he had to check in with his doctor periodically. But I think he could have surmounted these obstacles if it hadn't been for the estrangement between him and Hazel. With his illness she had moved into a separate bedroom in the apartment, and they began to go their separate ways outside the house as well.

The fondness for drinking that had been a bond between them became their major problem when it developed in Hazel into addiction. During the first decade of their marriage they functioned as a social unit like most couples. Increasingly during the second they stayed together by keeping themselves apart.

For some years Ring and Ellis and the Rices had made a practice of visiting Saratoga Springs, New York, during the summer racing season. John developed the same habit, driving up for a few days every August except when the war or his health made it impractical. In the early years it would be John and Hazel in their car, with John at the wheel, and three or four Bleeck's regulars as passengers. Hazel was a passionate horseplayer, of the hunch rather than the scientific-study variety. Once at Saratoga she had an overwhelming impulse to back a hundred-to-one shot named Alimony Kid but had to borrow the two dollars to do it. When it came in, she spent her entire winnings the same evening, treating the group and their local friends at Newman's Lakehouse, a restaurant in which Jack Bleeck was a partner.

In the 1950s she was no longer part of the annual pilgrimage, staying with the children on Fire Island while John drove up with a Formerly Club delegation that generally included Honey but was otherwise all male. And in the same period there was an unofficial property settlement between them involving the two bars, Bleeck's and Chumley's, in the Village, where they had done most of their New York drinking. From that moment on Bleeck's was John's territory and Chumley's Hazel's, and there was almost never a trespass by either of them.

The Formerly Club, organized some years after the war, began as a loose organization of people who gathered in Bleeck's on Saturdays to have lunch and play the match game for drinks. What they had in common besides varying degrees of devotion to alcohol, according to John Crosby, one of the members, was nonuxoriousness, which is to say they were all either unmarried or bound by somewhat elastic ties.

The majority of them were journalists of one sort or another, though even a banker who could drink like a newspaperman, Frederick T. Allen, was one of the more steadfast members during the entire life of the club. One of the founders was Walt Kelly, creator of Pogo, who came to be John's closest friend during those years. The membership fluctuated a bit but generally stood at about sixteen, of whom half would assemble on an average Saturday along with an occasional guest or two. Annual elections were gravely if not soberly conducted, and a 1956 announcement to the membership began: "The Formerly Club will meet at its headquarters on Saturday, September 20, to elect a president to replace the incumbent, to the extent that such a thing is possible." It was signed "Your beloved president, J. A. Lardner."

As an observer, once or twice at close range, of the organization, I am of the opinion that it wouldn't have survived nearly as long as it did if it hadn't come upon a supplementary function to fill those Saturday afternoons. This occurred after John had written a *Newsweek* piece in which he stated that a system for beating horse races was impossible and that if it did exist it would provide "riches beyond the dreams of avarice." Jacob A. Tolonen of Detroit, a reader and an attorney, wrote to say he was wrong on both counts.

In the first place, said Tolonen, while no one can beat a game of chance in which there is a fixed house percentage against the player, that doesn't always hold true when the odds are determined by human handicappers or pari-mutuel machines. "Overlays" were inevitable and all you had to do to win was learn to spot them and then place your bets where there was an overlay of better than 20 percent. "Suppose that a horse is $6.00 in the mutuels and its correct odds are 4 in 10, such a horse would show a profit in the long run. On betting ten times, your expectation is 4 winners at $6.00 each, which is $24.00. Your outlay was $20.00 leaving a profit of $4.00."

The profits from this approach, Tolonen continued, were comparatively small, and you had to have a reserve of fifty times your basic bet to guard against a streak of extreme bad luck. To win a million dollars a year would require a stake of $250,000, and in practice your bets would have to be so big they would depress the track odds enough to wipe out your profit. On a modest scale, however, you could beat the races by following his selections and he offered to prove this to John with a three-month free trial. He would make his predictions each day by 11 A.M. and mail them with a postmark not later than noon. John could check the results and see how he would have come out over the three-month period if he had made the recommended bets. Tolonen wound up by saying he wanted no recognition or publicity of any kind and had no intention of ever selling or giving tips or of writing a book on how to beat the races.

His selections turned out to be nearly as good as the advance billing promised and soon it became the first business of the Formerly Club sessions for John to phone Detroit and get the day's picks from "the wizard." The members would decide how much they collectively wanted to wager and a second call would be made to a bookmaker to place the bets. This routine continued for more than five years, with profits averaging close to Tolonen's projection of 20 percent. On a good Saturday the membership could walk out of the place, lunch and drinks paid for, with the same total capital they had had on entering, but redistributed by the match game.

The selections and the bettings ended when John and Tolonen died on the same day. Soon afterward the Formerly Club also died "of inanition" in the words of Frank Sullivan, a member of the Saratoga Springs branch.

In the spring of 1955 (Northern calendar) John made his second trip to Australia, where preparations were already under way for the Olympic Games the following year. According to his testimony in a subsequent letter to her, "the first words I spoke on touching Australian soil at Sydney were 'Where is Mary?' . . ." He wrote a few columns from Sydney and Melbourne (the answer to his question) and saw some of the people he had met in 1942, Mary Coles included. It was understood that he would be back for the games in the spring (Southern calendar) of 1956, so she wrote him the following January when she switched from the Melbourne to the Brisbane office of the *Australian Women's Weekly:* "If you detour at all when you come out later in the year I'll have a lamp lighted in the window—but if Brisbane has to be out of your itinerary I won't fuss because if threads can be picked up as neatly after 13 years as they were in May—another 13 years wouldn't matter much."

This kind of reasoning did not appeal to him. I am quoting from a letter that was never sent but which I take to be a first draft of one that was:

What do you mean, another thirteen years wouldn't matter much? There is a certain stony nonchalance about you, lovely as you are, that undoes me. It is almost certain that I'll be dead by 1969; there is a very fair possibility that I'll die if I don't see you in 1956. What in God's name do you think I am planning this journey for?. . . . I thought I made it clear, both in Adelaide and in Melbourne, how I feel about you. The only change was that last year, since you and I have been alive long enough to know our own minds—and I like yours as much as I do the rest of you—I was willing to be with you on your own terms. Still am, in fact. It is nice to be with you, whatever the terms are. So please make it a point to be in Melbourne in November.

John was forty-three when he wrote that, with all his tuberculosis symptoms gone. The reference to an early death could be taken as jocular in the context, but he did say on several occasions to different close friends that he didn't expect to make forty-eight, the age Ring died at. I don't know how seriously he felt that at this point in his life. Later on it became more plausible than pessimistic. But he frequently said at least one other thing about himself that was pure speculation at best: that he was part Indian. He didn't make the same claim, unlikely in light of the known genealogy, for anyone else in the family.

(I have reported that there were people who referred to me as "the Indian" and that the nickname was based more on a taciturn manner than on appearance. However, it may be pertinent that Ring, covering as one of his first assignments on the

Inter-Ocean, a football game between Chicago and the Carlisle Indians, heard one girl say to another in reference to him: "He must have some white blood in him.")

Walt Kelly was John's traveling companion on the next and final trip to Australia. I don't know what was involved in the negotiations, but Pan American Airways gave them a free trip around the world. Mary did arrange to be in Melbourne on vacation and she and John wrote each other occasionally for two years after that. She died five years after he did, of emphysema, at the age of fifty-two, and that is all I know of her except that she was born in Saddleworth, South Australia, in 1913 and was a pious Roman Catholic.

Kelly, an impious one, wrote later that John had what he called his first real heart attack in Darwin, Australia, on their way to Melbourne. They had come by way of Rome, from where John made a nostalgic excursion to Anzio; Beirut, where they were stranded several days by the outbreak of the Suez crisis; Hong Kong, where they picked up a local brand of Scotch called Old Gloomis; and Manila. They were sampling the Scotch in Darwin and trying to deduce its ingredients:

" 'For soy sauce,' John said reflectively, 'it's not really too bad.' It was then that he started getting pains in his left arm and chest. He blamed this on me, saying I had forced him to carry my typewriter while I carried the bottle."

A little later John inadvertently drank from Kelly's glass. "Oops," he said. "I'd better watch out. I'll catch your heart disease."

Ellis's doctor felt she would be better off with some family in the house, though his ideal prescription would not have called for children nine, eight and three years old. Yet it was the children especially and the obligation she felt not to inflict her gloom on them that brought back some measure of her old good spirits. It was part of her routine then to go upstairs after dinner and get into bed, and Katie and Joe, David's children in fact, but mine in practical effect, liked to spend their last hour before going to their beds sprawled on hers, drawing stories from her about the ancient world of her girlhood. Jim joined them when he grew old enough.

The strokes had left her with some paralysis and a few other impairments, but during the time we lived with her and for nearly five years afterward, she slowly recovered from those specific effects at the same time she was undergoing the normal aging processes of a woman in her sixties.

Sharing her house with us was hard on her in some ways. She wasn't used to the physical and emotional excesses of children and the attendant risk to some of her more fragile and valued possessions. But this was more than offset by the way in which they stimulated and diverted her and kept her on the alert with their questions. It was a good relationship on both sides, and all three of them still think of her as someone very special in their lives.

Frances and I also did our share to provoke her back into the contemporary world, sometimes deliberately, more often as unconscious of any therapeutic purpose as the children were. We were both in the middle of an extended re-examination of our views, particularly of how the Marxist-Leninist doctrines we had subscribed to for so long stood up in the nuclear era and against the pattern of postwar developments in Eastern Europe and the Soviet Union. It was interesting to contrast Ellis's more conservative reactions with our own to such events as the election of Eisenhower, the death of Stalin, the Army-McCarthy hearings and the Supreme Court decision on school desegregation.

I found in almost any discussion with my mother that we were pretty much in agreement on what the desirable goal was, and at odds about how to achieve it. She wanted, for instance, to see the wealth of this country distributed more equally and was sure that was slowly being accomplished under existing institutions; I thought the long-range trend was in the opposite direction. She felt sanguine about the steady progress in race relations during her lifetime; I said the improvements were so superficial and painfully slow that tensions would mount instead of decrease in the years to come.

At the same time I was becoming more aware as I approached the age of forty that there was soggy ground beneath some of my long-standing beliefs. The cause of socialism had been greatly fortified by the victories of the Chinese and Indochinese Communists. But what about the compatibility of socialism and democratic freedoms? It was no longer enough to say that abuses in Russia needn't be repeated in other countries; they were being repeated in other countries. And I had wildly underestimated the depth and persistence of delusions of superiority based on color and nationality. Build a rational society, I had thought, and irrationality will wither away.

Now I began to suspect what the two decades since have done so much to confirm: that very formula may be the grand and fatal delusion of our species. Now that we have devised two quite practical methods of extinguishing ourselves, nuclear war and chemical pollution, systems like capitalism and socialism have little relevance except as helps or hindrances to escaping our doom. But the problems of eluding extinction are clearly subject to rational solution. The only question, therefore, is whether we are capable of subordinating all the other forces within us to reason.

There is also the factor, however, that all situations are in a state of change and so, therefore, is the logic of the situation. If we fail to adopt a rational energy program now, for instance, soon the circumstances will require a drastically different solution. Project ourselves a couple of decades into the future and assume the United States of America is still doing as much to poison the air and the sea as the rest of the world together. The only reasonable choice for the rest of the world might be to join forces and bomb the United States back to the Stone Age. With clean warheads.

My main concentration our first year in New Milford was completing my novel. Frances was the one to go out in the world and look for work, not just because we needed money but because acting was her profession, her art, her way of fulfilling herself. She got a couple of minor jobs in the theater, but by far the most promising area was television. Shows were done live then and there was a freshness and vitality about them that disappeared with the use of film and then of tape. New York, not Hollywood, was where everything was happening. And a good many of the people making it happen were men and women Frances had worked with in radio. A couple of months after our arrival she was cast in a leading role on a show with as much prestige as anything then being done.

The series was Philco Playhouse on CBS and the particular play was *Holiday Song* by Paddy Chayevsky. Its content was appropriate to the Jewish high holidays and its presentation timed accordingly. The show and its cast, including Frances, were well regarded by the critics and within the organization that produced it. Her paycheck came with a note from the producer, Fred Coe: "You are now an official member of the Philco Playhouse." Soon she was told that Chayevsky was writing another show with a somewhat similar but bigger part that she would be ideal for; in fact, he was writing it with her in mind.

The second one was called *Marty* and everyone connected with it, short of Coe himself, told her the part was hers if she liked the script. The terms negotiated with her agent provided a 50 percent increase over *Holiday Song*. Then suddenly all signals changed. She was told, unconvincingly, that Coe had cast another actress without consulting or informing anyone else in the organization. He himself was unable to see her.

Frances and her agent had to accept the possibility that it had happened like that—that he had suddenly decided someone else would be better for the play. But then they started running into closed doors all over and we all had to face the likelihood that it was the blacklist operating in new territory. And though her own past politics, if known, might have qualified her for ostracism, the fact was that she hadn't appeared on anyone's list or been named in anyone's testimony. If it was her fortune to be unemployable, she had acquired it by marriage.

The last doubt was extinguished when Philco revived *Holiday Song* for the Jewish holidays the following fall. When the actors assembled for rehearsal, the other members of the previous cast were so shocked to see someone else in Frances's place they threatened to strike in her behalf. Coe persuaded them it would accomplish nothing except the loss of their jobs.

Not long after that Coe, a good man and clearly distressed by his role, finally agreed to see Frances and told her about the losing battle he had waged to clear another, better-known actor. But a man, he said, was no match for a network.

Most of the screenwriters on the Hollywood blacklist are no longer in the profession. Those who are never really left it; they managed to operate through pseudonyms and "fronts" on dubious projects for scanty rewards. There are perhaps a couple of dozen of us who have returned to the same level of success we occupied before or a higher one. I can think of three directors who managed to keep directing against all odds and who today are, along with one writer-director who kept on writing, "bankable" (to use a word bestowed on the language by Hollywood) as directors of major films.

But for blacklisted actors the damage to careers was in all cases more severe and in most of them fatal. There was no way their work could appear on any screen, theater or room-sized. When they were permitted to perform in theaters and nightclubs, it was not in important theaters and nightclubs. And during all the years they were denied a chance to work, the instruments they were trained to play—their physical persons—were changing, were aging, were becoming less familiar to the audiences that had once recognized and applauded them. If acting could be said to be a person's whole life, and there were some about whom this was not too great an exaggeration, such persons were suspended from living.

For writers it was easier without ever becoming exactly easy. When I finished the novel, I submitted it to a number of respectable American publishers in succession, which is the way you are supposed to do it. Some responded quite favorably at lower levels but never at the top. Each of them would take a month or so to say no and I soon realized it could be a lengthier process than I had patience for. As an experiment I sent it to a friend in London, Ella Winter, who passed it on to one of the older and more conservative publishers there, Jonathan Cape, who promptly accepted it. He added the comment that my being one of the Hollywood Ten might be helpful in the promotion since a fair amount of attention had been paid over there to "that curious affair."

After another discouragement or two in New York, I arranged to have it published in an obscure way by Angus Cameron, who had himself fallen afoul of the committee and lost his job with Little, Brown. Sales showed I was not going to recapture my Hollywood standard of living by writing novels, but the reviews it did get (most publications just ignored it) were balm to a bruised ego. One of these was a pleasant surprise because of both its content and its author. What it said in part was: "For wit, originality, style, and dramatic sense of plot, Mr. Lardner is second to no contemporary novelist." The reviewer, in *The New Republic* was Scott and Zelda's daughter, Scottie, whom I hadn't seen since she was a baby in Great Neck.

Meanwhile Ian Hunter and I had found ourselves an employer and a kind of writing work that was to sustain us and our families for the next five years. Our employer, under the name of Hannah Dorner, had been a pretty young neighbor of John and Dick Tobin and Tom Sugrue in the Peter Stuyvesant Hotel when she, too, was starting on a New York newspaper. Now she was Hannah Weinstein, divorced mother of three daughters and producer of a television series filmed in England starring Boris Karloff. That series was not renewed for a second year but she had ideas for other ones and we settled after a time on *The Adventures of Robin Hood.* Our pilot script and a prospectus sold the series to an American network, and the company began to turn out half-hour films in volume, starring Richard Greene as the outlaw leader.

We were commissioned to write, in strict anonymity, as many

episodes as we could devise, but the demand became more than we could satisfy and we had to bring in other writers, all blacklisted. Ian and I went on to develop another series called *Sir Lancelot* and then another called *The Pirates,* which had the good fortune to acquire young Robert Shaw as a star. At that point we had a record of three pilots written, three series sold to networks, which was as good as anybody in the business. Although we didn't do quite that well on some later ventures, which were sold by syndication only, everything we wrote, vast quantities of it, was filmed and shown on the tube.

The work called for discussions in person from time to time and when Hannah couldn't come to New York, Ian went to London on a passport he had extracted from the authorities with the aid of a Washington lawyer. But travel for me was deemed officially to be "not in the best interests of the United States." When after seven years of such denial, the Supreme Court ruled in 1958 that everyone was entitled to a passport, I was so eager to apply for one I went immediately to a neighborhood photographer who advertised passport pictures among his wares. But he couldn't meet my demand for a picture the same day. For that, he said scornfully, I would have to go to a coin machine or one of those assembly-line purveyors of pictures without negatives. But if I did that, he warned me, "You'll end up looking like a Communist."

I did get to London that fall for what turned out to be my last work for Hannah. In fact, after not having been abroad since the Swiss job in 1949, I now made three trips in less than a year. The last two came about after I was summoned to Hollywood early in 1959 by Carlo Ponti and his partner, Marcello Gerosi, to rewrite a script for Sophia Loren. The blacklist was collapsing by this time under a many-pronged attack led by Trumbo, who seized on every contradiction, and created a few of his own, to ridicule and discredit the now venerable edifice. The following year he and Otto Preminger breached it mortally with the announcement that Trumbo's name would appear on the picture *Exodus.*

But I was still pledged that spring to take certain precautions. One was to register in a hotel under a false name so there could be phone calls between the producers and me via the Paramount Studio switchboard without violating security. So I became Rick Spencer and when my daughter Ann, then a freshman at Stanford, came to visit me and share my quarters, a decent respect to the opinions of mankind required that she should register as Miss Spencer rather than Miss Lardner.

That picture ran into trouble shooting in Vienna, largely because, though neither he nor anyone else knew it, the director, Michael Curtiz, was a dying man. I went there, did some more work and returned to New York. Shooting was transferred to Rome, where Vittorio de Sica was enlisted as an anonymous codirector. I was needed again, enough so I could bring Frances along on the budget, and there in a Roman studio office, I learned something new about the blacklist.

The Paramount executives in Hollywood were concerned, with good reason, about the footage that was coming in. They wanted a certain key scene rewritten and reshot. A group of us sat around listening while the head of Paramount in Rome conveyed our collective and individual thinking to an executive in California. To my astonishment the man on our end would say now and then that "Ring" thinks so-and-so or "Ring" feels such-and-such. And I suddenly realized that Ponti and Gerosi would never have risked hiring me without the approval of Y. Frank Freeman, who not only ran the studio but was a leading spokesman for the Producers Association that had decreed the blacklist. The false name over the switchboard was protection not against him and the Paramount hierarchy but against a possible indiscretion on a lower echelon.

By the time John became forty-five in 1957, he was one of the best-known and respected journalists in America. This is a hard thing to gauge unless you conduct a survey and in his case the survey didn't come until after he was dead when his friend Roger Kahn, then sports editor of *Newsweek,* put together a collection

John in the 1950s, with no ailments showing

Ellis, 1959, the summer before her death

of his stuff. It was published, with a preface by Kelly and an epilogue by Roger, as *The World of John Lardner.* The reviews of that book were the first chance critics had to appraise his work since his last book in 1951.

They wrote mostly about the thoroughness of his reporting, the comic individuality of his slant on things and the craftsmanship of his sentences. Most of them made a point of noting how long Ring's shadow was, especially in the area of sports and humor, and how completely John had emerged from it as a distinctive American writer with a unique style.

Another way to judge where he stood in his last years was the increasing demand for his work, his reaction to which was to limit himself more and more to the two old stand-bys *Newsweek* and *The New Yorker.* He also began about that time to gather material for a book to be called *Drinking in America,* of which only seven short chapters were ever written. The first one began:

> Most of the early settlers of America had never touched water unless for hygienic or theological reasons, or because they'd fallen off a bridge. So they lost no time, once they were here, in rounding up as much liquor as possible and in forming rules and customs for disposing of it.

Nineteen fifty-seven was the year he made a big effort to cut out cigarettes, switching to a limit of ten cigars a day instead. He had been bothered by shortness of breath for about two years and Dr. Siltzbach had given him some pills for the condition. But now, with the pills and after stopping the cigarettes, the breathing problem grew worse. Along with it he had an attack of dizziness, nausea and vomiting. He also had trouble walking, tending to fall to the right, difficulty with certain speech sounds and double vision.

For the first time he told the doctor about an episode fifteen years before, during his first visit to the Pacific in 1942, when he had suffered paralysis of the right leg for two days and blindness of the right eye for two or three weeks. Occasionally in the intervening time he had had a recurrence of the walking problem.

Siltzbach put a patch on his right eye, but it was more than five weeks before his eyes returned to focus. His balance improved at the same time, but there was still unsteadiness. He was breathing better despite having started smoking cigarettes again. A little more than a month after that, he experienced numbness in the tips of his fingers and toes, in his torso and in his right leg, and he had another spell of difficulty in locomotion. After another month he was better and throughout 1958 he had only minor bouts with all these symptoms.

All the indications, including the fifteen-year history with long intervals of remission, made Siltzbach certain it was a case of multiple sclerosis. John told me right away and probably Kelly, but to other friends and relatives he acknowledged having a new ailment without giving it a name, playing it down as a temporary disturbance the doctor said would go away with rest and care.

That summer Wolcott Gibbs died and Shawn asked John, who had filled in as theater critic for more than ten years during Gibbs's frequent and occasionally prolonged absences, to take the post permanently. He told me he would have accepted it except for the image of himself making his way up the aisle after an opening in what might be an increasingly crippled condition. Instead, he asked for and was given a department to be called "The Air" in which he could write about emerging trends in television even if bedridden.

He continued to write that column on a quite regular basis until he died a year and a half later. That was only a couple of months longer than Ring, when he was bedridden, did for the same magazine the radio column that terminated with his death. Predicting he would die at approximately the same age was just an extreme example of how John modeled himself, unconsciously, I think, for the most part, on our father.

On December 8, 1958, Hazel summoned Dr. Siltzbach to the apartment, where he found John with a full-fledged coronary occlusion and dispatched him to Mount Sinai Hospital. Tests there revealed little more than that he had too high a count in both cholesterol and triglycerides, and a loss of hearing in his left ear. He told Siltzbach he had experienced discomfort in his chest about three times a year for about the last five years. Probably this didn't conflict in his mind with what he had told Kelly in Darwin; that may have been the first time he realized the discomfort was caused by heart trouble. A cardiac specialist was called in and he was kept in the hospital two weeks for observation.

Dr. Siltzbach believes there was no interrelation among John's three major ailments: tuberculosis, multiple sclerosis and heart disease. No one of them leads to another of them or makes its occurrence more probable. The odds against any one person's being smitten with all of them are staggering. But it could have been the early warnings he had on three separate medical fronts that made John think he wouldn't last as long as Ring did.

It went without saying between us that Ellis be given as little cause as possible to worry about his health, but there was no concealing his hospitalization because she was in the city at the time and in almost daily contact. What she wasn't told was that he had had previous cardiac incidents and that he was becoming more of an invalid than she was. One city block was about as much as he could walk without experiencing shortness of breath and angina pains. His hearing impairment vanished and he was able to drive himself to Florida for his annual look at baseball training camps, but after he came back he started having angina in the morning and stayed home more and more of the time.

Ellis, on the other hand, seemed in rather good shape on what she called her seventieth birthday that spring although she and I knew it was really her seventy-second. She even acknowledged her well-being herself by buying a new mink coat to replace one stolen six years previously. Up till then she had been saying she didn't have enough time left to justify such a purchase. That summer, when Frances had a two-week stint in a play in Chicago and I joined her for part of that time, we had no hesitation about leaving the children with Ellis. And shortly after that when we went to Rome on the Loren picture, Katie and Joe stayed with her while Jim visited friends on Fire Island.

In the fall, after an interval of eight and a half years, she had another stroke that left her with serious incapacities. She had decided to stay in New Milford that winter instead of taking a place in New York, and she was soon confined to her house there. Her sister Jane, also widowed now, came to stay with her and remained until Ellis's death the following February. Meanwhile the disease struck her twice more, leaving her at last in almost total paralysis and speechless.

John and I had gone to see her separately a few times that winter. The last time we drove up together in his car. A sudden thaw had turned the dirt road she lived on into a muddy morass and we couldn't quite make it to the top of a hill. I got out and pushed while he stayed at the wheel, and I almost managed to get it moving. Despite my protest John got halfway out, keeping a hand on the wheel, and lent some of his strength to the effort. I was so afraid of what it would do to his heart I pushed even harder, and between us we got it out of the ruts without any visible adverse effect on him.

The bedside vigil lasted nearly a week, Frances joining us for the final days. Ellis developed pneumonia, her fever soared, and the doctor took John and me aside. He could give her an antibiotic for the infection, he said, and if she responded she might linger for an indefinite period, but this time her incapacities were irreversible. We both knew what Ellis would want and we just needed to look at each other before we told him to withhold the medicine.

Less than four weeks after she died on February 15, John had another coronary and was hospitalized again for ten days. We had a drink together when I went to see him because one of his doctors had recommended a light highball before dinner, and we talked about how I could relieve him of some of the practical details of his job as executor of Ellis's estate. There was nothing unhealthy about his appearance, an electrocardiogram showed his condition had stabilized, his sclerosis was in a state of remission, and though both Siltzbach and the heart specialist, Dr. Field, would have preferred he stay a few days longer, they accepted his argument that he could rest just as well at home.

To Roger Kahn at the end of a visit, he said, "I'm getting sprung Tuesday, so I'll rest Wednesday, write Thursday, rest Friday, and see you in Bleeck's on Saturday." He carried out the first part of the schedule, but Thursday afternoon he called *Newsweek* to ask for extra time on his column. He was scrapping the one he had started because he had just heard about F.P.A.'s death and wanted to write about him instead.

Hazel called me around dinner time to say he had had another attack. I got there before Siltzbach did and found him barely conscious. His son Johnny and I lifted him into a better position and he thanked us. There were five drafts of his lead on F.P.A. around the typewriter. When Siltzbach and Field came, they sent for an ambulance but he was weakening fast. Siltzbach pleaded with him to pull through. "You're a noble human being," he said.

"Oh, Lou," John said, "that sounds like a quotation."

He lost consciousness soon after that and died before the ambulance came, six weeks short of his forty-eighth birthday. I was glad Mother had gone first. John took her death hard, but his would have been harder on her.

Hazel died two years later. They were survived by three children and David by two. I am the father of another three, and from that total of eight there is already a count of eight in a new generation.

The Hollywood blacklist lasted about fifteen years, seventeen in my case between screenplay credits. It had wiped out scores of careers and a few lives, but there were enough of us who survived it to create a whole new subversive threat to the content of American movies. The erosion so far is invisible to the naked eye, which is the way we prefer it.

There are a number of signs to suggest a revival of interest in the work of Ring Lardner. Bruccoli and Layman, the scholars who put together *Some Champions,* have also done an exhaustive bibliography; and both a collection of my father's letters and a new biography are in work. On an average of once a month a new anthology appears with one of his stories in it.

The most impressive development in recent years has been the spread of his work into foreign countries. During his lifetime and for thirty years after his death, he was practically unknown outside the English-speaking world; this year there are collections of his stories on sale in France, Italy, West and East Germany, Rumania, Norway, Czechoslovakia, Yugoslavia and a number of other countries. How full an appreciation of his work there can be in all these new languages, I am not competent to judge, but clearly some obstacles have not been surmounted:

The rhythm at least of "And he give her a look that you could pour on a waffle" is lost when it becomes *"E le diede un'occhiata che avreste potuto spalmarla benissimo su una fettina di pane."*

And the reader is not getting the same sense of the character speaking the line when "I've saw outfielders tooken sick with a dizzy spell" is converted to *"J'ai vu des joueurs de l'extérieur avoir une attaque de vertige."*

In 1975 I accepted an offer from Pakistan (of two hundred and fifty dollars, no less) for the amateur theatrical rights in the Urdu language to a revue sketch of Dad's that contains the exchange:

"Me? I was born out of wedlock."

"Mighty pretty country around there."

I'm still waiting to hear how this holds up in Urdu.

It's been a long time now, since 1960, that I have been the only one left of the family. Once a magazine editor suggested I set down some recollections of my father; later another one proposed a piece about the six of us. I complied in both instances, discovering in the process that there was more material than I had anticipated both in my memory and in the papers, mainly letters, which had been rather haphazardly preserved. But again it was on someone else's initiative that I undertook a book. Only in the course of writing it did I realize that my hesitation, even reluctance, went back to a defensive mechanism that began when I first understood that my name was, by no feat of mine, a famous one. All my life I had been trying to avoid any enterprise that bore the risk of inviting comparison with my father or the appearance of trading on his reputation. It was permissible, for instance, to write a novel but never a short story.

I rather expected the problems of carrying someone else's name would diminish in time, but in a curious way that hasn't happened. When I was a young man, it didn't matter whether I was introduced with or without the "Junior"; people who recognized the name realized at once that I must be the son of the man whose work or reputation they knew. But now, a generation and a half later, I meet people of all ages up to about fifty who know that Ring Lardner is a writer of some venerability whose stories they were exposed to in school and college textbooks. And seeing a reasonably venerable man who could easily pass for a writer, they think they are confronting the original, the author of "Haircut," "Champion," "Some Like Them Cold," "The Golden Honeymoon" or whatever else they remember, often dimly. It has an ambiguous effect on my self-image to be taken for a man who died so long ago, but I eventually came to realize there was nothing I could do about that.

As for exploiting the name, it finally seemed more important that there was a body of information about my family which I alone could put together, so I set about doing that. And in the course of it I found myself at long last weighing the advantages and disadvantages of bearing the name, with the balance coming out on the plus side.

Index

Lardner, Ring *(cont'd)*
163–165, 188, 190–195, 217; illnesses, 112, 113, 118, 140, 194, 201, 204, 205, 206, 217–218, 223; John resembles him, 125, 230–231, 334, 339–340, 351; magazine and newspaper writing, 135, 145, 217–218, 220; taste in reading, 137–138; in F.P.A.'s column, 141–142; income and finances, 149–150, 217, 220; stories become important, 153–159, 174–175; carelessness with papers, 154; attitude toward writing, 157–160, 174–176; affair with Dorothy Parker (possible), 189–191; syndicated column, 202, 206–207; political opinions, 219; play, unfinished, with Kaufman, 218, 221, 222; last days, 225–226; death, 226; sons resemble him, 249, 250, 287, 295; Broun praises him, 278, 280; continued interest in his work, 354–356; translations of his work, 355

Letters: to F. P. Abbott, 67; to Mrs. Abbott, 58–59; to Daniels, 7–8; to Ellis, 5, 34–37, 41–45, 47–62, 66–72; to Fitzgeralds, 145–146, 148, 151, 156, 170, 172–173, 188, 190; to Jim, 219–220; to navy recruiting station, 8–9; to Perkins, 154–155, 174, 194; to Ring, Jr., 206–207; to sons, 221, 222; to Walker, 229–230

Films: 150–153; *Alibi Ike,* 153; *Blonde Trouble,* 152; *The Cowboy Quarterback,* 152; *Fast Company,* 152; *The New Klondike,* 150, 151; *So This Is New York,* 153

Plays and Musicals: Elmer the Great, 176, 179, 181, film versions, 152; *June Moon,* 58, 140, 181–187, 198, 222, 237, film versions, 151–152; *Smiles,* 199–201; *Zanzibar,* 21; *Ziegfeld Follies of 1922,* sketches, 144–145

Songs: for family, 53–54; "Gee! It's a Wonderful Game," 53, 70; "Home, Sweet Home (That's Where the Real War Is)," 95; "Little Puff of Smoke, Good-Night," 53, 70; "My Alpine Rose," 53; "Prohibition Blues," 96–97

Stories: "Along Came Ruth," 94; "Back to Baltimore," 88; *The Big Town,* 83, 93, 149, 153, 160; "A Busher's Letters Home," 86–87; "Call for Mr. Keefe," 94; "Champion," 88, 154, 356, film version, 153; "The Facts," 88, 154; "A Frame-up," 156; "The Golden Honeymoon," 4, 153–154, 174, 175, 356; *Gullible's Travels,* 93, 160; "Haircut," 153, 174, 175, 356; "Harmony," 154; "Horseshoes," 88; *How to Write Short Stories,* 155, 157, 160, 172, 174–175; "I Can't Breathe," 152, 181, 237; *Lose with a Smile,* 217–218; *The Love Nest and Other Stories,* 4; "Mr. Frisbie," 176; "My Roomy," 88; *Own Your Own Home,* 93; "Poodle," 220; *The Real Dope,* 94; *Round Up,* 198; "Sick 'Em," 88; *Some Champions,* 94, 354; "Some Like Them Cold," 175, 181, 356; *Treat 'Em Rough,* 94; *You Know Me Al,* 82–83, 84, 87, 88, 152, 160, 218, comic strip based on, 135, 174; *The Young Immigrunts,* 102–104, 149

Miscellaneous: My Four Weeks in France, 93–94; prefaces, 155–157; "Sport and Play," 117; *The Story of a Wonder Man,* 156–157; "Symptoms of Being 35," 38; verses, 17, 34, 37, 42, 43, 45, 79, 83–84, 89–90, 96, 146, 162–163, 166–167; *What of It?,* 160

Lardner, Ring, Jr. (Bill), 3, 62–63, 81, 183, 189, 190, 196, 198, 199, 201, 217, 243–244, 248–250, 260,

Sorbonne, 199, 210
South Bend, Ind., 22
South Bend *Times,* 21
South Bend *Tribune,* 21
South Byfield, Mass., 220
Soviet Union: in cold war, 317; postwar developments, 341–342; Ring, Jr. in, 245–246, 255; U.S. Communist opinions of, 276; in World War II, 288, 289
Spanish civil war: Jim plans enlistment in, 261–267; Jim serves in, 267–283
Spanish Earth (film), 267
The Spider, 145
Spink, Charles, 65–66
Sporting News, 23, 57, 65–66
Stalin, Joseph, 255, 341
A Star Is Born (film), 190, 251, 253, 255
Starrett, Vincent, 225
Stearns, Dr. Alfred, 212
Stevenson, Robert Louis, 45
Stewart, Donald Ogden, 261, 330
Stock market crash (1929), 198
Strike Up the Band, 199
Stuart, Donald, 240
Sugrue, Thomas, 239, 345
Sullivan, Frank, 338
Supreme Court, 321, 325, 341, 346
Swain, Tom, 21
Switzerland, 326
Swope, Herbert Bayard, 117, 135–136, 147, 148, 163, 171–172, 251, 253
Swope, Herbert Bayard, Jr., 136, 251
Swope, Jane, 136

Taft School, Watertown, Conn., 125, 210, 216, 246
A Tale of Two Cities (film), 252
Taylor, Deems, 136
Taylor, Laurette, 141
Taylor, Robert, 323
Teheran Conference, 317
Television, 343–346, 351

Thackeray, William Makepeace, 137
Thanatopsis Literary and Inside Straight Society, 193
Thomas, J. Parnell, 322
Thomas, Norman, 219
Thompson, Dorothy, 296
Thompson, Jacob, 10
Thurber, Helen (Mrs. James Thurber), 261
Thurber, James, 18, 150–151, 159, 164, 261–262
Tilden, William T., 145
Time, 135, 184, 255, 262
Tinker, Joseph, 51, 52
Tobin, Anne (Toby, Mrs. Edward Willcox), 126, 142, 182, 192
Tobin, Anne Lardner (Mrs. Richard G. Tobin), sister of Ring, 6, 10, 13, 21, 29, 43, 48, 68, 78, 141, 162, 177, 215
Tobin, Blanche, 182
Tobin, Richard G., 43, 210, 215
Tobin, Richard L., 151, 215, 217, 220, 221, 233, 236, 239, 254, 345
Toledo, Ohio, 96
Tolonen, Jacob A., 337–338
Tombes, Andrew, 144
Tomorrow the World, 293
Tom Sawyer (film), 252
Torrence, George Paull, Jr., 133
Torrence, George Paull, Sr., 49
Tortosa, Spain, 266
Tours, France, 260
Tracy, Spencer, 289
Trotsky, Leon, 255
Truman, Harry, 317, 325
Trumbo, Cleo (Mrs. Dalton Trumbo), 330
Trumbo, Dalton, 309, 330, 346; in House Un-American Activities Committee investigation, 320, 322, 326
Tucson, Ariz., 204, 217
Tunney, Gene, fights with Dempsey, 145, 148–149

Twain, Mark, 159
20th Century–Fox, 291, 318, 319, 325, 326
Tyson, Dr. Cornelius, 218, 222, 226

United Press, 262, 263
Up Front (film), 315

Valentino, Rudolph, 178
Vanderbilt, Sanderson, 306
Van Loan, Charles, 87
Van Loon, Hendrik Willem, *Geography,* 221
Vereen, Lizabeth, 188, 223
Vienna, 347
Viertel, Peter, 292

Waco, Texas, 78
Walker, Mickey, 131–132
Walker, Stanley, 229, 233, 239, 246–247, 262, 284, 286
Wallace, Edgar, *On the Spot,* 201
Warner, Jack, 278, 323
· Warner Brothers, 152–153, 275
Washington, D.C., 142, 182, 187; *see also* House Un-American Activities Committee investigation
Washington Senators, 222
Watkins, Linda, 185, 187
Webb, Clifton, 291
Wechsler, Lazar, 326
Weinstein, Hannah Dorner, 345–346
Welles, Orson, 253
Werrenrath, Reinald, 173–174
West Baden Springs, Ind., 50
Wheeler, John N., 95–96, 140, 144, 198, 232, 236, 239, 298
Wheeler, Elizabeth, 285
Wheeler, "Tee" (Mrs. John N. Wheeler), 27, 140, 144, 198, 199
White, G. Harris (Doc), 53
White, Leigh, 272
Wilde, Cornel, 326

Willard, Jess, fight with Dempsey, 96, 145, 147
Willhite, Captain, 58, 59–60, 69
Williams, Bert, 20, 27, 95
Wilson, Edmund, 64, 157, 175
Wilson, Michael, 326
Winchell, Walter, 247
Windsor, Duke and Duchess of, 260–261
Winter, Ella, 345
Witkowsky, Ethel, 22
Wolfe, Thomas, 159
Wolff, Milton, 282–283
Woman of the Year (film), 289, 293
Won in the Ninth, 138
Wood, Gar, 144
Woollcott, Alexander, 136, 171, 193, 225
Wordsworth, William, 274
World Series, 22–23, 52, 56, 77, 85, 110, 145–146, 221–222, 285, 299; scandal (1919), 95, 146, 163, 286
World War I: Ring as correspondent in, 93–95; songs, 177
World War II, 288, 289; David in, 305–309; John in, 287, 295, 298–299, 302–305, 310–314; Ring, Jr. in, 289, 291; songs, 178
Writers Guild of America, 322
Wrubel, Allie, 63
Wyler, William, 320
Wynn, Ed, 27, 38, 140, 145

Yale, 286, 292
Yalta Conference, 317
Yankee Doodle Dandy (film), 176
Youmans, Vincent, 174, 200

Zanuck, Darryl, 291, 325–326
Zanuck, Richard, 326
Ziegfeld, Florenz, 27, 144, 175, 199, 200
Ziegfeld Follies: of 1917, 95; *of 1922,* 144–145